FLORIDA STATE
UNIVERSITY LIBRARIES

JUN 2 7 2001

TALLAHASSEE, FLORIDA

THE VIETNAMESE FAMILY IN CHANGE

NORDIC INSTITUTE OF ASIAN STUDIES

Recent studies of Vietnamese history and society

Authority Relations and Economic Decision-Making in Vietnam:
An Historical Perspective
Dang Phong and Melanie Beresford

Women's Bodies, Women's Worries:
Health and Family Planning in a Vietnamese Rural Community
Tine Gammeltoft

Thailand and the Southeast Asian Networks
of the Vietnamese Revolution, 1885–1954
Christopher E. Goscha

Vietnam or Indochina? Contesting Concepts of Space
in Vietnamese Nationalism, 1887–1954
Christopher E. Goscha

Vietnam in a Changing World
Irene Nørlund, Carolyn Gates and Vu Cao Dam (eds)

Profit and Poverty in Rural Vietnam:
Winners and Losers of a Dismantled Revolution
Rita Liljeström, Eva Lindskog,
Nguyen Van Ang and Vuong Xuan Tinh

The Vietnamese Family in Change:
The Case of the Red River Delta
Pham Van Bich

The Vietnamese Family in Change

The Case of the Red River Delta

Pham Van Bich

CURZON

Nordic Institute of Asian Studies
Vietnam in Transition series

First published in 1999
by Curzon Press
15 The Quadrant, Richmond
Surrey TW9 1BP

Typesetting in ITC New Baskerville 10/12
by the Nordic Institute of Asian Studies

Printed and bound in Great Britain by
TJ International Ltd, Padstow, Cornwall

Publication of this volume was assisted by a grant
from the Department for Research Cooperation (SAREC)
at the Swedish International Development Agency (Sida)

Copyright © 1999 by Pham Van Bich

British Library Catalogue in Publication Data

Bich, Pham Van
 The Vietnamese family in change : the case of the Red
 River Delta
 1.Family - Vietnam 2.Vietnamese - family relationships
 I.Title
 306.8'5'09597

ISBN 0-7007-1105-8

In memory of my father
and to my daughter

Contents

Introduction	1
1. The Traditional Family	7
The French Influence	7
Some Characteristics of the Traditional Family	17
2. Social Changes Affecting the Family, 1945–95	44
Planned Social Changes (or Social Steering)	45
Unplanned Social Changes	85
Conclusion	99
3. The Husband–Wife Relationship	103
The Husband–Wife Relationship in the Traditional Family	104
Conjugal Bonds in the Present Family	125
Conclusion	176
4. Reproduction and Its Socio-cultural Meanings	181
Reproduction in the Traditional Family	182
Reproduction in the Present Family	184
Conclusion	226
Conclusions	229
The State's Role in Changing the Family Patterns	230
Hierarchy and the Limits of Family Change	237
Confucian Legacy plus Marxist Bias on the Gender Issue	239
The Direction of Change within the Family	245
References	254
Index	265

Preface

This book results from a reworking of my doctoral dissertation at the Department of Sociology, the University of Göteborg, Sweden. I would like to thank Göran Therborn – my dissertation tutor – who went through the earlier versions of the manuscript in great detail. Thanks to his reading and commenting, my many arguments were reconsidered and reformulated. I have tried to incorporate many of his invaluable suggestions, but I am afraid that the results are not fully satisfactory. I should like to thank him especially for his encouragement.

Edmund Dahlström and Rita Liljeström provided a great many thought-provoking comments on my manuscript, suggesting numerous valuable improvements. I would like to acknowledge here that they have greatly influenced my thinking. Rita Liljeström not only read and commented on my manuscript, but also helped in the initial contact with NIAS Publishing and, even before then, brought me to Sweden.

Last, but not least, I would like to thank Leena Höskuldsson, Gerald Jackson and Janice Leon of NIAS Publishing. This book would probably never have come out if it had not been for their hard work and patience.

PVB

Introduction

The family was traditionally regarded as one of the key institutions of the Vietnamese society. Almost everybody among the marriageable population was either married or wanted to be. The family satisfied nearly all the basic needs of one's life from the cradle to the grave. Attachment to the family was so strong that everything, including the concept of nation, was subordinated to the family in Vietnamese culture (Woodside, 1976: 28). In the words of a Vietnamese scholar, if one takes into consideration the fact that the pivotal force of this society was neither a political nor an economic institution, but the institution of the family, then the essential trait of the society resides in the preponderant influence of the family in all realms: religious, cultural and social (quoted in Le Thi Que, 1986: 3).

However, that is about the pre-1945 period. The half century since 1945 (the date that marks a great turning point in Vietnam's history) has witnessed probably the most fundamental socio-economic transformation not only at village level (Luong Van Hy, 1992: 163), but also at nation-wide level. Since coming to power that year, the Communist Party has been carrying out its radical socio-economic programmes to change society in accordance with its ideas of modernisation, first of all in the north of the country, and since 1975, in the whole country. That has led to dramatic changes in every aspect of society.

What about the family in these circumstances? How has the family changed, especially as the Communist Party espouses, as part of its ideology, the Marxist theory of the family, which affirms that the family must be transformed? The core idea of this theory is that most problems in family life are rooted in ownership of private property. That is why great efforts have been made to eliminate the root of the problem; collective arrangements have also been made to replace and/or transform the family. In view of all these changes, one might suppose that all problems have been eradicated. As a hero in the well-known novel by Ma Van Khang (1985) puts it, for quite a long time, one has had the impression that there is no longer anything left to discuss in relationships between father and children, husband and wife, and siblings. Nevertheless, does that really resolve the problems of the traditional family? Are there any problems inherent in the present one? In fact, especially after the American war (since 1975) a number of family problems have come to the fore. Many of them are remnants from the old-style family; others have been brought about by the changes that the family has undergone.

This study is about the family and its changes in a northern part of Vietnam, i.e., the Red River Delta. The aim is to examine how the family has changed under the impact of the recent social transformations of the last half century (1945–95). The study first seeks to put the family in a wider socio-cultural context. It does this by situating the traditional family within the social matrix of the first half of this century, when the traditional culture existed together with French influence, and next by relating the contemporary family to recent social changes. Thus the Vietnamese family is related to the wider socio-cultural context, and should be understood in this context. In other words, if the family is usually associated with the home, this study attempts to place what is going on in the home into the wider context of major transformations going on outside it.

Next, the present study seeks to compare the contemporary family to the traditional one in order to highlight the differences. The changed and unchanged traits become clear when the dynamics of transformation are examined. What kind of change is taking place? What are the causes of the change? The purpose of this study is to try to answer these questions. However, the study does not claim to provide a comprehensive overview of the family in every respect, especially if we bear in mind the vitality of the extended kinship network in Vietnam.

It could be said that in Vietnam, the family is a group of people who are related by blood and marriage ties; who often live together; and who co-operate economically to satisfy the basic needs of their life: production, consumption as well as those of human reproduction – childbearing, childraising, caring for the elderly, etc.[1] In its most common form, the family usually includes a man and a woman and their children, whether their own or adopted. It may or may not include other relatives. However, it is only a link of generational continuity and often keeps close ties with other relatives to guarantee this continuity. We shall see later that the family is viewed by its members mainly in terms of its temporal dimension and location: people emphasise the temporal continuity of lineage and the family. The family is just a link in the lineal, generational chain that has to be continued forever. Family relations compose of relations across time. In this sense, the family is understood and seen in relations with other (previous/next) generations. The central concern is the overlap of generations. To the Vietnamese, the past never absents from the present and the future; the family is the connecting link of all these. So it is necessary to specify the areas of the Vietnamese family that will form the focus of this study.

To facilitate the research, I decided to choose a selective number of issues and restrict myself to the relationships within the nuclear family, i.e., to areas generally regarded as the core of family bonds, namely the husband–wife and parent–child relations. More precisely, the parent–child relationship is dealt with from the perspective of reproduction. If looking at the family in terms of a cycle of domestic development, i.e., the sequence of events which marks the growth and decline of the domestic group (establishment, expansion, fission, and decline), this form is 'relatively easy to describe because growth within and between generations is kept to a minimum' (Robertson, 1991: 12). That is why Robertson has called this particular version of the domestic development the compact pattern: it has no more than two generations.

In Vietnamese practice, although the perception of the family is broad, the nuclear family is the most common form. This gives a practical basis for restricting our analysis within the nuclear family relationships. As for polygamy (which was legal in the traditional family), this concept of the nuclear form is also suitable, because the family still consisted of the same two subgroups; except for the fact that 'polygamy brings in extra people in the parental generation and significantly increases the number of children' (Robertson, 1991: 12–13). Nevertheless, apart from the above relationships within the nuclear family (spouse:spouse; parent:child), there is another relationship (sib:sib) which is no less important, but remains almost unstudied so far. Therefore leaving it out is unfortunately inevitable.

To emphasise the changes, I shall try to see the traditional family and the contemporary one in comparison. By 'traditional' I simply mean the family form of the period 1900–45, which was mainly rural and closely connected with traditional agriculture, which had existed for generations and remained little changed in many aspects. I also mean the family that was influenced by Eastern religions, first

Confucianism and other religions in Vietnam until 1945. The date of August 1945 is chosen as the turning point because it marks the most important change in the country's history; since then many radical developments have taken place (The Vietnamese Government, 1972; Huynh Kim Khanh, 1982; Marr, 1995). The family during the period 1900–45 could be termed as traditional, as will be clarified in Chapter One. As for the contemporary family, the main focus will be on the period between 1953 and early 1990s, because evidence about the period 1945–53 and about the very recent past is not available.

However, that does not exclude from this study the dichotomy of history given by a great divide theory, which makes a contrast between primitive communalism vs. capitalism, or military vs. industrial society, or theological vs. positive (scientific) societies characterised by the so-called mechanical solidarity on the one hand and organic solidarity on the other. We shall find the dichotomy in the outlook of the government established in 1945, when they evaluated the existing social system and started their programme of modernisation. They made a sharp distinction between tradition and modernity, even juxtaposed them (see Chapter Two). That has left deep fissures in social life and the family.

As to the area of study, I chose the Red River Delta – described as being 'one of the most densely populated and least safe regions in the world' in terms of it being an uncertain and dangerous natural environment (Jamieson 1993: 5).[2] As it is defined at present (Vu Tu Lap *et al.*, 1991: 7–8), an absolute majority of the population of the Delta lives in the countryside. This study restricts itself to the Viet ethnic group in order to simplify the research and focus more sharply on the main subgroup that practised a mixed religion (but not Catholicism because up to now Catholicism remains a differentiating factor in Vietnamese society). The Catholic family is quite different from the other types of Vietnamese family and will not be discussed here. (For further information on Catholic families, see Mai Huy Bich, 1995).

The Delta is a large, densely populated area. In Gourou's (1936/1955: 9–10) words, the Delta has

> an area somewhat too great and a population somewhat too numerous, for a thoroughgoing ... study performed by a single person. The scope is too large for a single inquirer to be able to observe everything himself in a few years and to give a definitive answer to all questions raised.
>
> (Gourou 1936/1955: 9–10)

It is extraordinarily difficult to capture the essence of familial changes over an extended time-span solely through empirical surveys. Therefore this study relies on the findings of different research works. Moreover there have been very few studies on the topic we are now examining. We have to dig around in research materials that deal mainly with different topics, yet which contain some relevant information. Availability of data has therefore been a determining factor in the focus of this study. This poses a number of problems.

The first one is how to evaluate available data and information. This is especially true of materials concerning the traditional family. When evaluating materials that touch upon questions of our own time, it is easy enough to conduct surveys or interviews to elicit responses on present-day behaviour and opinions, but that is not possible when we examine the past. As for materials related to the present family, there are a lot of common practices among Vietnamese sociologists that make it difficult to evaluate the results of their studies. When we review the Vietnamese literature related to the family, seeking to identify the methodological approach employed, we find that most studies do not specify their methodology whatsoever. A clear majority of the documents just present research results in form of figures, tables, etc., which makes their validity somewhat difficult to judge.

The second problem is the lack of other research findings which might form the basis of a comparison of changes within the family. Moreover, most studies about the traditional family have up to now been carried out from a historical perspective without any investigative fieldwork, and that is not all: when researching the traditional family, some scholars seem to ignore distinctions between, for example, rules and norms about family relations in the teachings of different religions (Confucianism, Buddhism, etc.) on the one hand, and practices on the other. How to distinguish between them is another question. Meanwhile, most of the studies about the present family have examined it in sociological-statistical terms without an in-depth historical dimension. In brief, to find out changes through comparison is difficult. As a result, some of the family change trends that are traced in this study may well require empirical investigation.

This study consists of four chapters. Chapter One addresses the starting point of family change: the period 1900–45. It is supposed to act as a yardstick for comparison with the post-1945 period. As an expert on family sociology points out, to weigh the extent and type of changes now taking place, it is necessary to examine the recent past; otherwise no trends can be seen (Goode, 1963: 6).

From the above argument, the importance of bringing the broad context, or external structures into the picture of family change becomes apparent. Chapter Two examines the socio-economic transformations of the twentieth century that have affected the family and changed it. To paraphrase another expert on family sociology (Morgan, 1985: 56), we may say that the family, marriage and sexuality are continually constructed by outside forces, hence the need to place family change in a wider context. The aim of Chapter Two is then to find those forces.

In Chapters Three and Four I switch the focus of discussion away from the social context of family change and on to small-scale interactions between family members. More precisely, in Chapter Three we shall see how the conjugal bonds in different domains of family life have changed. Chapter Four tries to address the parent–child bond, but mainly in terms of the meanings of having children for parents. Finally, in the conclusions I try to discover which factors really cause change within the family, and how the family in a Confucian society changed when it encountered the Marxist theory of the family.

NOTES

1   In this working definition of the family, I just mention some activities that are, in my view, basic for an overwhelming majority of families during the period under investigation.

2   I was born and grew up in the Red River Delta. As a matter of fact, I have so far never been to the South of Vietnam. One of the sources used in this study is Luong Van Hy's book (1992). He regards Son Duong village that he investigated as being outside the Delta. However, according to Vu Tu Lap *et al.* (1991: 7–9), Phong Chau district in which the village is situated belongs to the Delta administration. Moreover, Luong Van Hy himself recognises perfectly well that the village is 'like virtually all other rural communities in the Red River Delta' (1992: 1), not only in its landscape but also in many other respects.

CHAPTER ONE

The Traditional Family

This chapter is about the family from the beginning of this century to 1945. The task of studying family change entails looking at the traditional family, but that is not simple for the reason that to date there have been very few studies about the topic. Moreover, the question of the validity of available data and evidence is difficult to resolve.

Based on fragmented evidence from different sources, chiefly studies by historians' and ethnographers as well as literary works, this chapter is designed to give a general view of the family during the period under consideration, a basis for comparison to find out the changes that the family has undergone. This chapter attempts to place the traditional family in the context of the French influence on the one hand, and the long-standing traditions on the other hand. In so doing it seeks to analyse and explain why the traditional family was criticised by a great many participants in the liberation movement that was well under way at the end of the period, as well as the new government established later.

However, the chapter does not exhaust the comprehensive evidence about the traditional family. A more detailed view follows in the subsequent chapters. Here we shall first examine the French influence on the family, then evaluate it in relation to the family form shaped by long traditions. From this general view of the family in this period we go on to examine how it later changes.

THE FRENCH INFLUENCE

The establishment of French rule at the end of the nineteenth century brought about some changes for which the Vietnamese paid a heavy price, especially between 1915 and 1925 (Buttinger,

1967: 160). These were the construction of roads, railways, and coal mines; the establishment of small-scale industrial enterprises; the peasant migrations; and an increased economic dependence on the world market. Under French rule, the old civil service examination system that recruited the members of the Vietnamese bureaucracy was eliminated, and replaced by the new education system based on the French curriculum and the romanised script (*chu quoc ngu*), not the Chinese characters (Nguyen The Anh, 1970). All those changes led to fundamental transformations in the social structure.

The traditional society is often said to have consisted of the following four categories: Confucian scholars, peasants, artisans, and traders. The scholars and peasants were of prime importance; artisans and traders were small in number, occupied low ranks, and played an insignificant role in social life. However, like many other agricultural societies, the traditional one in Vietnam consisted of mainly two categories: upper and lower classes. As Buttinger (1967: 160) has put it, precolonial Vietnam was a society consisting of a single class ruled by an educated bureaucracy. There was no middle class like in modern Western societies (Dao Duy Anh, 1938/1992: 373; Buttinger, 1967: 116). Under the impact of French rule, the Confucian scholars lost their predominant role, though their prestige was still maintained to some extent. As a result of the French colonial economic policy, since the beginning of this period, two new social categories gradually appeared in urban areas: the middle class and the working class (Dao Duy Anh, 1938/1992; Nguyen The Anh, 1970).

TWO NEW FAMILY TYPES

In terms of the family, this period saw some remarkable changes. The extended family ideal began to break down; the concept of romantic love blossomed among some young, French-educated people in urban areas; a new form of marriage (between French men and Vietnamese women) appeared; and some distinctive small groups – for example the Vietnamese women who served as wives, mistresses and prostitutes to French soldiers, and administrators – emerged (Woodside, 1976). Nevertheless, the most significant change was the appearance of two absolutely new types of urban family: the middle class and the working class.

According to the historian Dao Duy Anh's (1938/1992: 374–376) vivid description, middle-class families were wealthy (by middle class he meant senior officials, landowners, big traders, businessmen, contractors, medical doctors, lawyers and engineers). Many members received a French education and enjoyed a high social rank. They adopted a Western style of dress and housing, and had Western facilities in everyday life. They followed Western practices (greeting each other by shaking hands, embracing, etc.) in social communication. Many of them married freely, and lived separately from their parents after the wedding. A limited number of women from this class were French-educated. They adopted a Western style of dress which showed off their bodies; they freely embraced their male friends, or even danced with them – all this was previously unheard of in a society where the Confucian maxim *Nam nu thu, thu bat than* [Men and women should remain physically distant] was still powerful. Some of these women had jobs; so they were no longer under the control of their mothers-in-law and their husbands. The children of this family type were often sent to France for their education.

As for working-class families, they were a totally new phenomenon. Nonetheless, the study of Nguyen The Anh (1970: 257) has pointed out that those families were of peasant origin (they became industrial workers as a result of harsh recruitment measures brought in by the French), and that they kept in close touch with their relatives in the native villages. A great many workers did not bring their families with them; they often left them behind, and supported them by sending part of their wages home. They usually went back to their villages during the strikes that were caused by brutal working conditions and low pay, and also at harvest time (when labour was much in demand) or for festivals. Since working conditions in the towns were uniformly grim, there was a tendency to gravitate back to one's home village whenever possible (Marr, 1981: 29). We have little evidence to establish the accuracy of these accounts. They also tell us that only a small number of mineworkers and industrial workers became permanent members of the working class.

LIMITS OF THE FRENCH INFLUENCE ON FAMILY PATTERNS

There are conflicting evaluations of the French influence in general. On the one hand, Paul Mus, a French researcher well known for his book *Vietnam: la sociologie d'une guerre* (quoted in Nguyen The Anh, 1970: 228) holds the view that the traditional Vietnamese society was not affected strongly by colonialism; the latter just added some new elements. On the other hand, Buttinger (1967) supposes that the economic changes under the French rule destroyed the traditional Vietnamese society 'as effectively as the conquest of Indochina had destroyed the political structure of mandarinal Vietnam' in the sense that 'these changes resulted in the rise of social classes unknown in precolonial Vietnam' (ibid.: 160). By new social classes he means an upper class of capitalists that was, however, largely foreign and outside of Vietnamese society, a small middle class, a relatively large intelligentsia, and a working class.

Nevertheless, it would be safe to suppose that the French influence varied from domain to domain, and was seen mainly in the above social strata of urban areas. Different studies (Dao Duy Anh, 1938/1992: 376; Nguyen The Anh, 1970: 254) showed that the middle class was still weak; the working class bore many characteristics reminiscent of peasant origin. Buttinger (1967: 193) quotes the official count of workers in the whole country by the 1930s as 220,000; 'if this figure were correct, it would mean that only one person out of one hundred Vietnamese was a salaried worker.' Nonetheless, he points out that 'all its members were former peasants; what is more important is that the majority would sooner or later become peasants again' (ibid.: 194–195). As for the middle class, not only was it 'numerically small, but it also was of little social importance' (ibid: 196).

Altogether, the new classes were insignificant in comparison to the absolute majority of rural population. As late as 1936 it was not too difficult to find a large village, not too far from the town, where young children had never seen a single European face and where no French administrators had ever set foot since the beginning of the colonial period (Woodside, 1976: 118). New institutions coexisted with old ones. Confucian conventions still existed although they had lost much of their vitality.

As for the family relationships, one may say that during the period many old patterns changed very little among the overwhelming majority of population, even among the above-mentioned two family types. Marr tells us that although members of the middle class thought of themselves as urbanites, and tried to model themselves on their Parisian counterparts, complete with champagne, fashionable furniture and clothing, dinner parties, government medals, and advisory council positions, most of them still depended on rural income, many had concubines, and many arranged socially advantageous marriages for their children. The same source also tells us that in the countryside, despite the commercial character of relationship with tenants and wage labourers, most village landlords thought of themselves as inheritors of the traditions of the local literati and the village notables. They tended to be staunch upholders of status hierarchy, traditional festivals, rites for village tutelary deities, and patriarchal discipline (Marr, 1981: 26–27). We have so far no evidence to refute this; in fact what evidence we do have (including literary works), strongly supports this argument.

During this period, there was a gradual increase in the number of girls attending school, most of them came from a minority of upper- or middle-class families. By 1930, according to French administrators' recordings, there were 40,752 girls undergoing public or private instruction out of a total of 435,782 primary pupils (Marr, 1981: 206). Although these educational statistics demonstrate an unprecedented phenomenon, the significance is somewhat diminished when we remember that this was a country of about twenty million people. According to the above researcher, a new market had developed in textbooks written for female students in the new script. Nevertheless, the predominant topic of textbooks for female students were the traditional feminine norms 'three submissions' and 'four virtues', which were the dogmas taken from orthodox Confucian texts. The first textbook of this kind (with a print-run of 1,000 copies) was printed in Hanoi in 1918, entitled *Nu hoc luan ly tap doc* [Reading lessons in feminine moral conduct] by Phan Dinh Giap. In the next decade, about twenty-five other such texts, written especially for young women, appeared for sale; quantities ranged from 1,000 copies per edition to 10,000 (Marr, 1981: 207). In other words, the new educational developments and the new script were just the means to communicate the traditional norms to young, French-educated female students.

So in cities, many women received something that had eluded them in the past: an education. However, this did not always lead to free and self-determined marriages. By contrast, the custom of the bride-price[1] was maintained, even strengthened, in accordance with the education. A study by Woodside provides the following evidence.

 Thuy An, a female novelist and poetess, noted sardonically in a 1933 Hanoi journal article that the higher educational qualifications of these girls 'were simply absorbed into the mercantile ferment of old-style family marriage politics'. For those girls who have some learning, and a capacity of making their own living, the bride-price becomes increasingly expensive. In addition to computing the value of their own efforts at raising the daughters and giving moral instruction, their mothers count in addition the extra efforts at giving them some education ... If one adds together all these efforts, the bride-price amounts to a formidable sum of money, and terrifies the grooms when they hear it. In a middle-class family that has a daughter about to be given in marriage, 'the go-between bargains, the mother persists, and the daughter is no different from an article of merchandise displayed in a market, with sellers and buyers agreeing on a price'.

(Woodside, 1976: 99–100)

If this is accurate, in the lively description of the haggling there are some points indicating that the old family system had not yet been destroyed. First, married daughters – even without any level of education – were a net gain for the family they married into, because they no longer contributed to their family of origin. If they had some education, then that would be an extra merit. Second, although there was some modernisation in the rituals of the wedding (e.g. cars would be rented for the wedding procession), its purpose was to keep face and maintain the social standing of the bride's family with other people in the community, not to serve the interests of the young people concerned. Third, the go-between still played the same role in a marriage as before.

We can see the vestiges of the traditional family from other sources. It is no accident that this period witnessed the appearance of many novels and short stories based on family issues. A number of them were award-winning; in general they provoked an explosive reaction from readers for their realism. The typical plot often involved a young man and a girl falling in love, but then being forced to part due to social restrictions, and being driven into loveless marriages. Young people at this time were absorbing French ideas about romantic love, but they encountered the strong disapproval of older people. In the transitional period between the old and the new, the new ideas were not yet strong enough to vanquish the old. As a result, young people had to give up their romantic love or choose another option, like committing suicide or running away from home. Such events were not merely works of fiction. In big cities, there were often media accounts about parent–child conflicts; abandonment of the wife by the husband; young boys and girls running together away from home; and suicides committed by young people. That was why the historian Dao Duy Anh (1938/1992: 133) reached the conclusion that the Vietnamese family had to transform in step with the new era.

There were a number of reasons for the slow rate of change. The first one was the vitality and the persistence of traditional norms. Since the 1930s the traditional family as an institution had been encouraged by a number of French rulers. Its autocratic, hierarchical nature was useful for the colonial government because it provided them with a cheap source of social control and political stability (Woodside, 1976: 96–97). If we can lend any credence to literary works, it is worth pausing to consider the famous novel *Doan tuyet* [Breaking the Ties] by Nhat Linh (1935). In it the French-educated Vietnamese heroine has to struggle against an old-fashioned family. Finally she is taken to court, and made to face a conservative French prosecutor. The writer makes the prosecutor admit the growing identification of interests between the colonial government and the supporters of the hierarchical Confucian family (Jamieson, 1993: 143).

That may be open to question, but it cannot be ruled out that from the 1930s onwards, the French rulers deliberately kept the traditional family to serve their interests. Especially during the period 1940–45, according to one source, the Vichy slogan 'Work-Family-Fatherland' was hoisted on banners and splashed on walls because to the mind of the Governor-General Decoux, it corresponded marvellously with the deep-seated and traditional aspirations of the Vietnamese masses, and tallied with Confucian morality (Marr, 1995: 72–73).

FRENCH ECONOMIC POLICY AND THE PEASANT FAMILY

Probably the clearest impact of the French rule on the overwhelming majority of families was the colonial economic policy that aimed at the capitalist exploitation of land, labour, and natural resources. That exacerbated the problems the peasants faced in maintaining their precarious livelihoods. It should be pointed out that the colonial policy was not static, but changed in response to both the altering needs of the colonial economy and Vietnamese reactions. In the summary of Luong Van Hy (1992: 43), this policy included the following measures: direct and indirect taxation were introduced; the payment of taxes was converted from kind to cash; indigenous land was conceded to colonial settlers for the development of major cash crops; labour was appropriated through a corvée system, and repressive labour laws were introduced to keep down labour costs for capitalist agromineral ventures.

Meanwhile studies have emphasised the subsistence orientation of peasants in the Delta. In the precise words of Gourou, agriculture here is 'an agriculture of subsistence which is limited exclusively to feeding those who practise it' (quoted in Scott, 1976: 22). Scott has characterised it (ibid.: 25) as having little land, large families, highly variable yields (because of the vagaries of the weather), and few outside opportunities in overpopulated regions. To borrow the imagery of R. H. Tawney, the position of the rural population 'is that of a man standing permanently up to the neck in water, so that even a ripple is sufficient to drown him' (Tawney quoted in Scott, 1976: 1).

Therefore, the peasant family as a unit of production as well as a unit of consumption had to adopt the so-called 'subsistence ethic', as Scott has observed. In his view, unlike a capitalist enterprise, the peasants' 'hand-to-mouth' existence forced them to follow the 'safety first' principle. This meant that emphasis was placed on minimising the risk of disaster, not on maximising the average return (Scott, 1976: 17–18). Scott goes on to tell us that peasant families also had to look for ways to survive, including tightening their belts; making use of small trades, e.g. handicrafts; moving around as casual wage labourers; and relying on institutions outside the nuclear family. The last might include kinsmen, particularly bilateral kindred, neighbours, and villagers (ibid.: 26–27).

To avoid being left on their own, families often engaged in social arrangements, like patterns of reciprocity. First, labour was exchanged in a reciprocal pattern, not in co-operative production on a large scale. Second, families often participated in a complicated ritual system that was quite costly in terms of economically rational choice theory that French-educated people supported and promoted. Rites of passage that were often carried out by families became occasions for reciprocal exchanges between villagers according to the principle of give and take. Consequently, a lot of families got into heavy debt. That explained why there was a strong tendency among revolutionaries and reformists to transform radically the ritual system. Luong Van Hy (1992: 59, 85) has described how costly the rituals were and how the attempts at ritual reforms made by French-educated people failed. The reason was that those intellectuals saw the rituals only in terms of a waste of money; they neglected the social meanings that lay behind them. By the same token, rituals later came under heavy fire from the new government of 1945, as we shall see in the next chapter.

Nonetheless, the French rule made things much worse for peasant families. Most of the available sources tell us that taxes were a heavy burden; moreover the shift from taxes in kind to cash exacerbated the situation. Different researchers agree that in addition to the uncertainties of the weather (drought, flood, etc.), the peasant families were now forced to face the uncertainties of the local market and international demand for rice. At tax collection times, when almost all the desperate peasants sought to sell paddy and rice (even land if necessary) to raise the necessary money, the prices fell dramatically. As a result, a great number of land-owning peasants were turned into tenants overnight, while the emergence of huge individual landholdings became a common occurrence.

The social differentiation became more acute. In the words of Dumont (quoted in Popkin, 1979: 154–155), 'colonial rule and development did not simply bring wealth to a few ... they brought wealth at the expense of the majority of the peasants – the rich got richer, *and* the poor got poorer.' Available data (Buttinger, 1967: 168; Ngo Vinh Long, 1973: 19; Popkin, 1979: 155–156) may differ significantly but they have one thing in common: a great amount of the land in the Delta was owned by landlords; therefore most peasant families became landless; they had to work as agricultural labourers and as tenant-farmers and sharecroppers. Their working conditions were terrible; their wages were extremely low; and they had to live in constant hunger, culminating finally in the tragic famine of 1945. After the Japanese troops invaded Vietnam (1940), things went from bad to worse. As a result, two million people died of starvation in the whole country in 1945.

Paul Mus (quoted in Luong Van Hy, 1992: 48) reveals that peasants' livelihoods were sustained within a subsistence-oriented framework, but their taxes were calculated on the terms of the capitalist world economy. More importantly, as the different researchers (Scott, Popkin) have pointed out, the precolonial tax exemption and reduction in cases of natural calamity were no longer granted. The class relationship between landlords and peasants eventually deteriorated; instead of its traditional patronage aspects, it became quite arbitrary.

The studies of Ngo Vinh Long (1973), Le Thi Nham Tuyet (1975) and Eisen (1984) have demonstrated how brutal this class relationship was. Many peasants were forced to take desperate measures: the sale of children; the giving away of daughters as concubines and sons as slaves was often the only alternative to the complete break-up of the whole family, as Gourou and Dumont (quoted in Popkin, 1979: 152) observed. The following account of an old woman highlights the situation of just such a family in 1918. In her youth her father did not have the wherewithal to pay his poll tax. Consequently her parents had to mortgage her labour for five piasters to a wealthy relative for whom she worked for twelve long years (Luong Van Hy, 1992: 45). This was just one of the countless cases.

Thus social differentiation and class relationship penetrated the kinship network as well. It was common enough for relatives to exploit one another as landlords and tenants, masters and servants. That in part explained why some people, including communists, overreacted to kinship: in their view, class relation was the guiding thread of history. That would lead to extremes later. In fact, the evidence provided by Luong Van Hy (1992: 65) shows that although class differentiation reached its peak during this period, kinship was still an irreplaceable source of assistance in the form of mutual loans of money or rice whenever necessary. It was also an organising force even among the anti-colonial movement (ibid.: 95). It could be suggested that if the role of organising force was not common, the role of assistance source was quite widespread.

The historian Dao Duy Anh (1938/1992: 360) demonstrated that the tradition of mutual assistance and solidarity among members of the same lineage still persisted: *Co du thi bo vao ho, tung thieu thi nho vao ho* [Give the surplus to your lineage and rely on your lineage when in need]. In fact, apart from territorial and voluntary associations that were established in almost every village and offered some limited mutual help, the family and kinship were the main institutions of support during all the ups and downs of the human life-cycle. That was the main reason why people were concerned above all with family issues, not those of their country and society, as Dao Duy Anh (1938/1992: 363–364) complained. This irreplaceable role of the family and kinship in part explains many of the family characteristics that will be discussed later: the hierarchy which favoured the older generations, and the great emphasis on filial piety, etc. Robertson (1991: 68) has explained 'gerontocratic' tendencies – the concentration of political and economic control in the hands of the elderly – in the light of the need to assure adequate pensioning services.

Moreover, kinsmen still had to be responsible for one another when it came to the payment of taxes. If a poor peasant could not pay his taxes, another member of his family had to be responsible for his 'share'. If no member of the family could pay, the delinquent taxpayer's possessions were auctioned off, then his family's possessions. In case all these measures failed, the peasant or one of his children would become enslaved to anyone willing to pay his tax (Popkin, 1979: 146). Another source has confirmed this: if a man failed to pay in time, his brother or adult family member would be arrested and tortured in the communal house courtyard (Luong Van Hy, 1992: 64). That meant that even under French rule, the traditional principle of mutual responsibility of the whole family community continued to exist; the system of personal responsibility before the law was not recognised. In other words, with the principle of mutual responsibility, the authorities continued the long-standing traditional communitarian character of the family, whereby if one of the members broke the law, all the others had to be punished. This feature of the traditional society was not undermined even when the French law (which incorporated the principle of individual responsibility) was introduced in some areas.

In this context, it is understandable that the failure of numerous peasant revolts and isolated violent acts against the French resulted in the emergence of modern anticolonial movements. The collapse of these movements in 1930 reinforced the prominence of the Communist Party, whose founders were able to work and study in France, then bring back to Vietnam the Marxist–Leninist theory with its strong emphasis on the class dynamic. Their targets were dual: first, the French colonialists and second, the landlords together with everything that could be defined as 'feudal' (*phan de, phan phong*). Their aims were national independence and improved socio-economic welfare.

In sum, the French influence on family patterns could be seen mainly in the two social strata in urban areas; moreover, within these strata, some of the old features continued to exist alongside the new ones. As for the overwhelming majority of population, they lived in the countryside and remained attached to their traditional family patterns (Le Thi Que, 1986: 6). The French influence was seen in the appearance of some new family types, but not in the change of the family patterns among the population as a whole.

SOME CHARACTERISTICS OF THE TRADITIONAL FAMILY

We shall turn our attention at this point to some general characteristics of the traditional family that could be seen in the majority of population, especially in rural areas. However, we need to keep in mind that within the overall patterns described here, there may be differences resulted from the diversity of social groups.

COLLECTIVE COMMUNITY

The most marked feature of the traditional family was the collective community. The hazardous natural environment and the often uncertain social one demanded the subordination of the individual to the collective discipline of the family and, to some extent, the village. The collective community was highlighted by the absolutely dominant influence of the family as a whole *vis-à-vis* every one of its component members. The individual was not an independent entity; there was no individual in the Western sense, and certainly no free individual. Every facet of life was bound up with the family to which a person owed complete allegiance. While the *raison d'être* of the Western family may be to produce and support the individual, whose maturity will signal the attainment of its objective, in the Vietnamese family the *raison d'être* of each individual member was to continue, maintain, and serve the family, and first of all people of the older generations.

Ideally members of a family were expected to subordinate their personal interests to those of the family as a whole. Personal interests could not run counter to the family interests but should comply with the latter. Each person had to discipline him- or herself, and subdue his or her personal desires and aspirations if those ran counter to the communal standards. Communality was upheld and individualism was negated: therefore conformity was emphasised. Senior members of every family repeated again and again the following proverbs to the younger members: *Khon loi sao bang gioi dan* [Individual excellence is not as good as group success]; *Xau deu hon tot loi* [Equal mediocrity is better than exceptional goodness]; *Tha chet mot dong con hon song mot nguoi* [Better for the whole group to die than for one person to survive]. From childhood everyone was trained in the sense of communality, considering communal assessment the highest standard, and modifying their behaviour and attitude accordingly, not by reasoning out for themselves what was right or wrong. Otherwise a person would be subject to 'social disgrace' and 'losing face'. The opinion of people around was very important. Disciplines were based on what the surrounding people, particularly the 'significant others', approved or considered appropriate (Mai Huy Bich, 1993: 43–45; Dao Duy Anh, 1938/1992: 363).

Within the family a sense of solidarity was strong. The family members would help one another in times of need and adopt a united front *vis-à-vis* the outside world, whatever their internal differences might be. Woodside (1976: 95) has penetratingly observed that the traditional family was a little like a modern business corporation: it survived the deaths of its individual members or 'shareholders' at any point in time. It was designed to be a permanent corporate group. Each individual member had to serve it first and foremost.

It must be pointed out that the communitarian character of the family found expression not only in the relationships between living members, but also in those between dead, living and unborn ones; between generations along the temporal axis. The family was understood as a human community stemming from ancestors often going back four or five generations, or as long as Vietnamese families could remember and worship (Do Thai Dong, 1991; Nguyen Tu Chi, 1991). This community extends through the present into future. In this sense, the family was more than a group of people; it was a continuing entity carrying on from generation to generation. This human community was of a special kind that could be called a diachronic and generational community. Each member was not an independent person, but a link in the generational chain. (S)he had numerous obligations and limited rights in this diachronic community, which may be summarised in a few words: to serve this community was the first and foremost virtue. By dividing these obligations (and rights) into the ones directed towards the older generations on the one hand, and the ones directed at the younger generation on the other, we may say that the primary duties were towards the older generations (Mai Huy Bich, 1993: 48–50). The main obligations and rights are presented below.

Everybody should be permeated with the concept of origin. Everything that an individual enjoyed in his life was not the result of his individual efforts, but an inheritance from, and blessing of his ancestors. That was why a young student who obtained an academic degree of French education after trying three times supposed that it was thanks to his close relatives, including his father's progressive attitude, his senior mother's kindness, and his intelligence inherited from his mother's father, who was a mandarin and a doctorate degree holder (*pho bang*) (Luong Van Hy, 1992: 68). That meant that the French education did not liberate him from the traditional view.

Traditions stipulated that everybody should take care of and obey the older generations while they were alive, then worship and revere them with appropriate rituals after their death (in addition to supplying them with some symbolic necessities to enable them to survive in the other world). Each family member should take care of the tombs of his or her ancestors and ensure that they were covered with 'green grass and incense smoke' (*xanh ngon co, do nen huong*). It was a sin of filial omission to leave a tomb in a state of neglect or without a carer. Filial piety then was a paramount responsibility but in response, the older generations – even after their death – would continue to protect and bless the younger ones in different ways. For instance, based on geomancy, people held the view that a certain locational co-ordinate of a tomb would render either blessing or disaster to future descendants of the deceased person.

Those standards of behaviour towards the older generations served as the social adhesive connecting people not only with their forbears, but also with their native land, where the tombs of their ancestors were located. This sometimes resulted in a person feeling unable to leave his or her native village, no matter what the reason. Although natural disasters, economic crises, and so on, continued to happen, and the population pressure increased, not only did the unemployed refuse to move and uproot themselves in the search for a job, but young people, too, looked for work in their overpopulated home areas. Having lost ancestor tombs in their native villages meant that there could be no memories and no sense of roots, even imaginary ones, anywhere else. That would make them miserable. By staying in their own areas, they could take care of their parents, their ancestors' tombs, and remain in their native cultural milieus.

To fulfil his duty towards the older generations and his ancestors, a man not only had to meet all his present obligations, but also had to produce male offspring to continue in the future all the tasks he was currently performing. Otherwise the older generations would be anxious until their last breath. As for the obligations towards the younger generations, there was a cause-and-effect relation between generations in the sense that what one member did would affect the whole generational community. Because of this, the social behaviour of one person was deemed not to be his own responsibility; the consequences were not only rendered to himself, but also to future generations in the diachronic community. A Vietnamese saying went: *Doi cha an man, doi con khat nuoc* [When the father eats too salty food, his children will be thirsty].

So everybody should, in their lifetime, accumulate virtues, store up merit (*tu nhan, tich duc*), be benevolent, show piety to others, and strive to do good deeds, in order to hand down blessings to posterity. Moreover, a person should avoid bad or irresponsible acts, which would bring disaster to the future generations. That was why rich parents tried to leave lands and properties to their children, and scholars tried to leave a good reputation as their legacy. Those who had little to leave also did their best to help their children to build up a home. If they were too poor to do so, they tried to improve themselves, accumulate virtues, and avoid committing sins in order to pass something on to the younger generations. They did so because they not only hoped to be supported by their children later, in their old age, but also thought that this was their responsibility to their children.

This belief could be seen in people with little formal education, particularly old Buddhist women. The following narrative is about the belief of an old woman.

> Her son had received two death sentences from the French authorities for having participated in an anticolonial uprising. After learning the news of his two death sentences, his senior mother consoled him by telling him not to be afraid because she believed that their family had accumulated a lot of merit through their compassionate Buddhist acts. That, in her view, would save her son from being beheaded. Upon hearing this, a French investigator laughed in disbelief.
> (Luong Van Hy, 1992: 114)

The Frenchman, from the other side of a cultural abyss, failed to understand her way of reasoning. This story, with its idea of storing up merit for one's descendants, tells us how the transgenerational community was understood in Vietnam.

The next story shows how strongly embedded was the communitarian character at the family level.

> In 1929, there was a fight between a landlord and the labourers whom he had hired. It had been agreed that the wage was to consist solely of a day's food. The labourers claimed the right to share the evening meal with their families, but the landlord argued that if they did not eat the meal themselves, they would be less able to work the next day. In other words, the men thought not only of themselves, but also of their families; they even denied themselves for the sake of their families. At last, the landlord had to give way because the men acted according to the customs.
> (Popkin, 1979: 157–158)

It could be said that the family ties were still quite close-knit despite the economic hardship and crisis endured under French rule.

In response to the individual member's submission to the strict, sometimes arbitrary, control by the family, and the sacrifice of individual interests to the supreme interests of the whole family, the latter tried to satisfy all the fundamental needs of its members, and serve as a reliable support base for their whole life, from infancy to old age and death. In other words, the family performed all the basic functions for its members. That was why people were so attached to their families.

Hierarchy

But despite the communal solidarity among the family members, the family structure was also characterised by a sharp hierarchy. Everyone occupied a certain position in the order of precedence based on generation, age, and gender. Furthermore, the hierarchy was very clear-cut, and strictly defined. Father, mother, older brother, and older sister were at the top of the hierarchy; children and younger siblings occupied a lower ranking. This could be seen in the relation between discursive practices and power structure within the family: unlike the English language, in Vietnamese a sharp distinction based on the order of birth is made between siblings. There are separate terms of kinship and terms of address for older brother (*anh*) and older sister (*chi*), while there is only one term for younger siblings (*em*) to express the lesser importance of those people, although the term needs a double clarification by adding a gender word in each case: *em trai* for younger brother, *em gai* for younger sister. Those who were older must be addressed and treated with respect, and they really exerted some power over the younger ones. Otherwise, it would be quite confusing, disordered and therefore unacceptable. However, when translated into English, these subtle distinctions of rank are often lost entirely by their rendition as simply 'brother' and 'sister'.

The order of precedence thus imposed heavily on two kinds of people: first, those who belonged to younger generations and ages (children, younger siblings) and, second, those who belonged to the female sex (wife, daughters, and sisters). This was not confined to the nuclear family, but extended to the lineage. Everyone was connected not only with his parents and siblings in his family of origin, then with his spouse and children in his family of procreation, but also with other people in his lineage through the older generations. All those relationships were woven together, creating a complex network of relatives. Everyone must know who his parents, grandparents, and forebears were; their places in the order of precedence; where his own place was, and how to behave appropriately to each family member. For instance, from early childhood everyone was taught to know who this male or that female relative was; whether they were of superior, inferior or equal rank; whether a close or distant relative; how to address them and refer to oneself in relation to them; etc. (Nguyen Hong Phong, 1978).

The terms of address denoted exactly the other person's order of generation and family rank, and whether that person belonged to one's maternal or paternal side. The kin terminology also included various self-referential terms, which differed according to the person whom one was addressing, and the relationship with that person in terms of hierarchy. Vietnamese people considered that the proper usage of terms of reference to family members involved not only order and social etiquette, but also real behaviour and sentiments. As Le Thi Que (1986: 16) has explained, correct terms of address were an expression of family solidarity, and a proper observance of order. If a family member used a wrong kinship term when addressing other relatives, that would be considered an indication of lack of family order, and therefore a lack of filial piety.

It is interesting to point out here that the term of the first person, I (*toi*), was rarely used in reference to oneself within the family, particularly by the inferior to the superior. To refer to oneself as *toi* was to tell the other person that one was not pleased with him, or that one did not consider him to be a family member. The term *toi* destroyed the bilateral relations between the interlocutors. Just as the pronoun 'I', as used by English-speaking people, served to individualise the user, the pronoun *toi* as used by Vietnamese had the reverse effect (Le Thi Que, 1986: 17). Thus, a child never referred to himself as anything but *con* [your child] when speaking to his parents, and *chau* [your grandchild] when speaking to his grandparents. By doing so, the person continually reminded himself that he was in a specific order to others, symbolising thereby that he existed only in relation to others (Le Thi Que, 1986: 17). Even in late adulthood a person had to continue to use *con* [your child] for self-reference in speech interaction with his parents. Luong Van Hy (1992: 228) is correct in his remark that such a linguistic usage highlights the hierarchical nature of the interaction.

In brief, the hierarchical character of the Vietnamese family could be presented in a few words: age-respecting and mainly male-oriented. As a proverb puts it, you had to know exactly who was above you and who was below in the family order so that you could yield to those below, and respect those above (*tren kinh, duoi nhuong*). A popular saying went: 'Above has to be above, and beneath has to be beneath' (*Tren phai ra tren, duoi phai ra duoi*).

We can see through the following story what kind of behaviour the hierarchy of the traditional family caused.

> A man joined a secret movement to fight against the French rule in 1929–30. His comrades wanted to use his house to make bombs but they had to persuade his senior mother to agree, because they knew that she was the most senior family member in the house at the time. Once she had agreed, nobody in the family could object. Other members of the family, including not only the females, but also junior male ones, did not dare to object, although they knew it was dangerous if the colonial authorities discovered what was going on. As for the wives, they had to follow the Confucian maxim of the three obediences: 'When at home, obey your father; after marriage, obey your husband; after the death of your husband, obey your sons'.
>
> (Luong Van Hy, 1992: 92)

Typical examples of family community and hierarchy could be found in family rituals. The Vietnamese culture is characterised by a large number of rituals, often performed at the family level. For instance, on the anniversary of a parent's death, all the sons and their families had to get together at the eldest son's home to celebrate. It was the duty of every family member to keep in mind the dates of the death anniversaries to gather together with other relatives and worship their common ancestors. Forgetting those dates or being a wilful absentee on such occasions showed a lack of piety to dead ancestors and an arrogance to living relatives. Those death anniversaries were very meaningful to living relatives. For the adult members they provided an opportunity to get together, perhaps to patch up quarrels, to recall the old days, or to relate to the younger generations the past glories and deeds of their common ancestors. This was the chance for the young to be involved in family rituals, to get acquainted with one another, and to learn of the numerous ties that bound them together.

> In other words, they served to renew and strengthen family ties, promote intrafamily relationships ... One has to attend one of these family gatherings to understand the intense emotional attachment that Vietnamese feel for their families.
>
> (Le Thi Que, 1986: 22).

That means that the sense of community was quite strong here. At the same time the hierarchy was also strict. Le Thi Que continues:

A member, whatever his social status, finds his place in front of the ancestor altar and at the feasting table determined on the one hand by the place he occupies in the order of generation, and on the other by the order number he holds in his own family. (ibid.)

Nevertheless, it must be said that while there is some truth in this picture, it cannot be the whole truth. The author has forgotten the other side of the coin: in some cases there was a contradiction between siblings, things did not go in the way described here. However, community and hierarchy in those rituals were undeniable.

The ritual meals were another example. At the usual family meal, everyone would wait for the absent members to return so that the whole family could eat together. Even in poor families where there was less emphasis on rituals, children usually did not start to eat until they had said a few words respectfully to request (*moi*) all their superiors around to start the meal. They made this request according to the established order of precedence; they must not reverse or break this order, for instance they must not mention the parents first. Instead, they must mention the grandparents first, then the parents, etc. When leaving the eating place, they must say a few words to excuse themselves. According to Phan Thi Dac (quoted in Mai Huy Bich, 1993: 51), those rituals were carefully observed in all families. In well-to-do families or those of high social status, children were not allowed to start to eat before the adults. In this way they were trained to control their hunger, a natural instinct, and to learn the proper way of taking a meal, in an atmosphere imbued with communitas and a sense of generational hierarchy.

Very often the whole family sat around a tray of food with a big pot of rice. Each person possessed only a pair of chopsticks and a bowl as their individual things. All the rest, including various dishes and sauce, were for common use (not divided into personal rations). The senior members approved of the junior members' respectful requests, gave small children the best dishes, and received their thanks. This picture served as a concrete and familiar symbol of the harmonious, ordered family community, and represented the strong attraction of the home to every Vietnamese. On the other hand, it should be pointed out the obligations of this family hierarchy weighed most heavily on the younger generations and women.

Patrilineal family

Following the system of tracing descents that has prevailed until now, kinship is attributed through the father. It is through this system that ancestor worship is performed (see Chapter Four). Consequently, in the traditional family, polygyny was practised to continue the male line, and having son(s) was emphasised. Resources were located in favour of sons and other patrilineal relatives. The strong emphasis on the clear-cut distinction between patrilineal and matrilineal relatives was obvious in the kinship terminology used in reference to 'uncle' and 'aunt'. In some areas there was a strong terminological distinction between the father's and the mother's siblings. Luong Van Hy (1989: 745) has noticed that one used the term *bac* for father's elder brothers; *chu* for father's younger brothers; and *co* for father's sisters. Meanwhile, one used the term *cau* for mother's brothers and *di* for mother's sisters. That is correct, but there might be variations depending on the region.

However, each Vietnamese still kept his relationships with the people of his mother's lineage. He belonged to two *ho* [lineages]: *ho noi* ['interior lineage' or the father's] and *ho ngoai* ['exterior lineage' or the mother's]. Of course, the lineage on one's paternal side was accorded priority in its claims upon one's affections and service, etc. Nevertheless, that did not mean the Vietnamese family neglected the kinship network of the mother's side. Morals and customs required everybody to respect the members of the mother's side and give them certain considerations in terms of observance of mourning rites, visiting, moral support, and financial help.

In return, one could call on members of both lineages for moral and material support. The popular saying *say cha con chu, say me bu di* [When your father passes away, there is still the paternal uncle for you to rely on; when your mother passes away, the maternal aunt will nurse you] has been quoted by Le Thi Que (1986: 15) to demonstrate one's affinity with both lineages. By the same token, another saying goes: *chau ba noi, toi ba ngoai* [The child is the descendant of the paternal grandmother, but it is the maternal grandmother who bears the greatest burden of care]. The woman maintained not only contact with her natal relatives, but also the surname of her father upon marriage, and kept ritual obligations towards the members of her natal relatives. For example, she was expected to bring her children to her parents' home to attend important death anniversaries in her natal family (Le Thi Que, 1986: 20). In this sense, the male-oriented model in the Vietnamese kinship was not absolute; there was also the non-male-oriented model (Luong Van Hy, 1989: 744–749).

Patrilocal residence pattern and its variant

Marriage required a bride to go and live with the groom's family. In general, once she married, she severed the ties that attached her to her parents. From the moment she entered her husband's home and was presented to his ancestors at the altar as the climax of the wedding ceremony, her status changed. From being an outsider, still belonging to her natal family, she started to become a member of her husband's family. She and her husband often lived in the same house as the husband's parents and unmarried siblings for a certain period of time. The married sons were allowed to remain in the parental home until they reached agreement with their parents to set up households of their own. If there was only one son in a family, he often stayed in the same house as his parents, when there were several sons, one of them (often the eldest one, but in some areas, the youngest) stayed with the parents, the rest moved away some time after their marriages. However, their households were often in the vicinity of their parents' ones. Thus they established the patrilocal residence pattern, or its variant.

The primary reason for this was that sons preferred to live in the same village as their parents and siblings. It meant that they could keep in touch with their relatives more easily, and retain the intense attachment to their natal place that they called *que cha, dat to* [father's natal village, ancestors' land]. This traditional attachment was still so strong in the period under consideration that Desrousseau, a French Inspector of Mines, wrote a report addressed to a Governor General that the peasants would leave their villages to work only when they were dying from starvation. Therefore the way to overcome the difficulty (in getting enough people to work the mines) was to impoverish the countryside (Ngo Vinh Long, 1973: 116).

The second reason for the patrilocal residence pattern lay in the disincentives to move away. If a person left his native place, he would find nowhere to put down roots. Anywhere else he would be treated as *dan ngu cu* [a refugee] who lived on *dat khach, que nguoi* [other people's land, other people's natal village] (Le Thi Que, 1986: 18). In almost every village there was a written code that made a sharp distinction between *dan noi tich* [insider] and *dan ngoai tich* [outsider]. The discrimination against the outsiders – people coming from outside a given village – was undeniable. The village insider status was granted only after a family had settled in the village for several generations. That was why sons and their families often resided near their parents' home: there were social constraints which prevented their moving away to establish their own households after marriage.

In some areas, daughters of wealthy families might be able to stay on with their natal families to help their parents for a short time after marriage (Luong Van Hy, 1992: 74). As a vestige of the old custom, after the wedding, a bride sometimes went back to her natal family for some years (Le Thi Nham Tuyet, 1975: 121). However, this rarely happened. In this period patrilocal residence was taken for granted; there were only certain situations whereby a bridegroom might live at the future wife's house.

One such instance was if a rich family accepted a poor young man as a suitable marriage partner for their daughter. He then had to live and work in the fiancée's house for three years before they could marry. This was called *lam re* [living and working as a fiancé]. However, he lost his freedom, and in spite of his hard work, the bride's family sometimes drove him out of the house and married her to someone else. Moreover, people around the young man often sneered at him. There was a popular saying: *O re nhu cho chui gam chan* [To live and work as a fiancé is to lead the life of a dog that has to make do with the limited space under the low cupboard].

A rich family might also accept a promising but poor young man who could not afford to pursue an education. They created favourable conditions for his studies. By being studious, becoming successful, and earning both a good reputation and the praise of the society, he brought honour to himself, his parents, and to his parents-in-law. Nevertheless, this was not common practice.

When living in the parental house, sons were supposed to take care of parents in every way possible, to comply with their wishes and instructions, and receive in return mutual help from them. Even if sons established households of their own, they were supposed to continue this tradition. The main thing here was not the residence pattern itself, but the way sons treated their parents. Probably not being aware of that, when trying to get an operationalisation of Confucian concepts in their empirical survey, Hirschman and Vu Manh Loi (1994) identified the Confucian family with the patrilocal residence pattern. Nonetheless, I would disagree with them on this point; otherwise a subtle theoretical concept has been reduced to a crude indicator. Perhaps we should recall here the words of Confucius on how to understand and interpret the basic Confucian concepts? Somebody asked Confucius what filial piety was; whether to feed one's parents was filial piety or not. Confucius is reported to have answered:

> Filial piety nowadays means to support one's parents. But dogs and horses are nourished too. If care for parents is not

accompanied by respect, what is the difference between them and the animals?

(Quoted in Lang, 1946: 24)

Confucius, then, particularly emphasised the devotion of children to parents, i.e. filial piety. He demanded from a son not merely the cold formal fulfilment of obligations but an attitude of warmth and reverence. In other words, the Confucian family stressed the respect due to parents by their offspring, not just patrilocal residence pattern. This tells us how complicated it is to relate the subtle Confucian concepts to data.

The patrilocal residence pattern exerted a profound influence on the position of daughters and daughters-in-law. First, daughters were regarded as 'flying ducks' in the sense that one raised them, but when they grew up, they moved away from one's home. Feeding a daughter was an unprofitable investment. There was a popular saying that went: 'To raise your daughter is to raise her for others' (*nuoi ho*). A folk song noted: 'Your daughter is someone else's child. Only a daughter-in-law is your true child for whom you have paid.'

Second, daughters-in-law were often placed in difficult situations. For a young woman, being married meant *ganh vac giang son nha chong* [shouldering the burden of taking care of everything in your husband's family]. If the bride was the eldest son's wife, her obligations were much heavier than those of the other daughters-in-law. She was expected to set a moral example in serving the whole household's interests. To be able to play such a new and arduous role meant changing all her habits and way of life. Although she would have received training since childhood on how to live and work as a bride, that was just the anticipatory and primary socialisation into her new role.

On stepping into her husband's house, she was a 'stranger'. To integrate herself into a new family, she had to undergo a secondary socialisation, a crucible trial. She had to submit to the judging eyes, the severe training, and often the ruthlessness of her mother-in-law. 'It was considered routine for mothers-in-law to haze a new arrival mercilessly' (Marr, 1981: 193). The daughter-in-law had somewhat similar obligations to her mother-in-law as a son had to his father, but she could not expect from the mother-in-law what a son could expect from his father.

The relationships were totally unbalanced and tense. They were often so tense that in many areas there was a custom whereby on the wedding day, when the new bride first arrived at the groom's house, the groom's mother would avoid meeting her for a while. It was believed that the mother-in-law had already anticipated and prepared for the tense conflict that would inevitably ensue between the two women. By postponing meeting the new daughter-in-law, the mother-in-law hoped to delay the conflict that would accompany their coexistence under the same roof (Le Thi Nham Tuyet, 1975: 151–152). Of course, this custom may have been disregarded by some, but those who did disregard it were often blamed for the conflict if it developed.

The incompatibility between mothers and daughters-in-law often surfaced during the first days of the marriage and started with the custom of setting the daughter-in-law different tests. For instance, the mother-in-law would pretend to drop some money, then ask the daughter-in-law to sweep the floor in order to discover whether she would keep the money or not. Or the mother-in-law might measure out some paddy (of course in secret), then ask the daughter-in-law to grind the paddy into rice. Then the mother-in-law would measure the rice to see if the daughter-in-law had stolen any. If the mother-in-law was not satisfied with her daughter-in-law, she would begin to scold and ill-treat her (Le Thi Nham Tuyet, 1975: 152). That was not always true but gave us some ideas about the tests.

Folk songs frequently dealt angrily with these relationships. One of them went: 'Once you are the buffalo trader, you certainly are dishonest; once you are the mother-in-law and daughter-in-law, you definitely do not love each other' (there was a strong prejudice against traders because it was believed that they were dishonest). Another song concluded that mother-in-law and daughter-in-law 'can never have anything good to say about each other'.

Why did mothers-in-law often mistreat their daughters-in-law? One of the reasons was that with the patrilocal pattern and its variant, a woman was incorporated into an alien patrilineal family who bought the rights to her fertility, sexual services, and domestic labour by the payment of a bride-price. As a part of the wedding ceremony, the bride's family often asked the groom's family to deliver pork, chickens, glutinous rice, wine, and sometimes cash. The quantities demanded were often large; consequently the groom's family representatives generally negotiated to reduce the amount. As a result, the mother-in-law often thought that after having paid the price of buying her daughter-in-law, she had the right to regard and treat her however she liked. The treatment meted out often equated to the amount of money she had paid for her 'possession'.

The second reason for maltreatment was that the relationship between the two women was not based on a blood tie, unlike that between mother and son. The two women competed with each other to win the son's affections. In a society that emphasised blood ties, of course the mother–son relationship had to come first. In the words of O'Harrow (1995: 170–171), a woman often regarded her daughter-in-law as 'archival' because in the context of Vietnamese culture, her son was the only male she could possibly dominate, the only male who could look upon no other woman in the same way as he looked upon her. When her son married, he left her private space, betrayed this most intimate connection for another woman, his wife.

To keep the balance between the blood ties and the marital ones was a very difficult task for the groom. If a conflict occurred between them, because of the norm of filial piety, the husband could not act against his mother and in favour of his wife. On the contrary, he had to obey his mother; moreover, he also had to teach his wife to respect her mother-in-law, otherwise, a mother could ruin her son's marriage.

> Indeed probably nowhere in the world's folk literature is there a richer mine of sayings than the one found in Vietnam about mothers-in-law, and especially regarding the hatred that arises between the husband's mother and the young wife.
>
> (O'Harrow (1995: 167–168))

Conflicts of this kind often formed the basis of the plot for novels and short stories. Literature thus held up the mirror to life. Such conflicts were commonplace and especially tense in this period because an increasing number of young women began to discover the Western concept of romantic love and individual freedom, and they started to oppose the old order.

Nonetheless, such conflicts stemming from patrilocal pattern did not last indefinitely. Except for sons who were supposed by local custom to stay with their parents for good, or who lived in rich, upper-class families, a great many left the parents' home a certain time after the marriage. In fact, if we take a snapshot of family patterns, existing literature has suggested that in the period under consideration, families were diversified: some were in the extended form; for the rest, the most common pattern was not the extended patrilocal family, but its variant: the nuclear family. However, it was not far, let alone isolated from patrilineal kinship network.

According to Phan Ke Binh (1915/1992: 26–27) those parents who were well-off and healthy often lived separately from their children;

only the infirm and the poor co-habited with their adult offspring. Nevertheless, children were mindful of their parents and often presented them with delicious food; even those who lived far away offered them monthly allowances or gifts. One must remember that Phan Ke Binh was only offering his opinion, no hard evidence.

Nguyen Tu Chi (1980) made the assertion that the Vietnamese family has long been, in the main, a nuclear one. The reason for this may have been connected to the techniques of wet-rice cultivation, which were most suited to the nuclear type of family. Similarly, the researcher also failed to provide precise data to confirm this view. Do Thai Dong (1991) claimed – but presented no substantiating evidence – that the most common family pattern was what he has called the 'semi-nuclear family'. By that he means what in the sociological jargon is termed the 'stem family': parents lived with the eldest son's family, and other sons established their own households after marriage. He has offered no explanation for this development, but there are good reasons to apply Robertson's arguments (1991: 15) and suppose that the existence of the stem family pattern was associated with scarcity of development opportunity. Living space and economic resources were so limited that the only way one household could replace another was by taking over the residential space and economic assets of its predecessor.

Though they present different pictures about the family patterns, these authors are of one mind in their claim that the extended family was not common. There is no objective method to validate their claims, but if they are accurate the following conclusion may be drawn: although until the 1920s and 1930s the three-generational family (under one roof) remained the social ideal for most rural Vietnamese (Marr, 1981: 25), the extended family was not common in Vietnam this period. It existed mainly among the upper classes, as the evidence by Luong Van Hy (1989) has shown. For the majority of the population the family was almost nuclear. Owing to the harsh living conditions prevailing among the lower classes, death and widowhood were common occurrences. Consequently, the one-parent family was not rare.

In sum, then, families at this time could take the extended, stem, nuclear, or one-parent form. Furthermore, if one does not lose sight of the repetitive cycle of domestic development, one can say that at certain stages in its development process a nuclear family may derive from an extended one, or come to take the extended form.

Gender separation and women's status

This period witnessed the decreasing influence of Confucianism, one main characteristic of which was patriarchy (i.e. male domination), but its vestiges were still obvious. On the other hand, so-called matriarchy, with its emphasis on the high status of women, that was said to have existed in the remote past of Vietnam (Le Thi Nham Tuyet, 1975: 27–40; Wiegersma, 1988: 28) also left some impressive traces. As a result, we can see both sources of influence in family life. Let us look at men's domination first.

This can be seen in the gender separation that has been created by men and served their interests. It found clear expression first of all in the division of activities and labour.

Division of activities and labour. In the family, there was a division of activities and labour. For the upper class, the husband–father was the head and had the absolute power over his wife and children if his family existed in the nuclear form. In the extended family, the eldest man was the head. With Confucianism's 'three obediences', the wife's role was insignificant in comparison to the husband's. In accordance with the Confucian tradition, a sharp distinction between mental and manual work was made. Men in this family type were often the privileged and educated ones, the gentlemen. They were supposed to play a vital role in social leadership. To fulfil this mission, they did not get involved in manual labour; that left the domestic economy largely in women's hands. Consequently, women had to do everything, including rice production, housework, and trading. They worked from early morning until late at night, while men were exempted from all that. Men even were accustomed to rise very late in the morning, as related by a man from an upper-class family (Luong Van Hy, 1992: 68–69).

The narrative revealed the significant contribution of women in the upper-class family: their labour was effective and essential not only in wet-rice cultivation, but also in housework chores and trade. Thus the old tradition that held commerce to be unworthy of men's respect, and therefore the purview of women, was still very much alive under French rule. So it was the women who spent much of their time and energy in the marketplace and who brought their families a significant amount of cash income. In fact, women predominated in the market: they not only formed the overwhelming majority of all active merchants, but also made up the mass of customers.

The narrative reminds us of the similarity between the position of the daughter-in-law in Vietnam and her counterpart in China:

they both had to get up earlier than anybody else in the family and serve not only the men, but also their mothers-in-law (Lang, 1946: 233). The gender-based division of labour is also revealed by a folk song that voices the women's dissatisfaction:

> You dress in your best gowns and loaf around
> While I have to soak in sweat working in the paddy.
> (Vietnam Resource Centre, 1974: 34)

Moreover, in this family type, even the sons were prohibited from getting involved in manual work (Luong Van Hy, 1992: 68).

It was also this family type that was most likely to practise polygyny, which was designed to exploit women's labour. Rich landlords might get concubines by purchasing daughters of poor peasants who could not afford to pay their debts. In the eyes of those men, buying a concubine was cheaper than paying the wages of a servant for life. Among those families there was a saying: *Thu the, mai thiep* [A wife is married, but a concubine is bought]. Except for concubines who were their husbands' favourites, many husbands and concubines had little contact with each other.

The situation in the lower-class family was different. Wet-rice cultivation was extremely hard work; it required co-operation. It was this type of family that functioned as the production unit. Couples had to share the rice cultivation and housework at different levels; nobody had reason to feel superior or inferior, and women were the irreplaceable helpers of their fathers and husbands. This was especially the case if the family had no buffalo and could not afford to rent one. Then women and their children sometimes had to act as draft animals, pulling the ploughs on the front while their husbands pushed on the ploughs behind, as an agronomist described vividly (quoted in Ngo Vinh Long, 1973: 46). That was why a common ambition and dream of all peasants was to acquire a buffalo.

As soon as children could make a contribution, they started to work under the supervision of their parents. The parents exerted guidance and control over their children's work to some extent. In the beginning, the labour of children was just supplementary to that of the parents, but the important thing was to utilise the labour force of the whole family to the full, be it the labour of the young or old. If grown up, but not married yet, children still worked according to their parents' plans.

However, the gender-based division of labour could also be seen clearly in this family type. Wet-rice cultivation comprised the following stages: ploughing, harrowing, transplanting, weeding and reaping.

Ploughing and harrowing were jobs for men; but the transplantation of the rice seedlings to other fields was the exclusive task of women (Nguyen Tu Chi, 1991). This interesting fact was of a symbolic significance. Women were – because of their biological reproductive affinities – believed to be best suited to perform transplanting. Although women participated in the cultivation process as indispensable and irreplaceable labourers, the gender division was undeniable. As in the upper-class family, in this family type the housework was not done by men. Women were responsible for the most of housework chores.

Apart from the division of labour, the division of other activities was also clear-cut: it was the man who took part in outside-family activities; women were absent in village organisations. It was the man who received guests, especially the important ones.

Spatial separation. In the house, each sex had separate locations. There was a room named 'the room for the honours' in every house. It was here that the altar for the ancestors stood and important visitors were received; therefore the place was a male domain. At celebration times it was women who prepared special foods, but they could not enter the male domain; it was men who made the offering to the ancestors.

The extent of spatial separation between the sexes varied between the classes. According to Luong Van Hy, women in an upper-class family were not allowed to enter the main room of the house in the presence of guests. They also had to cover their faces with conical hats if passing through the courtyard in front of the ancestral room, if male guests were present (Luong Van Hy, 1989: 745). There were often rooms or places for women which most female members shared, but those places were semi-dark (Gourou, 1936/1955: 326). In general, the place of women was at home, in the darkest, wettest locations (Le Thi Nham Tuyet, 1975: 89–90) and in the kitchen.

By tradition, the kitchen was regarded as the women's place and had a low status. This was expressed both in the vernacular and in the very construction of the area, which was a separate outhouse. The traditional house was always built higher than the ground (this was as much a precaution against flooding by the Red River as a symbol of status), however the kitchen was built directly on the ground. The house was often built with care and sometimes with art, but the kitchen was a pitiful hut of lower height, made of poor quality material, as Gourou described. However, the kitchen was more than a place for cooking: most of the housewife's guests (relatives, neighbours who came to talk to the housewife, therefore unimportant from the household head's point of view) were received here.

In the common parlance, people created a hierarchy of spatial locations between the house and the kitchen. In Vietnamese a sharp distinction was drawn between the two places; therefore the phrase 'go to the house' was phrased *di len nha* [go up to the house], and *di xuong bep* [go down to the kitchen] (Tran Hoai Anh, 1993: 2–3). That may reflect to some extent the status of women.

In upper-class families, the gender separation was rigidly applied – to the extent that men and women ate separately. According to one of Luong Van Hy's case studies (1989: 744–745), the most privileged members of one particular household were the household head, his three sons, and the three senior women of the family: they were served meals together in the family's main room. The household head's niece and three daughters-in-law ate separately with the children. This again reminds us of a story related by Lang (1946: 161). She recounts how Western guests organised a communal dinner for a rich Chinese family: this marked the first occasion that the women ate together with the men. However, there was an important difference: in Vietnam, the senior women of this upper-class family could eat meals with the men; it was only the junior women who had to eat separately. In other words, although Vietnamese women were secondary to men, they started to gain status and influence with increasing age. A woman who had progressed in status, from a new bride in the patrilineal family to a mother-in-law experienced a turning point of power.

There was even a separate place for women to wash, hang and dry their clothes because, as Gourou (1936/1955: 298) mentioned, women's skirts (not solely after childbirth and during menstruation) were generally considered as particularly unclean. Men were advised to avoid touching women's clothing; some husbands would not even help their wives bring in female attire from the drying place when it rained.

As for the lower-class family, the house was often overcrowded; therefore the spatial separation between the sexes was less obvious. The problem here was that women often enjoyed very little privacy and were supposed to cover themselves well at all times.

Double standards of conduct. The gender-based segregation could be seen most clearly in the double standards of conduct. Women had long been considered as the property of men. To keep their property secure, men imposed and continuously enforced rules guarding women's chastity. Women were supposed to value their chastity above all things. If, on the wedding night, the groom found that the bride had already been deflowered, it would be perfectly justified to return her to her family immediately. Another example: an unmarried woman caught in sexual relationship was punished with 100 lashes according to the Gia Long Code that was still in effect during this period. At the village level, an unmarried mother brought so much shame to her parents' family that she and her parents had to pay a fine to the village (Eisen, 1984: 16).

O'Harrow (1995: 175) may be right when he claims that in Vietnam extramarital affairs outnumber premarital ones, yet men took stringent measures to discourage adultery by their wives. A man was encouraged to have many wives, while a woman could only have one husband. The unfaithful wife suffered brutal punishment, but official law never mentioned adultery as a crime for men and they were never punished for it either. Two measures dealing with an unfaithful wife were often reported: first, her head was forcibly shaved and plastered with lime; then she was led around her village while villagers did whatever they liked to humiliate her in front of everybody. The second and more extreme punishment was to tie the wife to a raft of banana trunks, then let the raft float on the river until she died.

An author (Toan Anh) gives accounts verifying the use of both measures. Both accounts seem to be generally reliable. He has an example of the first measure (humiliation) being used in 1930 in Hanoi's First District. Le Thi Nham Tuyet (1975: 133, 162) also tells of this measure being applied in Dinh Bang village, Ha Bac province. Descriptions of the second, more severe, punishment have been received from eye witnesses now living in Ha Bac province, also by Demoutier, a French researcher whose book was published in 1907. Toan Anh's account is from a district now belonging to Ha Nam Ninh province. An unfaithful wife was caught in the act. She was charged with adultery and punished severely. Villagers made a raft of banana trunks and tied her to it, then put a board beside her, where they wrote down her name, age, native village, and her sin. The villagers left the raft floating on the river until she died; nobody rescued her (Toan Anh, n.d.: 197–198). The date of this second story is uncertain but seems to have been in 1917–18.

It should also be pointed out that it was mainly men who had right to initiate divorce; women had no parallel right to do so. Women could appeal to a court only if their husbands had abandoned them for more than six months.

In brief, women suffered from numerous male prejudices and conventions. The gender relationship deteriorated particularly during the period under consideration as a result of the impoverishment of the overwhelming majority of peasants on the one hand and the enrichment of a minority of landlords as well as the French on the other. It became a fertile soil for the growth of the idea regarding men as exploiters, and women as the exploited.

The evidence from the studies of Le Thi Nham Tuyet (1975) and Eisen (1984) strongly suggests that it was women, particularly those from the lower class, who suffered most under French rule. Although some upper- and middle-class women in the 1930s talked about women's rights, peasant women interviewed by a female reporter stressed that the real problem they faced was extreme poverty, not sexual inequality or polygamy. Later, the upper- and middle-class women also came to realise that to improve the lot of women they had to eliminate all the contradictions in the current society because 'the women's issue is only one aspect of the social question' (Vietnam Resource Centre, 1974: 17, 39). In other words, the contradictions of the colonial society obscured the gender oppression. Therefore the aims of the women's liberation movement would be defined later in a special way, as we shall see in the next chapter.

However, it would be wrong to say that women were regarded as absolutely inferior to men. Women had their own separate sphere of influence, in which they wielded quite a lot of power. Different researchers (Yu Insun, for example) have demonstrated the wife's prominent position in the family prior to the twentieth century. Many Western observers and tourists (René Crayssac, Diguet) had already pointed out that in the traditional Vietnamese society, women enjoyed more economic and social independence than their counterparts in China; they never suffered from footbinding, for example, as did the Chinese women (Vietnam Resource Centre, 1974: 9). Actually, the position of women in lower-class families was much higher than that of women of the upper class. Generally speaking, if a family was poor, because of difficult living conditions, the husband and wife were more likely to rely on each other, to cooperate, and to pay no or little attention to the superior–inferior structure. A wealthy family often had more opportunity to retain the extended family form, and therefore needed a clear-cut role differentiation and vertical organisation.

We can see the relatively high position of women in the following spheres of lower-class families. Whereas farming provided a family with rice, the cash income of the family depended totally on small trade, which was almost entirely in women's hands. The wife made the decisions regarding not only most money issues, but also the use of the harvested rice, in the production of which she had played such a large part. According to Nguyen Tu Chi, before the arrival of the French, the currency unit was a round coin with a square hole in the middle for threading on to string. During the French rule, metal coins were still used together with paper notes issued by the French. In the family, strings of coins were kept in a strong wooden trunk locked with a key. It was the wife who had the key; nobody else could open and lock the trunk. The husband – the head of the family – seldom knew the sum of coins kept by his wife. He could ask her for money for various expenses, but the final decision rested with his wife. A popular saying went: 'The wife holds the key to the cash trunk' (Nguyen Tu Chi, 1991: 66). However, the researcher had no definitive facts and figures.

As for rice, apart from daily domestic needs, the family head had to obtain his wife's consent before taking any rice from the container. If after a long discussion, the wife did not agree, the husband had to give up (ibid.). Again, the researcher seems to be relying on hearsay evidence. By the same token he described how women could still exercise their influence on organisations outside the family which had a traditional patriarchal basis and interests, and from which women were often excluded. That was because, he contends, the husband's behaviour in village social life was influenced by the wife's opinion even though she stayed at home.

The wife also played an important, even decisive – in the words of Tran Dinh Huou (1991: 45) – role in the socialisation of children. Ideally, the father had to be severe; otherwise he might lose his authority. The mother taught her children differently, through playing on the sympathy of the children, through tenderness and gentleness. As the above researcher put it, 'by his strictness, the father inspired fear in the children; by her gentleness the mother instilled love in them; and they did not dare to, or have the heart to misbehave' (ibid.). We need to add that by his discipline the father was often the chief judge of the family: all misbehaviour was reported to him; therefore the threat of telling a child's faults to the father was one of the most effective methods of preventing the child from getting into mischief. So the husband and wife complemented each other. She often tried to intervene if her husband beat the children; by doing so she reduced the tension in the home.

As a result, the children's attitude towards their parents was often bifurcated. According to Le Thi Nham Tuyet (1975: 91), in upper-class families, there was some psychological distance between the father and the children; the children usually displayed a negative attitude towards him (fear and a desire to avoid him). Nevertheless, there was no such distance between the mother and the children, particularly between the mother and daughter. Sons might go to school, but the education of daughters remained in the mother's hands. The mother often offered companionship to her daughter. She also acted as an intermediary between the father and the children, especially when arranging a marriage for her daughter. On the other hand, the mother's views also had most weight in the choice of her daughter-in-law. Tran Dinh Huou noticed that the mother did not pay as much attention to selecting a husband for her daughter as selecting a wife for her son. If this is correct, it must be because it was primarily her responsibility to deal with the new daughter-in-law. If we understand how important the selection of a daughter-in-law was in continuing the family, we will understand too the prominence of the mother-in-law's role in this process.

If we turn to the vernacular as well as folk culture in an attempt to discover more about the position and status of women in family relationships, we see that wives were often referred to as *noi tuong* [general of the interior]. This was a hidden, but real position, as Nguyen Tu Chi (1980) put it. In describing the relationship between a married couple, one always mentioned the wife (*vo*) first, the husband (*chong*) second (*vo chong*). Any attempt to reverse this order would not only make the speaker a laughing-stock, but also show that he or she could not speak the Vietnamese language correctly (Vietnam Resource Centre, 1974: 30–31). Of course, local parlance does not really reflect the power structure; however, it can lend some insights. Peasant men showed their high esteem for their wives in the following adages: *Nhat vo, nhi troi* [The wife comes first and the king of heaven second], *Lenh ong khong bang cong ba* [His kettledrum cannot sound as loud as her gong].

In brief, we may say that in spite of the persistence of the Confucian doctrine of 'three obediences', the Vietnamese women played a significant role in the family, especially among the lower classes and families where the husbands were incompetent or irresponsible. It is generally agreed that it was because of the original Vietnamese folk culture that the rigid Confucianist concepts about women were softened. If we make a distinction between the East Asian cultural world, which is characterised by the male-dominated character, and the Southeast Asian one, which is characterised by the relatively high status of women (Taylor, 1983), we can recognise both elements within Vietnamese society. However, the Vietnamese form is less stringent in its characteristics than the East Asian and

Southeast Asian models. The Confucian vestiges found expression not necessarily in the patrilocal residence pattern, as some researchers have interpreted crudely, but in the communal character of family relationships; the hierarchy of sexes, generations, and ages; and the way in which children had to behave to their parents (filial piety).

Although the clear system of oppression for women nurtured and refined by men varied from class to class, and although women of a certain class enjoyed a degree of status, up until this century there was ample reason for women and young people to challenge the status quo. This protest grew in tandem with the spread of new ideas about individual freedom, social justice, and so on. The dissemination of Western ideas of freedom and self-expression led young people, particularly French-educated urbanites, to recognise the oppression and to take a stand against it. As Jamieson (1993: 107) noted, those youths believed that 'the old Vietnamese family system had to be overturned'. In fact, the above-mentioned important conclusion was voiced by Dao Duy Anh: the traditional family had to transform.

However, to adopt this view, one first had to decide the direction in which the family should be transformed. That depended in great part on how the existing family was evaluated, and what socio-economic transformation programme was chosen. From everything that has been presented so far, it is clear that the family during this period was still quite traditional. Being heavily hierarchical and male-dominated, the existing family was a fertile soil for the growth of imported ideas about liberation, freedom, equality and modernisation. Nevertheless, when accusing the traditional family of oppression of the young and women, the reformists seemed to lose sight of its deep cause: the concerns about protecting old people against the ups and downs of the human life course in a society where family and kinship were the main support mechanisms. Moreover, in the context of the urgent need for national liberation, in the eyes of revolutionaries and reformists, the traditional family nurtured only one kind of person who was too narrow-minded in his or her preoccupation with the family (that was understandable because the family was the only thing people could rely on for their needs). This prevented them from widening their horizons to participate in the struggle for national independence.

At last the Communist Party with its Marxist theory came to power and carried out its radical socio-economic transformation programme, a crucial part of which was aimed at the family. The communists evaluated everything at the time as old-fashioned and backward, and saw the key solution to the problem in radical transformation. They viewed everything that they wanted to achieve (the elimination of private property; the restructuring of the traditional family; collectivisation and large-scale production; industrialisation; rationalisation; and so on) as modern – as not only antithetical to but also superior to traditionalism. As we shall see in the next chapter, apart from some major achievements, they also made many extremist mistakes. A major reason for this was their erroneous evaluation of traditions, which led to a misconception of their programme.

Of course, if the native soil had not been fertile for the growth of the Marxist ideology, for instance if the class relationships had not worsened seriously during the period in question, then the Marxist theories would not have taken root so deeply in Vietnam. Nonetheless the communists have lost their sight of the fact that class relationships did not totally prevail over kinship. Not so long ago, a researcher wrote:

> Class contradictions entered the hearts of the patrilineage organisations and created complications for the kinship system, making it difficult for insiders to realise where their family feelings rested and whence class contradiction arose.
>
> (Nguyen Tu Chi, 1980: 41)

That may be true of distant relatives, but not so of close ones, at least within the immediate family, or what some social scientists call household. The reason is twofold: first, social classes divide whole societies but do not divide households (Robertson, 1991: 102). Second, because of the precarious circumstances of the majority in Vietnam, people were well aware of the phases of poverty in the life course. In other words, however rich a person might be, he knew he would grow old and be incapable of supporting himself. Therefore to secure his old age, he had to support – not to exploit – his children. Contrary to the communists' misconception, the family and kinship still played an essential role in almost all aspects of life. The communists' misconception led to dramatic transformations of the family later. Meanwhile the class issues seemed to have obscured the gender ones for them.

NOTES

1 The concept 'bride-wealth' has been used to avoid the implications of 'bride-purchase', but I use here the concept 'bride-price' instead of 'bride-wealth' because the latter 'goes to the bride's male kin (typically brothers)

in order that they can themselves take a wife' (Goody *et al.*, 1973: 5). In the Red River Delta, that is not the case. By contrast, people who have more than one wedding during a short period of time for their children of opposite sexes often try to avoid that. They usually make arrangements so that the marriage of the son is held first, then that of the daughter. Otherwise they would be open to public criticism that they were selling their daughter to get money for their son's marriage. Furthermore, the bride-price is often used to covering the wedding expenses of the bride's family, not for anything else.

Moreover, in the Vietnamese language, the concept *ga* (to marry off one's daughter) is sometimes accompanied by the word *ban* [to sell out] in the saying *ga ban* [to marry off and sell out one's daughter].

CHAPTER TWO

Social Changes Affecting the Family, 1945–95

In September 1945 in Hanoi, Ho Chi Minh declared the independence of Vietnam, and the formation of the Democratic Republic of Vietnam (DRV). This is a great turning point in Vietnamese history and marks the rise to power of the Communist Party.

Just over one year later, the French colonialists began to reconquer Vietnam. After the armed conflict with the French in the so-called first Indochinese war (1946–54), the country was divided into two parts. In the North, including the Red River Delta, there was a decade of peace during which the Communist Party and its government carried out their socio-economic policy that resulted in profound changes in many aspects of social life. Since then Vietnamese society has been undergoing the most fundamental socio-economic transformation in its history. Step by step, the second Indochinese war involving the American invasion began and spread. The American air forces bombarded the North. The fall of Saigon in 1975 marked the end of the American presence and the reunification of the country. Attempts were made to continue the government's socio-economic policy on a national scale. However, this policy led to a deep socio-economic crisis. As a result, in December 1986, the government had to start a reform programme.

All these transformations resulted in unprecedented changes in the family. This chapter is intended to provide a brief summary of how the changes have affected the family during the period under consideration. It is supposed to set a wider socio-economic context to the more specific chapters that are to follow. In a relative sense, I differentiate two main sorts of social changes: the planned ones that have been carried out according to the government's programmes (or social steering), and the unplanned ones that are beyond their social steering. During the period a number of changes were designed by the government in accordance with its ideas of equality, democracy, social justice, liberation, and so on, as well as its conceptions of modernisation: the class struggle, collectivisation, industrialisation, etc. Those changes can be viewed as the planned ones (social steering in the broadest sense of the concept). Behind the changes is the leadership's belief that people can be improved and society perfected by well-planned social transformations provided that the masses go through some proper ideological indoctrination and consciousness-raising activities. The planned changes can be regarded as a set of policies towards the family, understood in the sense that it is the nation's principles and planned procedures that are intended to influence or alter existing patterns of family life. These policies towards the family are divided further into two subcategories: first, *social changes* aimed at creating the so-called socialist family (ideological campaigns, laws on marriage and the family, women's liberation movement), and second, *socio-economic policies* not aimed directly at the family, but affecting it strongly (class struggle during land reform, collectivisation of agriculture, household registration, housing and distribution policies in industrialised areas).

Wars as well as the so-called 'open door' and renovation policy are regarded as the changes that are beyond the social steering programme. They are objective in the sense that they are not available for change at the will or caprice of any particular group. The 'open door' and renovation policy is so classified for the reason that it is started from the bottom upwards; the leaders have to accept it when they have no other choice. Moreover, when carrying out it, they are always afraid of deviating from their programmes, and try to keep it under control.

PLANNED SOCIAL CHANGES (OR SOCIAL STEERING)

A process of social steering has two sets of actors: the directors and the directed, and requires four basic components: a goal, steering media, implementation structure, and feedback mechanisms (Therborn, 1995). Although there are many differences between Eastern European countries and Vietnam, a few similarities can be found; therefore the discussion of social steering in those countries may also be applicable to Vietnam to some extent.

A few words must be said about the goal of the planned changes, that is 'something good (or better) in this world, which does not currently exist but which those doing the steering know about', which is 'attainable', but 'not being reached by the current activities and strivings' (Therborn, 1990). That could be presented briefly in one word: socialism, and all that is viewed as socialist by the directors. Ho Chi Minh (1977: 252) affirmed that 'only socialism and communism can liberate the oppressed nations and the working people throughout the world from slavery.' Socialism is not only good, but also juxtaposed in sharp contrast to all that currently exists: the so-called nonsocialist systems like feudalism, colonialism, and capitalism. For instance, Le Duan, the General Secretary of the Communist Party (1960–86), compared socialism to capitalism:

> Unlike capitalism, which was born and developed in a spontaneous way through anarchic production and competition, the whole socialist regime as well as economy came into being in a planned fashion through socio-economic transformations that were planned right from the outset.
>
> (Le Duan 1984: 53)

> Similarly, the objective of the capitalist mode of enterprise is profit; its method is anarchic competition, while the aim of the socialist mode of enterprise is to encourage the producer and the manager to fulfil and surpass the targets of the state plan, and on that basis to serve the interests of the whole society, of the collective and the individual producer.
>
> (ibid.: 58)

So the government has unwittingly followed the historical dichotomy well known in sociology that contrasts tradition and modernity. They have regarded tradition as something bad and backward, and modernity as good and pre-eminent. There is also a dogmatic faith among the leadership that Marxism–Leninism is the apex of human thought; once armed with it, they can achieve everything, be it victory in the war against the foreign aggressor or the establishment of socialism. As they put it, 'a people, however weak, who have risen up in unity to struggle resolutely under the leadership of a Marxist–Leninist party to win back independence and democracy, have sufficient forces to vanquish any aggressor' (The Vietnamese Government, 1976: 91). After analysing briefly some characteristics of social steering in Vietnam, we shall turn to its concrete programmes.

SOCIAL CHANGES AIMED AT CREATING THE 'SOCIALIST FAMILY'
Ideological campaigns

Changes in the family must be studied against the background of the ideological campaigns continuously launched by the government, because these campaigns have affected the family directly and deeply during the last half century. It should be pointed out that the government's perception of the family has changed considerably during the period 1945–95.

In 1930, a few founding members of the Communist Party perceived the family as a conservative institution which kept people within their patriarchal home, and prevented them from participating in the revolutionary struggle for the country's independence. Armed with only a rudimentary knowledge of the basic principles of Marxism, they urged the adoption of the slogan *tam vo* [the three no's: no religion, no family, no fatherland] (quoted in Eisen, 1984: 180). This came from the Marxist theory of the family that has stated that in the future society, the family would wither away because of its internal structure. To the Vietnamese people, 'no family' was really shocking: family relations have always been sacred and very close, as a leader of the Women's Union puts it (ibid.). Later, realising that the slogan went against the aspirations of the people and did not help the struggle against French colonialism and feudalism, the communists dropped it. Since then the main idea has been to transform the family dramatically rather than destroy it.

To the communists, the traditional family deserves condemnation because it creates enormous friction, hampers the development of personality, and leads to the oppression of young people by their elders. However, the fundamental criticism is that the traditional family is an obstacle to the establishment and defence of the new society; that Vietnamese people need to organise themselves on a national scale, but they lack a national perspective and capacity to do this. One of the reasons is that everything is subordinated to the family. Moreover, the government supposes that the traditional family is based on irrational customs; it must be transformed according to a new culture that means a 'national, scientific, and mass-oriented' culture. Since 1960 the government has related the transformations of the family to the third of the 'three revolutions':

- revolution in the mode of production;
- revolution of technology; and
- revolution of culture and way of thinking.

After 1945 they began to follow a more elaborate Marxist theory of the family, which proclaims that the family model founded on private property ownership must be uprooted.

Based on an excellent presentation of the theory's core principles by Geiger (1968), the Marxist theory of the family may be summarised as follows: The family originated from a stage of primitive communism, and assumed many different forms as it evolved. Those forms roughly corresponded with the principal stages of social development. Property has played a central role in civilised society, and the family form known to the present (monogamous) is designed to satisfy the need for private property transferring from one generation to the next and remaining within the hands of a small number of families.

From those general concepts, the Marxist theory goes on to deal with the family contemporary to Marx and Engels. Here a sharp distinction is made between the bourgeois family and the proletarian family under capitalism. The bourgeois family – in which the husband was the bourgeois and the wife was the proletarian – was viewed as quite corrupt. It was associated with exploitation, greed, boredom, adultery, and prostitution. It was private property ownership that was deemed to have a corrupting influence on family ties. As for the proletarian family, although it was poverty-stricken, on the positive side it embodied true love, marital equality and the freedom to divorce where necessary. The absence of private property – the original source of all the trouble – in the proletarian family can have only a salutary effect. If there are negative aspects (e.g. brutality towards women in the family), it was just pure survival, with no roots in the conditions of proletarian life.

According to the Marxist theory, in the future society where the 'abolition of private property' would be carried out, such activities as property-holding, work, consumption, and the rearing and education of children should be taken over by society because they breed inequality and oppression within the family in one way or another. In the choice of a marriage partner, there would be no other motive left than mutual inclination. Love, free from all economic calculations, would exert the most powerful influence (Geiger, 1968: 11–40). Thus the theory has markedly emphasised the importance of property in the development and changes in family structure, and has adopted a class perspective on this issue.

The Marxist theory of the family has been criticised for its view that all mankind progressed through the same stages of evolution, and for the reason that 'Marx and Engels conducted no field studies' (Geiger, 1968: 16) on family matters. However, this theory has been accepted as the official one, and has become canonised and integrated within family policy in Vietnam. Later in this chapter we shall see some concrete examples of how the classic Marxist–Leninist principles on the family and women's issues were applied wholesale in Vietnam without due consideration of the specificities of the Vietnamese reality.

So over time, the government's perception of the family has changed, partly as a response to the attachment which Vietnamese people have accorded their families, partly because the government has come to understand and develop further the Marxist theory of the family. From an initial opposition to the family institution in general, they have come to recognise that the family cannot be dispensed with entirely. They have therefore drawn a distinction between different family types, and support the type that conforms to their image of the so-called socialist family. Before their social steering programmes, they opposed the family mainly because it was a basic property-holding institution. After private property ownership was eliminated, the so-called socialist productive relationships were established in the late 1950s and early 1960s; however, the family did not seem to be any better off, contrary to the Marxist predictions. Further development of the Marxist theory of the family was deemed necessary to transform the existing family into the so-called socialist model. Stable marriages and self-disciplined families would be important for the regime, but the actual family came to be seen increasingly as a vehicle of discord and disharmony between individuals and socialist society. To become socialist, the family had to overcome this discord. The government's ideological principles in family issues are applied differently for Communist Party members and non-Party members. We shall look at them in turn.

For Communist Party members, the aim is to gain control over family matters, especially in the choice of marital partners. According to Hoang Van Chi (1964: 145), in 1951 the Party issued a regulation, stating that cadres of village level and soldiers must inform the Party before they married; that cadres of district and provincial levels and non-commissioned officers must get the Party's agreement to their marriages; and that the marriage arrangements of high-ranking officials in the Party and of officers in the People's Army were the Party's affair. This state of affairs has lasted for a long time. Eventually, the regulation was relaxed a little, but remains in force for Party members, for instance in the security forces. One typical example was the writer Tran Dan who 'was victimised by the Party for falling in love with a girl who was classified as a class enemy because her parents had been property-owners and fled to the South in 1954' (Bui Tin, 1995: 34). Young people of both sexes, when they fall in love and intend to get married, have to report this to the Party's organisation where they work. If they do not follow this regulation, they are punished in different ways. In Viet Hung commune, Dong Anh district, on the outskirts of Hanoi, there was a man who had been dismissed as Chairman of the commune's administrative committee. He was also expelled from the Party; the reason was that among other things, he had been married to a woman whose relative migrated to the South during the American war (Mai Huy Bich, 1993: 77).

It could be said that the class approach predominates in marriage and family issues. The regulation is aimed at establishing a strict class endogamy, and strengthening political loyalty to the ruling Party. In fact, it greatly narrows the scope of choice for young people. This is the replacement of marriage control by the family with that of control by the political organisation. Love is deprived of its social and emotional qualities; it is totally subordinated to political requirements. Apart from controlling their members in choosing their marriage partners, the Party also intervenes in divorces, viewing these as harmful and immoral. So after the removal of the traditional barrier between men and women (i.e. the traditional family), couples became subjected to the rigid surveillance of the Party cadres.

For non-Communist Party members, the government carries out its socialist indoctrination related to family issues in two directions: the campaign for the so-called New Cultured Family (*gia dinh van hoa moi*) and ceremony reforms. It seems that the terms 'socialist family' and 'New Cultured Family' are used as synonyms, but the latter is applicable in everyday language.

The New Cultured Family Campaign was introduced after the American war (1975), led directly by the Party in close co-operation with the ministries of education and culture, the Trade Union, the Women's Union, and the Youth Union. It is designed to create a new family that ideally is based on unity, equality, and mutual affection. Husband and wife should help each other to work and to study so that both make progress, and share the responsibilities of family life and the education of the children (Eisen, 1984: 193). The campaign particularly emphasises building and restoring harmony between couples, and raising well-educated children. One of its major objectives is to break down the resistance of husbands to women's participation in social and working life outside the home. To help women to do that, and to achieve matrimonial harmony, men should share the housework.

Another objective is to encourage the family's stability, to strengthen it, and hence, most importantly, speed up the desired social change. The family must be stable, otherwise family problems interfere with work and study. Particularly emphasising harmony, the campaign tries to persuade 'disharmonious families' to reunite. Family conflicts are resolved first by the so-called groups for the New Cultured Family at local level; it is only when the involved parties are determined to split up that the conflict is referred to the divorce courts. Just as happened in the former Soviet Union some decades ago (Geiger, 1968: 95), people seeking divorce were faced with substantial ideological, moral, and judicial barriers. It is only relatively recently that these barriers have been removed.

A long-term objective of the campaign is to urge families to socialise their children into the role of good citizens, i.e. worthy successors of the revolutionary cause. It is believed that the children's unformed minds are still suggestible, and that they represent the future; therefore their rearing and education must not be entrusted to the individual family without their being given proper instructions. Those activities are best organised around a collective work: namely schools and other social organisations. In 1961, on the twentieth anniversary of the children's Pioneer Organisation (the one designed, among other things, to indoctrinate young children and control them) Ho Chi Minh addressed all children and asked them (quoted in Nguyen Khac Vien, 1971):

- to love the fatherland and their countrymen;
- to study well and work well;
- to promote unity and discipline;
- to observe the rules of hygiene; and
- to be modest, frank, and courageous.

Thus his five teachings concentrate only on civic qualities, not family ones; there is no mention of the 'filial piety' that was proclaimed 'the root of all virtues' in the traditional family. In fact, Ho Chi Minh reused the concept, but instead of applying it to family relations, he appealed to all soldiers 'to be loyal to the Communist Party, and to be filially pious to the people'. Thus he changed its meaning completely. There are also no longer rituals symbolising subordination, age, and generational hierarchy that the traditional family regarded as the first things to learn ('Rituals are the first things to learn, then literature is the second one', as a saying puts it).

The new Cultured Family Campaign also encourages family members to participate actively in production while practising thrift, and to apply correctly the policies and directives of the state and the Communist Party (Molander, 1977). This is essential. A new family cannot be good in itself; it must benefit the new society by conforming to the new *mores*.

To communicate these objectives to people, the propaganda apparatus often arranges meetings at local level, informs people about the campaign, arranges discussions, then delivers to each family a proforma letter to sign, in which they promise to participate in the campaign, and to satisfy the criteria of the New Cultured Family. The media are used to present a certain image of the family. If we look at the popular literature, these criteria are highly visible. Moreover, the 'Five Good' emulation movement (1961–65) for women specified these criteria as follows (in Le Thi Nham Tuyet, 1991):

- good solidarity, production, and thrift;
- good observance of government policies;
- good knowledge of politics, culture, and techniques;
- good handling of one's own family and children; and
- good participation in economic management.

It should be emphasised here that the second criterion is of prime importance; in fact, it encourages women to adopt a conformist attitude towards everything that the government does and prescribes. In other words, a new woman is always depicted as a working (moreover, hard-working) and strong-willed citizen. The official position of the regime is that a good woman should work; it is never quite legitimate for a woman to be just a housewife, particularly in cities. Especially valued are women who perform extremely well both at work and at home – things that are, in fact, well beyond reach of an overwhelming majority of women. Being a good wife, such a paragon is able to manage the household, and to help her husband to devote his whole mind, heart, and energy to building and defending the socialist fatherland. She is also able to bring up children as revolutionary successors of the country. In brief, everything in the family is harmonious, and aimed at getting more time and energy for work and study, in the interest of the socialist fatherland. Family members are not only relatives, but also comrades in the revolution. Thus in the eyes of policy-makers, who emphasise the importance of public life, the traditional family with its concentration on the personal sphere must be transformed into the public-spirited, socialist one.

After signing the letter, families send it back to a group that is responsible for the campaign at local level. The group monitors and reviews the results of the campaign, and rewards deserving families with the title 'New Cultured Family'. By so doing, the government tries to establish a set of values that they call 'revolutionary and socialist', and to encourage people's adoption of it. As for the children, at the end of every term, the title 'Well-behaved nephew (niece) of Uncle Ho' is given to pupils who have performed well the so-called 'Five Teachings of Uncle Ho'. However, the families that are awarded the title are not able to replace the decent traditional family that was revered by other families for their good manners and conduct. In reality, very few people pay respect to either the title or to the families that receive it (Molander, 1977).

The second target of the socialist indoctrination is the replacement of the old system of rituals with a new one. During the two wars, in the name of national salvation and wartime economy, the government continuously launched an attack on these age-old ritual practices. When the wars were over, the traditional rituals continued to be attacked as a hindrance to scientific progress and a waste of resources needed for national reconstruction. Until the early 1980s, the government was still actively pursuing their strategy as part of the socialist reconstruction. Promoting a modern scientific worldview as well as collective economy measures, they outlawed many 'superstitious' and costly practices which, in their view, ran counter to modern science, and were the remnants of a feudal system. They imposed a simplification of many other consumption-oriented rituals (Luong Van Hy, 1993). Their sharp attack is based on two main arguments: economic and scientific rationality.

Ancestor worship is regarded as supernatural, antithetical to the materialist and scientific worldview. As a communist in the best-selling novel *Paradise of the Blind* by Duong Thu Huong puts it, 'we live in a materialist age. No one cares about all this ancestor worship. After death, there's nothing' (1988/1991: 49). Lands for incense and fire (i.e., to defray meal expenses incurred at gatherings of the whole lineage) were collectivised. In most localities the chiefs of lineages were solely responsible for offerings to the ancestors.

The attack was aimed not only at the annual cycle of festivals that were often celebrated beyond the kinship domain, but also at another set of life-cycle rituals performed mainly by the family, *viz.* weddings, funerals, and other rites of passage. The changes include the elimination, or at least simplification, of the traditional rituals related to the family, and their replacement with new ones.

Houtart and Lemercinier (1984: 171–176) have looked at a document called 'Agreement about a new mode of life' of Hai Van commune, Ha Nam Ninh province. This is based on governmental and presidential directives about religion. In almost every commune, there is a similar agreement dealing with different ceremonies. The only available evidence about the reformed rituals comes from a detailed study of Luong Van Hy (1993) which is based on data gathered by different collaborators. Let us first examine the data on the wedding rituals.

In Son Duong, for instance, in 1987 the village administration issued a ruling to limit the wedding banquet to sixty guests. It also eliminated the cash bride-price and financial sponsorship of the wedding banquet. It was decreed that the engagement ceremony should require no more than five packets of cigarettes, half a kilogram of tea, and a few dozen areca palm fruits (instead of much larger amount formerly expected by the bride's family). A new wedding ceremony had to be held in the village office (Luong Van Hy, 1993).

In Hoai Thi, in 1955, the local leadership also discouraged lavish consumption by organising weddings for five couples simultaneously at a communal house. After receiving tea and tobacco from the families involved, the Youth Organisation took charge of the event and organised the entertainment for the occasion. There were only singing performances by participants, no formal reception by the bride, and no bride-farewell ceremony. The bride-price came under attack. Only a small meal for close relatives of the bride and groom was allowed. In 1986, after the interruption by the American war, the village administration attempted to revive the village-hall weddings and to eliminate wedding feasts by making a simplified village-hall ceremony a precondition for registration of the marriage (Luong Van Hy, 1993).

We need to clarify here that before 1945, a marriage was considered legitimate providing the couple made some contributions in cash or kind to the village fund. The villagers were the witnesses to the establishment of a legitimate sexual relationship between the husband and the wife. The new Law on Marriage and the Family

(1960) ushered in the obligatory registration of all marriages, whereby every couple has to register for marriage with the local government. All applicants for a marriage certificate have to undergo an investigation to make sure that traditional practices are stopped, and that people obey the propositions of the law. To do so, each of them has to obtain a document from the authorities of the workplace or place of residence, confirming that they are eligible for marriage. In urban areas, if they are state employees, it is only after they register for marriage that they earn the right to buy some essential furniture at a subsidised price. These rights existed at least until the early 1980s when the economic crisis deepened.

What about the funeral ceremony? According to Luong Van Hy, before 1945, the family of a deceased person had to invite all male villagers to a funeral feast. In return, the guests were obliged to offer cooked food to the deceased. Under the communist government, the funeral ceremonies had to be simplified for economic reasons to different extents in different areas. The elaborate offerings of the past were reduced to incense and flowers, and later, at the suggestion of Son Duong administration, to incense and a funeral banner loaned by the village. In both Son Duong and Hoai Thi, children of the deceased no longer walked on canes during the funeral procession (Luong Van Hy, 1993).

How were these regulations carried out and received? It must be noted that they were warmly welcomed as progressive changes by quite a few people. In the past, many poor couples could not get married because they were unable to afford the costly wedding ceremony. Many other families sank heavily into debt as a result of wedding and funeral expenses; now there was an easing of these burdens. However, other people took a different view, and did not welcome the changes, even though they were under pressure to observe them. According to Luong Van Hy (1993), who studied weddings in Hoai Thi, village officials put pressure on parents through a local government ruling and through visits to families that were rumoured to be preparing to slaughter pigs for wedding feasts. They dealt with funerals and other life-cycle ceremonies in the same way. In spite of that, the ceremonies have become considerably more elaborate as certain rituals are revitalised and imported, and as the size of the banquets increased, especially since the late 1980s, after the government launched its reform and renovation programmes.

The same source also reveals that although officials in Hoai Bao imposed a heavy fine on hog slaughter for a wedding, many well-off villagers ignored the ban and willingly paid the fine. Son Duong village administration issued in 1987 a ruling to limit the wedding banquet to sixty guests, but by 1991 the banquets had grown to at least 120–180 guests. Moreover, villagers considered the community-hall wedding ceremony imposed by the local government to be a meaningless burden, especially when the weather was inclement. Therefore when there is no longer pressure from above, villagers give up this additional step. As a result, 'in the late 1980s, the national and local leadership finally had to give in to the resistance to their tight control of ritual practices' (ibid.). So the state's efforts in this area were unsuccessful. Why?

It could be suggested that by reforming ceremonies, the government wanted to avoid the extraordinarily high costs. However, they looked at the ceremonies only in financial terms; they did not recognise the inherent social meanings. For the people involved, life-cycle ceremonies served as the markers of socio-economic status in that one could identify a person's standing in the community by asking how many guests and what guests attended his (her) ceremony. Moreover, the ceremonies were linked to an elaborate network of gift exchange, and the reciprocal assistance system of people who could not seek help from anywhere else, especially after the collective assistance from the co-operatives had been reduced.

However, for the family, the life-cycle ceremonies mean more than that. They are the occasions for interaction between dead parents and living family members: in those ceremonies, the head of a family reports to his ancestors about the event, and prays for their blessing. It is here that we can discover the function of the rites of passage: to summon the ancestors' blessing, to alleviate the anxiety, and to share the joys in the life-cycle transitions of daily existence. Here we see the profound connections between the rites of passage and the family: the strength of family bonds. That was why people were ready to pay any price to keep the ceremonies, and to keep family bonds. People responded to the authorities' arguments on the need to economise by saying that it was their own money that was being spent, not government funds (Luong Van Hy, 1993). To sum up, economic rationalisation was supported and encouraged by the government, but was not welcomed by many families.

Apart from the new Cultured Family Campaign and ceremony reforms, one should also mention the so-called *ba khoan* ['three postponements'] campaign by the media, i.e., the encouragement by the propaganda apparatus to put the needs of the country before personal needs during the American war. If a couple fell in love, they postponed their engagement; if they were engaged, they postponed their marriage; and if they were married, they postponed having children (Eisen, 1984: 190). There was another version of this; before all those postponements came the first one: if young people were not yet in love, they put this off too. According to a writer, in schools there also existed a slogan 'Three Don'ts', 'which forbade sex, love or marriage among the young people. Love affairs for ninth- or tenth-formers were regarded as a disgrace, unpatriotic' (Bao Ninh, 1991/1993: 121). All this was designed to meet the requirements of war. That may have been deemed necessary for the survival of the whole country; however, it also leads to some extremes in which love is not encouraged because it may interfere with work and study as well as civic duties. Premarital sex may be strictly punished if known to officials. One must practise self-restraint and abstinence. The effects of that on the family and gender relations are unknown for lack of scholarly evidence.

Laws on Marriage and the Family

After colonising Vietnam, the French first applied the law of the Nguyen dynasty, then French legal and administrative practices were gradually introduced in various fields. In the view of Ta Van Tai (1997), the new civil codes that were promulgated in the North in the 1930s were fashioned after the Napoleonic Code. The researcher supposes that the new civil code improved women's status to some extent, but in other ways marked a retrogression. However, the traditional society never absorbed the colonial legal culture, therefore the two systems of norms existed parallel to each other (Nguyen The Anh, 1970: 148). So until 1945 the Gia Long Code that had been introduced in the nineteenth century still held sway in family matters. Though the forces of colonialisation started to have an impact on behaviour from the beginning of the twentieth century, and the discussions of family problems had their effect in cities in the 1930s, the family patterns of most Vietnamese had not changed fundamentally when the Communist Party took control.

As some Vietnamese authors (quoted in Eisen, 1984: 193) have identified, in the revolutionaries' view, the traditional family is the last bastion of feudal ideology. That was why immediately after the 1945 revolution, the 1946 Constitution and later decrees laid the foundation for changing the family, first of all outlawing polygamy and forced marriages. Many new leaders realised the necessity of changing the family system in order to change the political order.

The new Law on Marriage and the Family came into force in 1960. In 1987, yet a new one was introduced.

In contrast to the traditional patterns, the 1960 law banned the following: polygamy, arranged marriages, child marriages (the permitted age of marriage was 20 upwards for men, 18 and above for women), the bride-price, the dowry, and wife-beating. It did not allow any spouse to exercise more power than the other. Each partner was guaranteed the right to choose freely an occupation, and an equal right to divorce, but a man was not allowed to divorce his pregnant wife. If she herself did not wish to divorce, he had to wait until a year after the birth. Widows were permitted to remarry. Women's rights to child custody and communal property were protected. As for the children, the law guaranteed the right of daughters and sons to equal treatment in the family. Children born out of wedlock had the same rights as children whose parents were married.

Thus the law eliminated many articles of the Gia Long Code, which was based on the Confucian principle 'men are to be respected, women despised'. The 1960 law emphasised first of all the principle of free choice of marriage partner, monogamy, equality between husband and wife, and the protection of women's and children's interests. In brief, it stated that women are equal to their husbands in controlling the family and that women should receive help from their husbands in bringing up children. Both husband and wife have equal rights to the ownership and use of property before and during the marriage, and both are free to take part in social and political activities. All these provisions, which were not included in the Gia Long Code, demonstrated the fundamental changes.

The law was quite progressive in comparison not only to the Gia Long Code, but also to the law in the South of the country. According to Eisen (1984: 182), the Law I/50 'on the Family' under the Saigon regime in South Vietnam at the time made the husband the legal head of the family and forbade divorce unless it was especially authorised by the 'Head of State'. If that was correct, the 1960 law clearly favoured women compared to the law in the South.

The 1987 law has not only followed but also developed further the main principles of the previous law, and has added some new articles to deal with recent developments (e.g. marriage to foreigners, etc.). Among the new articles are the ones about family planning. The fact that contraception is widely available and family planning has become an official policy is a fundamental change (see Chapter Four). However, the most marked change is that the 1987 law is designed to overcome a shortcoming of the 1960 law in which, among other things, the question 'of relations between family and society have not been dealt with in a concrete and comprehensive manner', as an editor of the English translation of the law text puts it (The 1987 Law on Marriage and the Family: 28). In other words, now the family is seen not as contradictory to socialist society, but as too narrow: it must contribute to building the socialist society. Many other changes of the 1987 law are technical and aimed at greater legal clarification.

Although some see a link between Vietnam's family legislation on the one hand, and China's 1950 Marriage and Family Law and 1979 one-child policy on the other (Goodkind, 1995), there is no doubt that the laws of Vietnam signify a radical break with the Gia Long Code. It is needless to speak of their revolutionary significance and effects on family relations. In the new family, progressive and relatively democratic relationships are appearing and have been generally welcomed by the public. In theory, if a husband beats or abandons his wife, and neglects his family responsibilities, the wife can have recourse to the law, and get support from the Women's Union to defend her rights and happiness and those of her children. Many women have not hesitated to seek divorce at the tribunals. These changes are fundamental, but what about the real family? How are the laws implemented?

Alterations of family codes in the Delta by no means prove that the population has accepted the new stipulations in either attitude or behaviour. In fact, the implementation of these laws has not been simple, and the social reality is often a far cry from the ideals posited by the law-makers. A massive effort is needed to modify people's thinking and to establish in the minds and behaviour of the masses the new ideas about marriage and the family. This requires education, and the elimination of not only long-standing traditions, but also misconceptions, and even strong opposition. The question is how to educate people to renounce the traditions of polygamy, child marriages, arranged marriages, etc.

Ho Chi Minh himself took an active part in the debate. At a meeting about the draft of the Law on Marriage and the Family in 1959, he replied to the challenge that, as a bachelor, his knowledge of the subject might be somewhat limited by stating:

> Though I have no family of my own, yet I have a very big family: the working class throughout the world and the Vietnamese people ... To enjoy concord in matrimonial life,

marriage must be based on genuine love ... The Law on Marriage and the Family aims at emancipating women, that is freeing half of society. The emancipation of women must be carried out simultaneously with the extirpation of feudal and bourgeois thinking in men.

(Eisen, 1984: 180–181)

Ho Chi Minh was fully cognisant of the Vietnamese love of the family, therefore he tried to combine it with new notions about equality. However, he interpreted the concept of family in too broad a sense, which is often seen as the revolutionary interpretation. His all-embracing definition of family includes working-class people all around the world, but not concrete relatives. The class criterion and not kinship is emphasised as the bond. In fact, for Vietnamese people, it is hardly imaginable that the family could be understood in that sense. Moreover, he also viewed the male domination from a class viewpoint by relating it to the so-called feudalists and bourgeoisie. Le Duan had this to say: 'In socialist society the family is built on equal relations and genuine love. The family is no longer an economic unit' (Eisen, 1984: 181). The influence of the Marxist theory of the family is obvious here.

From all that Ho Chi Minh and Le Duan said, as well as the description given in the 1987 Law on Marriage and the Family, we can see how the so-called socialist family is defined:

In the socialist family, husband and wife are equal, love and help each other to make progress in all aspects, actively participate in socialist construction and national defence, and bring up their children to become useful members of society.

(1987 Marriage and Family Law)

Thus the socialist family must be of working class (not feudalistic or bourgeois) character; and be based on equality and genuine love. It has to fill in the gap between the personal sphere and the public one to make contributions to the public cause of socialist construction and national defence. There is clearly a remarkable transition in evidence here, from the early negative ideas of the communists about the family as a source of oppression and exploitation to the more positive ones about the socialist family.

According to Eisen (1984), shortly after the 1960 law was enacted, a directive from the Central Committee of the Communist Party urged the necessity to carry out permanent and long-term propaganda and educational work to ensure a correct application of the

Law on Marriage and the Family among cadres, Party members, and other people. A retired member of the central committee of the Women's Union recalled how she led a group of Women's Union cadres in a campaign that brought the law to the rural strongholds of patriarchy. Sometimes her group had a fierce struggle with people who had arranged and forced marriages, and those who continued to flout the new law were fined. In spite of that, in her view, by 1974 polygamy and forced marriages were virtually abolished in the North (Eisen, 1984: 182–183).

This evaluation is an exaggeration even at the moment, and contradictory to the factual evidence (see conflicting data on polygamy given in Chapter Four). It is not easy to abolish the centuries-old institutions of polygamy and arranged marriage. These institutions have not disappeared completely, and they are often skilfully camouflaged, even among state employees and high-ranking government officials. During the American war, the government and people could not put enough effort into applying the law. That was one of the reasons why the 1987 law is promulgated to strengthen and develop the previous one. However, even if state control and supervision have been tightened up, old-fashioned habits have been continuing to re-emerge, especially after the reforms of the late 1980s. A similar situation often occurred in the past, when for centuries certain customs were followed in the face of official disapproval. Many historical studies of Vietnamese legal decisions concerning the family (Yu, 1990) have shown that clearly.

The new Laws on Marriage and the Family allow women to take the initiative in asking for enforcement of the law. However, before any law can be effective, women must understand their rights. As Women's Union cadres often put it, no one forces a woman to divorce her husband, even if he is a polygamist. That is up to her; she must do it voluntarily (Eisen, 1984: 184). Nevertheless, in a society with a patriarchal heritage, not every woman knows what her rights are. Therefore it is not surprising that opposition to the new laws has come not solely from men. For example, as Eisen (1984: 181) has demonstrated, some women – fearful of their husbands taking concubines – opposed the provision of the Marriage Law that granted equal rights to children born inside and outside marriage. Some women, even though they know that their husbands are having an affair, dare not oppose them for fear of being abandoned (as will be discussed later).

To conclude, we may say that the laws have laid the legal foundations for the new family that is supposed to be more equal, democratic, and progressive. Nonetheless, great efforts must be made to transform the family in social practice.

Women's liberation movement

In Communist Party eyes, one of the aims of the Vietnamese revolution was to overthrow feudalism. They recognised that to achieve this, the government had to gain women's support and participation. To mobilise women, they supported and spread the principles of 'women's rights' that had been debated among the small groups of French-educated women in urban areas since the 1930s. More than that, they promoted the principle of gender equality immediately after they came to power; it has become the institutional right (Article 9 of the 1946 Constitution) (Le Thi Nham Tuyet, 1975: 210–211). This is repeated again, in a more elaborated form, in the 1959 and 1980 Constitutions. Compared to the traditional society, the change is very fundamental. To reiterate Ho Chi Minh's words: 'If women are not free, half of the nation is not free' (quoted in White, C. P., 1989: 175).

The so-called women's liberation movement emerged in Vietnam. 'Women's liberation' means the right to health protection, education, economic security, a job that will not break their back, the opportunity to rest, equal constitutional rights, and freedom from polygamy. The concept also aims to put an end to the ideological and psychological subordination of women that was holding women in contempt (Eisen, 1984: 8). However, the crucial objectives of this were to restore women's social dignity, self-respect, social consciousness, and through all those aims, to release their potential for national goals under the Communist Party's leadership (Le Thi Nham Tuyet, 1975).

An organisation for women, the Vietnam Women's Union, was established in 1946. Its functions are, among other things, to represent women's right to equality; to take part in state administration and management of all aspects of life; to educate and mobilise women in building and defending the country. It has branches at all administrative levels. Let us take a look at some achievements of the movement in the most crucial fields, namely education, employment, and political participation.

Whereas the traditional education system banned women from learning, the present one recognises women's right to study. As a researcher (Luong Van Hy, 1990: 92–93) tells us, in the male-oriented model, the middle name was a gender marker according to the rule of rigid distinction between males and females. *Thi* was always used for females and simply meant 'person', while the most popular male middle name, *Van*, meant 'literature'. It was no coincidence. When the mastery of Confucian literature was the main route to power, this middle name applied to males only. During the first half of this century, some changes took place: the French administration drew up a plan to train a few female functionaries. As a result of this, some women of middle-class background gained a French education, but only a few.

However, since 1945, more and more women have received an education. Although Vietnam is one of the poorest countries in the world, its literacy rates and educational levels are relatively high. According to the 1989 census, the literacy rate for the whole population was 88 per cent and for women 84 per cent. The gender difference in literacy has been steadily reduced; there is no significant difference between the genders among the 10–25-year-old (The Vietnamese Government [CCSC], 1990).[1]

As for women's employment, if we keep in mind the relative significance of statistics in Vietnam, the census also shows that more than half (52 per cent) of the total working population is female. Nevertheless, except for some new domains (education and social service), where women's employment has achieved impressive rates (67 per cent and 64 per cent respectively), sectors in which women play a major role are agriculture (73 per cent of employed women work in agriculture), and trade (over 70 per cent of people engaged in business are women) (ibid.). In other words, those traditional domains still belong chiefly to women. The most remarkable change in those domains is that of women's status. In every village before 1945, there was a list of village members who could have access to public land, the most common means of production; this list included only men, even young boys and old men, but never women (Wiegersma, 1988: 53). This meant that women were barred from the village membership. Now as citizens, they have the right to participate in this means of production.

Ten per cent of women work in industry where they constitute 43 per cent of the labour force (CCSC, 1990); in theory, they are supposed to work in light industrial occupations (textiles), but in practice, an unknown number of them have to do heavy work. The principle of equal pay for equal work is applicable. To help them in their professional roles, the government established not only a wide child daycare network, but also a health care system. Both these measures to some extent eased the caring duties of working women, although there was no doubt that the provision of those institutions (especially pre-school ones) lagged far behind the needs. The former was extended to the village and hamlet levels; the latter to commune level in rural areas. Nonetheless, it must be pointed out that behind the social rearing lay the rationale that the upbringing of children by society would not only free the women for work, but also produce better citizens. Thanks to buying paddy at a low price from co-operatives, society could afford to share the family's caring functions. In this sense, the well-known proposition according to which at least some of the family's functions were shared with other social agencies was true of Vietnam during collectivisation, though to a very limited extent.

However, it must be emphasised that in this domain the Communist Party has followed the principles laid down by the classic Marxist–Leninist assumption that women in the pre-revolutionary period were not involved in public social production. Therefore women's entry into social production has been seen as a precondition for their liberation. For instance, Le Duan said that women under the feudal regime were cloistered and completely isolated; that for 'thousands of years women's activities had been confined to the narrow circle of their family', that women 'must have a clear class position, take part in public activities and think more collectively' (quoted in Mies, 1986: 203). A researcher comments:

> This statement is simply not true; only in the upper-classes did the Confucian theory that 'men live outside, women inside the family' apply. Ordinary Vietnamese peasant women, the overwhelming majority of the population, were neither cloistered nor limited to working in the house.
>
> (Mies, 1986: 203)

This incorrect evaluation of the crucial role played by women in social production has led to a situation where women frequently have to do everything. White says:

> In this context, the Leninist route to women's emancipation by drawing women into productive labour seems a cruel joke, a formula for total exhaustion rather than for liberation.
>
> (White, C. P., 1989: 175)

In fact, the significant change is that before 1945 most women worked, but since then they have been earning a living independently of their men on a nation-wide scale.

In political life, women have been rather well represented. Eisen (1984: 244) gives the following figures: in the national assembly, the percentage of female representatives was 18.2 per cent in 1965, 32.3 per cent in 1975, but declined to 26.8 per cent in 1976 and 21.8 per cent in 1981. At the village and district levels the percentage of women in people's councils in 1967, for example, reached approximately 45–47 per cent (Le Thi Nham Tuyet, 1975: 296). Compared to the pre-1945 period, this is a marked change. Probably women's participation in political life reached its peak during the American war. As men were mobilised, women played an even greater role than both before and after the war in the production processes, and other aspects of social life.

However, it would be an oversimplification to believe that women have achieved full emancipation as they define it. Though being impressive, the above data do not do fully portray the real situation. Many aspects of the traditional and patriarchal practices remain both inside and outside the family. This can be seen in women's working conditions and the opportunities (or lack of them) for upward social mobility.

Although women work, their working conditions are very poor. In farming labour, all stages of production are done by hand; in other occupations, working tools are primitive. Most management and administrative positions are occupied by men. There has been only one woman in the Politburo of the Communist Party up to now (Werner, 1997). Except for the President of the Vietnamese Women's Union, who is always a woman, and Madame Nguyen Thi Binh, who was Foreign Minister during the American war, and later took over the ministry of education, the highest official is always a man; a woman is often vice-chief. In other words, the highest management position to which a woman can aspire is to assist a male boss (Gammeltoft, 1997a: 205). Apart from the position of President of the Women's Union, the highest one that the well-known female General Nguyen Thi Dinh could take was Deputy Commander-in-Chief of the Southern Armed Forces during the American war.

Few women are promoted to top positions; the resistance they face comes not only from their male colleagues, but also their husbands and husbands' families, as is revealed in the following story.

> This is about the daughter of a poverty-stricken illiterate woman, named Thep, who became the head of a village in Hai Hung province. When she was first promoted, her husband's family was her most militant opposition. The reason was that they were reluctant to see their daughter-in-law with more power than their son. As a village head, Thep

met many people. Therefore the family spread the news that she had committed adultery when her husband was away in the army. By so doing they attacked the woman's most sacred virtue – her faithfulness to her husband.

(Eisen, 1984: 189)

The story has a happy ending, but in fact, the same source also recognises that the husband in the story must have been exceptional in his willingness to support his wife's leadership. Male intransigence is revealed in the following words: 'You may be the boss of the cooperative, but at home, I'm the boss. Even a woodcutter is master in his own home' (Eisen, 1984: 180). That is far from unique. Asked to sum up the most important quality a woman should possess to ensure family happiness, a woman doctor (who is reputedly a very happy wife) says:

> Forbearance. Yes, because every husband, even the best one, wants to show that he is 'master' of the house, a wife must, in the first place, be forbearing. This is my experience.
>
> (Ngan Tam, 1988: 53)

Given the present climate of opinion that it is better for a couple to stick together than to divorce, a wife has to be very flexible, conciliatory, and diplomatic at home. Women learn to keep silent, avoid confrontation, and never contradict their husbands directly. They behave in this way in the hope that after a while, the husband will get used to being with a strong wife (Eisen, 1984: 190). That sounds rather like a vain hope. Those stories show the pressure put on women who are superior to their husbands: to be successful in marriage, they have to be extremely tactful and avoid any action or word that might hurt the masculine pride of their husbands.

As we shall see later (Chapter Four on reproduction), it is still considered a woman's duty to marry and have children. Spinsterhood and failure to have children, (especially sons) equate with failure in the most crucial aspect of life, no matter how well a woman may perform her role at work, or in other spheres of family life. If an unmarried woman gets pregnant, she suffers greatly from the treatment meted out to her by society (this will be discussed later). In many families a wife is regarded primarily as a baby-making machine, and sons are more desirable than daughters. When a couple succeeds in producing a son, it is the husband who claims that it is his 'success'; by contrast, if they fail to produce a son, it is the wife who is blamed. In practising family planning, women have to take the prime responsibility, even if the contraceptive device used has damaging side-effects to her health. Sons are given more opportunity to pursue their studies than are the daughters. If there is any chance to migrate from agricultural areas, priority would be given to sons.

If a family row breaks out, it is the wife who must back down. She is always supposed to remember: 'If your husband is angry, refrain from talking back. Boiling rice does not burn when you lower the flame', as a folk song puts it, and fathers and mothers repeat this to their daughters. Women's work in the countryside ranges from weeding, transplanting, wood gathering, water carrying, sewing, cleaning, washing, and the rearing of domestic animals to shopping, cooking, and serving other family members. Women's work never carries with it the prestige of men's work and the men generally take the most important family decisions. In a lot of families, the wife alone is responsible for all the manual work; her husband does nothing. Household chores and childcare are still largely carried out by the wife, with little help from her spouse, even if she has an outside, full-time job. Moreover, household chores are not only unpaid, but also manual and time-consuming.

To get a concrete image of the daily life of women, we can recommend the Vietnamese film *The Scent of Green Papaya* (directed by Tran Anh Hung) 'which is crowded with subtle ethnographic data', as an American film critic puts it (Mason, 1994). The wife in the movie governs everything in the household: she cares for her three sons and runs the family business. By contrast, the husband is very passive: he lives off his wife's earnings and leads an idle life. Every now and then he disappears for long periods with the money his wife has brought home. The long-suffering wife has to bear all that, but eventually he leaves, taking all the family's money and jewels with him. The wife cries; her mother-in-law blames her for 'having a husband, but you do not know how to make him happy'. Although the wife is a very good human being, selfless, hardworking, kind, and obviously undeserving of blame, this reaction of her mother-in-law is quite telling. In the words of the same film critic, it creates 'a feeling for how life was for women and their time and situation'. Put another way, it is not rare to hear the following criticism of a wife: 'When your husband does wrong things [has an affair, for instance], you should admit that you are to blame. If you had known how to satisfy him as a good wife, he would not have done that!' Only by watching such a movie, can foreign viewers get an insight into what it must be like to be a woman in Vietnam.

Although women work in state-run factories and offices, they are the last hired and the first fired. One reason for this is that they have to take maternity leave and often days off to care for sick small children. Unfortunately there has been no study on this subject. On farms and in other trades, they are often used for much of the backbreaking labour. Another reflection of the strong domestic orientation of women is the recent decrease in their participation in social life, although there has been some improvement in basic education for girls. As the above-quoted data given by Eisen (1984: 244) show, the percentage of female deputies in legislatures of the national assembly has fallen recently. At the commune level, in Hai Van, when soldiers returned from the American war, the number of women in the active local workforce decreased by 20.3 per cent during the period 1975–78 (Houtart and Lemercinier, 1984: 31). This suggests that the great gains made earlier by women are being gradually whittled away. Why?

One reason might be that during the war, by necessity, women's roles were greatly expanded; now that these conditions no longer apply, women are being gradually eased back into their traditional role in the home and marketplace. Another reason may be that women's responsibilities at home limit the opportunities for further training and promotion. One may also posit the theory that the government – the instigator of the movement – launched it simply to get women's support, not with the aim of achieving real emancipation. As the government often states, women play an enormous role in the revolutionary cause; without them the revolution would be unsuccessful (quoted in Le Thi Nham Tuyet, 1975: 187). Therefore it is necessary to do everything that makes it possible for women to carry out fully their historical role (Truong Thanh Dam, 1995).

Meanwhile Son Duong village leaders explained the decline of women's public status in terms of the return of the war veterans and women's lack of rhetorical skills (Luong Van Hy, 1992: 215). This explanation is surprising; the ramifications will be discussed later in this chapter in the section on land reform.

Though these explanations are plausible, none of them is totally satisfactory. The real reason is rooted in the patriarchy, the vestiges of which are very difficult to eradicate. It is generally believed by the Communist Party and government that the obstacles women face in Vietnam stem principally from living in a country devastated by feudalism, colonialism, and wars rather than from gender inequalities *per se*. Women's oppressors are often identified as feudalists (i.e., the class enemy), colonialists, imperialists and other foreign invaders;

male power is rarely mentioned. The leaders of the Communist Party and the government have over-emphasised the class issues at the expense of the gender ones. That has reached the extent that not only women's struggle for emancipation must be subordinated to the task of national liberation, but feminist ideas about equality also have been denounced as 'bourgeois ideologies' (also a class label). In the first full Communist Party programme in October 1930 the leadership emphasised that it was necessary to distinguish the Party's position from the views of 'bourgeois feminism'; the programme called for, among other things, the liberation of women from bourgeois ideas (White, C. P., 1989: 177). This is repeated again later:

> The Party must liberate women from bourgeois ideologies, eradicate the illusion of 'sexual equality' advocated by bourgeois theories. At the same time it must make women participate in the revolutionary struggle of workers and peasants. ... [T]o achieve this, it is necessary to ... give female workers and peasants a serious political education, raise their class consciousness and make them participate in working-class organisations.
>
> (Mies, 1986: 189).

Le Duan insisted that one should look at the women's issue from the class viewpoint (quoted in Le Thi Nham Tuyet, 1975: 16). This took root in the earlier conceptions (see 'Gender separation and women's status' in Chapter One) and explains in part why the country's progress towards female emancipation has met with only limited success: instead of defending and building on the gains made, after the wars the women's emancipation movement seems to be slowing. This has become more apparent under the impact of the socio-economic reforms since 1986.

Apart from confusing the gender issue with the class one, the Communist Party leadership has taken the attitude towards women's roles that is, as White has pointed out, 'a mixture of foreign and indigenous, as well as modern and traditional, views' (White, C.P.,1989: 179). The researcher quotes the male poet Luu Trong Lu, who admired the role that Nguyen Thi Dinh played in the fight against foreign invaders, but preferred to see her in a traditional service role in her relationship to her male comrades: 'In the assault you command a hundred squads. Night returns, you sit mending fighters' clothes' (ibid.: 180). Some of women's traditional roles have also been also encouraged, particularly their responsibility to care for their husband's parents: that would liberate men to leave their villages to serve in the army or in modern economic sector (ibid.: 184).

In other words, there are variations in the way that the women's liberation movement and its goals are perceived and defined, depending on who is defined as the target. Gender relations are 'lost in officialist complacency' (Therborn, 1995: 340) in the countries of the so-called 'socialist camp', but in Vietnam, gender problems are much more acute, as we have seen. Gender equality is understood and interpreted differently in each society. In Vietnam, it can include, among other things, an equal right to education for boys and girls, and equal responsibility for family planning, etc. However, even with regard to those minimum rights, there has been still too little equality. All this reveals the plight of a woman in Vietnam even today, long after the birth of the women's liberation movement.

To conclude, we can say that the government's ideas about the family have changed with the passage of time, and at last have become clear. In their current view, there is a big gap between the family and society, or between the existing family form and the so-called socialist family. Once the so-called socialist production relationships and many other parts of socialist society are established, family members must bridge the gap, work hard in the state-run enterprises, the co-operatives, and teach their children to become good citizens of the socialist society. Thus the government seems to have been taking a view of normative functionalism of the family that emphasises the importance of integration and harmony between different parts of society. An efficient social system requires its parts to fit smoothly. We shall examine later whether this view is accepted by families or not.

SOCIO-ECONOMIC POLICIES AFFECTING THE FAMILY

In this section we deal with different socio-economic policies that are not aimed directly at the family, unlike the ones cited above. However, their effects on the family, even though unintended, are significant.

Class struggle approach during land reform (1953–56)

By the end of the first Indochinese war, poor and landless peasants still constituted 60 per cent of the population (Houtart and Lemercinier, 1984: 13) – that is the data of the whole country; no data about the Delta in particular is available. To the government, this state of affairs was no longer acceptable. In 1953, Truong Chinh, the General Secretary, made a self-critical statement on behalf of the Communist Party for having concentrated up to then only on the struggle against French imperialists, while neglecting the issue of class struggle (Moise, 1983: 181). To mobilise the peasant mass in the decisive period of the war and pave the way to their socio-economic policy, the government started to implement land reform in the North. This campaign aimed at land redistribution by confiscating landlords' properties, giving poor peasants access to the land, creating social justice, liberating the forces of production, increasing production, and improving living standards. These new ideas introduced into Vietnam were supported strongly by the government. In fact, the campaign's most important result was the egalitarian basis of the land distribution, from which a clear majority of families benefited. That meant the rationale of social justice, which lay behind the land reform, had largely been achieved.

However, in 1992, more than thirty years after the land reform, when villagers of one commune were asked what they regarded as the obvious difference between the present and the past, most pointed to the land reform as the period of great fear. Even those people who had benefited from land distribution and who were granted land for the first time in their lives, expressed their anger about the political atmosphere of the period (Kleinen, 1993). Another source (Luong Van Hy, 1992) also mentions these feelings. Why is it paradoxical? It must be said that the campaign also attacked the family relationships among the so-called landlords to an unprecedented extent.

Based on an oversimplified view of rural society, it was estimated that 4–5 per cent of the rural population were landlords (Luong Van Hy, 1992: 188). The land reform cadres had resolutely set out to find the given percentage of landlords per village. To achieve that, they used all means, including the ones that overemphasised class relationships at the expense of the kinship relationships. In fact, many people who were actually members of other classes were misclassified as landlords. We shall see concretely how the campaign affected the landlords' families.

The policy and attitude towards landlords and their families were very controversial. On the one hand, land reform cadres not only distinguished between landlords and their children, but also encouraged children and wives to denounce the landlords. On the other hand, when the land reform was over, landlords' children suffered from strong discrimination because of their family background. We shall examine first the two forms of differentiation between landlords and their families.

Children's isolation from parents. Those who had been labelled as landlords were boycotted and isolated by their fellow villagers. Cadres did not permit their children to visit them and help them, regardless of how old and weak they were. For that reason, a lot of children did not dare to perform their filial duties towards their parents. For example, according to the Communist Party's newspaper *Nhan dan*, one son of a landlord family had been afraid to visit his parents for three years for fear of being vilified as 'connected with landlords' (Moise, 1983: 215). Perhaps that was only one of many cases.

By the end of the reform, the newspaper published advice on how people related to landlords should treat them. *Nhan dan* said that if people visited their landlord relatives during the land reform, they could harm both the mass struggle and themselves. After the reform was over, it would be acceptable for people to visit their relatives who were classified as resistance or ordinary landlords, but the relatives of other landlords were advised to limit themselves to writing letters rather than visiting (Moise, 1983: 215). This is a verified fact.

How did this affect the family relationships? Why is it said that the land reform seriously undermined family relationships? Contrary to the mutual responsibility principle of the traditional law and custom, the land reform movement carried out a policy of differentiation; in fact it urged children to safeguard their own position by not acknowledging the family relationships.

Children's denunciation of parents. This represents the second and more extreme form of differentiation. In many areas, those who were classified as brutal landlords were brought to the so-called people's courts. On such occasions it was not uncommon to see the accused's own daughters or daughters-in-law denounce him publicly, using the pronouns *may* [you] and *tao* [I/me] that were very seldom used in the Vietnamese family and kinship network. This can be seen in a story of a so-called brutal landlord's son about his traumatic experience during the land reform.

> In the story, the old man did not own enough land to rent to anybody, but was classified as a brutal landlord for the reason that he had been a land manager for one of the wealthiest villagers, and had occasionally beaten villagers during his term as a village administrator. The son, who was a *Vietminh* cadre at the time, was ordered to return to the village. The land reform cadres told the son to advise his father to re-

imburse the excess rent that the latter had collected. They also wanted the son to address his father with the pronouns *may* [you] and *tao* [I/me], which implied a total denial of the kinship relation. However, not having the courage to use this form of address, the son looked away from his jailed father, and said quietly: 'Sell whatever possible for the rent reimbursement', thus avoiding totally the use of the offensive pronouns.

However, other relatives did not succeed in avoiding the behaviour expected of them by officialdom. On the trial day, under pressure from the land reform cadres, some close relatives and even the daughter-in-law denounced the father, and addressed him with the pronouns *may* and *tao*. In the end, he was imprisoned. Some years later, after the daughter-in-law passed away, her children moved her tomb away from that of her father-in-law. This action was a direct result of the bitterness in their relationship after her public denunciation and her indirect rejection of their kinship tie by the terms of address she had used during the trial. More than three decades later, the son still does not feel comfortable in the presence of the relatives who denounced his father and addressed him with the terms *may* and *tao* on that trial day. The involved people still feel embarrassing to interact.

(Luong Van Hy, 1992: 189)

We can trust this story because it was told thirty years after the land reform, when people were no longer under pressure from the land reform cadres. Perhaps it is only by reading this story that we can understand how the land reform damaged the landlord family ties. The man and his wife as well as other relatives in this story were expected by the land reform cadres to act in a way contrary to the traditional moral norms and values, and to look for individual security at the expense of their very close family relationships. What they were supposed to do ranged from giving priority to social class position, instead of family relations, to addressing their relatives with the terms denying kinship relations. Why would using such terms entail a denial of kinship relations?

Earlier, in the discussion on the hierarchy of the traditional family (see Chapter One), we mentioned that the proper usage of terms of address was paramount to the hierarchy. Therefore the tasks of socialisation were to teach children four basic skills that were summed up in the popular saying: *Hoc an, hoc noi, hoc goi, hoc mo* [to learn how to eat, speak, wrap things up, and open things]. Learning to speak meant speaking properly according to one's position in relation to other people. Everybody in Vietnam knows that using the pronouns, instead of the kinship terms in the family and kinship network, would destroy the kinship. In this sense, the denouncing of one's relatives and using the pronouns meant the total denial of kinship relationships. This denial was unprecedented in a society where kinship relations were considered to be sacred, or at least undeniable. Moreover, as Ngo Tat To, a North Vietnamese writer since the pre-1945 period, pointed out correctly, the pronouns *may* [you], *tao* [I/me] can be used only by uneducated people, and they imply not only the lack of deference towards the addressee, but also the negation of stable solidarity (Luong Van Hy, 1990: 131). These pronouns are used only by social equals, or by people of superior status; if used by children to address parents, they imply the utmost disrespect because the hierarchy between parents and children is totally broken. (By contrast, parents can use them to address children, but that means the negation of solidarity, and is not seen as good practice.)

The son in the story above chose a novel form of address: to delete the subject and avoid using the pronouns *may* and *tao*. To the Vietnamese, the deletion of the subject in speaking to senior people (*an noi trong khong*) also showed disrespect, but it was not of the worst kind. His wife hurt her close relative and the kinship relationships so deeply, that after her death the children had to separate her tomb from that of the relative whom she had hurt. To understand this action fully, we need to interpret it in the Vietnamese cultural context. As will be pointed out in Chapter Four on reproduction, death is believed to be a continuation of existence, but in another form; so family members are often buried close to each other. Tombs are always so sacred that traditional laws even stipulated that people who intrude upon tombs or graves must be severely punished (Toan Anh, n.d.: 381–385). The removal of someone's tomb is carried out only when (s)he is an immoral person. That means people who implemented the class struggle orthodoxy at the expense of kinship were regarded as immoral.

Usually the denunciations took place in public areas, in the presence of a lot of other people. Their impact were not limited to the landlords' families, but wide-ranging on the family ties in general. One might say that by forcing children to deny the traditional principle of mutual responsibility, the authorities tried to replace it with the new one of individual responsibility, and to liberate children.

However, the traditional principle of mutual responsibility seemed to continue. Children of the landlords were also ill-treated, regardless of their innocence. According to Moise, who has read and verified different sources, there were two sisters aged 17 and 20, both with good reputations in their village as strong and enthusiastic workers in the rice field. Their father had been arrested, and the land reform cadres were trying to undermine the prestige of the whole family. They were assigned to do corvée labour wearing hats labelled 'despot' (Moise, 1983: 216–217).

It could be said that the differentiation principle was applied during the land reform campaign only; after the campaign was over, the other principle was put into effect – that is to say the discrimination against landlords' children based on the principle of mutual responsibility. Landlords' children, regardless of how bright, were not admitted to institutions of higher education, though they were employable in nonsensitive positions in the state apparatus (Luong Van Hy, 1992: 195). This state of affairs lasted for a very long time. In this sense, the differentiation was used not to liberate children from their landlord-fathers, but just as a means to achieve the desired goals of the land reform (to reach the given 4–5 per cent of population as landlords). The principle of mutual responsibility was kept and continued.

When the government recognised the serious errors committed in the land reform, and tried to retreat from extremism by carrying out the so-called 'correction of errors', wrongly classified landlords took revenge against those who had wronged them. That created a widespread climate of tension and dread in a good number of places (Moise, 1983: 250-258).

In sum, the land reform was a response to genuine demands from the poor peasants. In fact it made a radical effort to provide adequate landholdings for this sector of the population and gave them what they had always dreamed of – lands and buffaloes, that was to say, the economic basis to earn a secure living. However, as an unintended consequence of this, the landlord family ties were seriously undermined. Although only those families classified as landlords came under heavy fire, the land reform brought about wide-ranging repercussions in society at large.

By applying the policy of differentiation between landlords and their children during the land reform, the cadres tended to see the class enemy everywhere, even within their own families. That was why they made the landlord family members into the political opponents, class-based enemies, and why they pushed them to deny the family and kinship relationships. This damage to the family ties was undeniable. It is argued that class is a concept of internal division in societies where kinship relationships are relatively weak (Therborn, 1995: 6), but when coming from Europe to Vietnam, it was regarded as a scientific discovery, a new idea, even 'the thread guiding the development of our society' (Bui Tin, 1995: 66). In this class struggle orthodoxy there is something reminiscent of the Marxist theory of the bourgeois family, in which the husband is seen as the exploiter, and the wife as the exploited (i.e., class enemies) (Engels, 1972: 82), and the parent–child relationship is tainted with exploitation (Geiger, 1968: 53). The class approach brought about gains to landless and poor peasants, and losses to landlords. However, the losses were so heavy that their psychological effects persisted, while the material gains seem to be neglected even by the beneficiaries.

Economic development policy in agriculture during the central-planning economy

After the country's division (1954), the government began the task of economic reconstruction and social development in the North. The development strategy was the central planning aimed at rapid industrialisation, collectivisation of agriculture, and strong state control of the whole economy. In their view, large-scale production was always preferable to small-scale. To achieve that, industrialisation was urgently required. As they put it, 'the primary duty of the entire transitional period in the North is socialist industrialisation, of which the key is the development of heavy industry' (quoted in Fforde *et al.*, 1987: 38). This mimics the Soviet model which was based on assumption that collective production was superior to private production. Again, here we have new evidence about how the imported ideas of social change and of modernisation were taken up and imposed on the family.

Believing in the Marxist theory about the necessity of abolition of private property, and hoping to get resources for an accelerated industrialisation within a centrally planned and collectivist economy, the government started collectivisation of agriculture in the late 1950s. Moreover, they were afraid that private property and production would mean that many peasants who had got land during the land reform would once again become landless.

Many co-operatives were established. All the means of agricultural production, including fields, buffaloes, cows and farm instruments, became the co-operatives' property, and were pooled, except for the 5 per cent of land that was left for household use as residential, gardening, and animal husbandry land. At the beginning co-operative members received their share of the crop according to their labour input and their contribution of land and draft animals to the co-operative. Gradually the methods of agricultural production and of crop distribution changed. Co-operative members received points for the work on contract to the task-specialised brigades under the co-operatives' management. For the peasants, this meant that the family no longer functioned as a production unit. Rather than farming in the small family units as in the past, family members worked on different tasks and in different places in the collectivised production.

There was no doubt that the co-operatives had some strong advantages. Apart from paying for production costs and taxes to the state, the co-operatives put aside portions of their total yearly products for collective use – such as the accumulation funds and social security funds – and used the rest to pay the members for their labour. Thanks to those funds, families who lacked labourers, or elderly people whose children had been killed during the wars, or families of disabled soldiers and so on, received some subsidies and managed to survive.

Women in general also benefited greatly from collectivisation: as Le Thi Nham Tuyet (1991) has summed up, a large number of them transferred from agricultural production to non-agricultural services. They caught up with men with regard to their standard of primary and secondary education; they were able to comprehend and apply new techniques to boost production. They also improved their social position: from being private peasants, a great number of them have become the members of managerial boards of the co-operatives, heads of the co-operatives, production teams and other leading positions. Social services were instituted widely in rural areas: dispensaries, maternity homes, crèches, kindergartens, schools, clubs, libraries, cultural houses, amateur art groups, and mobile projection teams. All of these benefited women.

However, besides these advantages, there were also many disadvantages attached to the co-operatives. Work for the co-operative became increasingly less attractive than work for one's own plot; consequently people began to turn their attention to the household garden. They showed up late and tried to finish the work for the co-operative on contract as soon as possible so that they could take care of their gardens and other economic activities for themselves. This could be seen in a number of concrete examples.

In fact, many families who agreed to breed water buffaloes on a contractual basis with the co-operatives that now owned them, failed to look after the animals in a responsible manner. This was a profound change. In the past, as Gourou (1936/1955: 461–462) pointed out, a buffalo represented a considerable investment that was beyond the means of many country people; that was why they used to care for them quite well. Under collectivisation, buffaloes were badly fed and overworked. The animals became exhausted and then died. There was a simple reason for this change of attitude towards the livestock: families who bred buffaloes no longer owned the animals themselves. As a result of this, there was an endemic cattle shortage that undermined the Vietnamese economy. A man who grew up in Vietnam before 1945, but then lived abroad for long time before coming back for a visit in 1979 said that if the collectivist economy continued, the buffalo would all die in Vietnam (Luong Van Hy, 1992: 207).

Another example: in Hai Van commune in 1979, when questioned the peasants said that the work done on their private plot of ground was definitely more intensive (two or three times more intensive) than that done on collectively held land. It was the same story with the use of fertilisers (Houtart and Lemercinier, 1984: 40). Of course, the type of production employed on the private plot of land was different from that used on collectively held land, but the estimation given by the peasants was rather conservative. In fact, the work invested in the private plot of land was almost certainly much higher than claimed. As for incomes, the average proportion of cash revenue of families yielded by domestic economy was said to be 45 per cent of total income (Houtart and Lemercinier, 1984: 40).[2] Again, this figure would most probably have been an underestimate since, if the peasants were to reveal the true figure, they would no doubt suffer all kinds of trouble.

Why did family members work in a lazy way in spite of the advantages that the co-operatives offered to them? The main reason was that under collectivisation, it was the collectives (brigades) and not the individuals that were directly connected to the end products of their labour. As a result of this, people felt they were being underpaid. However hard-working they might be, their incomes were much smaller than what they had invested. On the one hand, they had to feed the bureaucratic apparatus, which demanded too much and took a significant share of the crops even though it contributed little to output. On the other hand, the state's policy was unfair. The purchase price for paddy that the state commercial apparatus offered to the co-operatives fell increasingly behind the black-market price and the inflation-prone cost of living. So the share of the crop that each and every peasant received from the co-operatives became smaller and smaller.

For that reason, members of the co-operatives became alienated from their products in co-operative production. Though Marx was regarded in Vietnam as the greatest thinker, his ideas were not implemented. According to him, work is the humanising activity *par excellence*; it is meant to connect us to the products of our minds and bodies, to nature, and to other people. Under collectivisation work lost that meaning and failed even to connect family members together. When the family was no longer the independent production unit, family members lost the co-operation and material basis that they had earlier enjoyed. The main thing they had in common now was consumption. In production women and older children earned income in kind (mainly) as well as in cash under their own names, similar to the male labour; i.e., they might be paid independently for their work, so that they could see what their contribution to the family income was. In this sense women were supposed to become equal to men. However, the labour norm was set by male work: if a day's work for a male labourer was usually 10 work points, for instance, the rest of labourers (women, older children) were listed on a lower scale; thus the maximum for women was usually 8 work points.

Nonetheless, family members had no choice. Let us take Son Duong village, Vinh Phu province, as an example. At the beginning of the collectivisation, quite a few villagers were unenthusiastic. Under the guidance of the Communist Party, its members were instructed to take the lead in persuading their families to join a co-operative as well as in convincing their relatives and other villagers. As a result, most villagers eventually joined, but up to 15 per cent of members withdrew at one point (Luong Van Hy, 1992: 197). However, the first achievements in co-operative production, and the policy of discrimination against those who did not join, left the villagers no option. So they had only one way to take action and express their dissatisfaction: they worked lazily in the co-operatives.

This happened not only to Son Duong, but to many other co-operatives in the Delta. That was the price paid for the imposition of the co-operative mode of agricultural production, which deprived the family of its function as a production unit. Nevertheless, the government misinterpreted this behaviour as the pure survival of the outmoded private ownership relations. It is believed in orthodox

Marxism that small-scale, private production gradually leads to capitalism; that is why Vietnam's pre-1986 governemnt did not accept private production

If feedback mechanisms in social steering are always a special problem for communist regimes, the situation is much more acute in a Confucian society. The leaders here always regard themselves as the perfect gentlemen, and the masses – just as the subjects of their teaching. Therefore, public opinion polls are very few and far between, their results are not published; they are known only to high ranking leaders, but interpreted in completely wrong ways. Those leaders who do pay attention to feedback mechanisms are criticised as promoting 'excessive democracy', and of being led by the nose, like a buffalo. That was one of the main reasons for the acute food shortage which reached a peak in the late 1970s.

Industrialisation, household registration, and housing policies

To accelerate industrialisation, the government started to eliminate the social structure inherited from the French rule on the one hand, and to recruit the members of the new industrial labour force from swarms of young, inexperienced peasants on the other hand. In urban areas, the middle class with its way of life was considered to be exploitative, high-living, degenerate, or at least isolated from the working masses. Middle-class property was confiscated, or they were forced to sell it through compulsory purchase. Their way of life was discredited in the eyes of nearly everybody. As a result, this class disappeared after some years. Poor urban residents and state employees became the real masters of cities.

Concomitant with the disappearance of the middle class was the passing of the elegant ways of dressing, the polite ways of behaving, and even the courteous ways of addressing and speaking which were characterised by the standard accent of the thousand-year-old capital. This is recalled and described by a reporter (Pham Thi Thu Thuy, 1994) in the fortieth celebration of the French troops' retreat from Hanoi.

The state urbanisation policy placed a limit on migration from rural to urban areas through the state planning system, comprising two clear policies: (a) the household registration scheme and (b) the distinction in urban areas between state and non-state employees. Lacking research data about that, we cannot be certain about how those regulations affected the family, but we may say that the household registration system had far-reaching social consequences in family life. It created not only a spatial hierarchy and gave priority to the city over the countryside, but it also prevented population migration from place to place (a resident of city or town may freely get permission to move and work in rural areas, but someone from a rural area cannot readily obtain permission to move to a town or city). It was difficult to move even within the countryside.[3]

The system fixed people in place on the basis of their birthplace or, in the case of women, of their husband's residence. In fact, its far-reaching effects accentuated the distinction between insiders and outsiders in traditional villages. In urban areas, residence became associated with sharply differentiated socio-economic benefits. Without registration one could not establish eligibility for food, clothing, shelter, employment, schools, medical facilities and other essentials and amenities of life. Therefore it was quite difficult for ordinary migrants to bring their families with them.

It also became difficult to migrate within the state sector for the state employees even as individuals. A study of Liljeström and Ohlsson (1988) tells us that if a state worker wants to relocate, (s)he has to find a new workplace and obtain written approval from there (this is given after an investigation into the worker's personal file has been carried out), then get an approval from the present workplace by submitting an application for transfer. If (s)he is a good worker, and the present workplace needs him (her), and therefore does not want to approve of the application, then objections may be arise. The worker has to delay the transfer for a while in order for the present workplace to find a substitute. Only after the new, prospective workplace gets a signed document from the head of the former workplace can it give the new employee food rations, etc. If the worker leaves without permission and wants to continue to work as a state employee, (s)he would face major difficulties in gaining access to food, housing, hospitals, and so on in a new workplace (ibid.: 58). We need to clarify that those rules were applicable to all state employees, not just to forestry workers.[4]

Another point needs to be made: in many cases if the present workplace did not like a worker, it may or may not approve of his (her) application for transfer. Every year each state workplace got a *chi tieu bien che* [quota] of its staff set and fixed by a higher organisation; this curtailed its ability to recruit new blood exceeding the quota. In general, there was very limited freedom to move from job to job.

In fact the new social structure in urban areas made a distinction between state and non-state employees; often treating the latter as the second-class citizens (existing literature has never dealt with this issue!).[5] Because state employment played a welfare role in the sense that it was closely related to many social services, the size of state-run labour forces was systematically limited as if there was a huge barrier around it. As a result of this, the social differences between the families of different social categories were obscured, except the one between the state employees and the non-state employees. In this respect the Vietnamese leadership follows the Chinese model which Walder (1986: 6) has named 'communist neo-traditionalism'. A central premise of this ideology is that 'political loyalty is rewarded systematically with career opportunities, special distributions, and other favours that officials in communist societies are uniquely able to dispense' (ibid.).

The above-mentioned process also transformed families in cities and towns into the units of consumption. However, the living conditions of families were very poor. This can be seen first in the housing crisis. Between 1955 and 1965, an estimated 650,000 peasants were transferred from their villages to non-agricultural assignments in industry, construction, transportation and commerce (Woodside, 1976: 261). Although the rural–urban migration was carried out according to the state's plans, it led to a housing shortage. The housing crisis was so deep that in Hanoi that 'whole families slept together in one bed' as a Frenchman who had lived in Vietnam much of his adult life described vividly (Shaplen, 1986: 81). The observation by a southerner visiting Hanoi reinforces this picture: 'In each house I visited, several families lived. Often a curtain stretched across the room was all that separated one family's area from another's' (Truong Nhu Tang et al., 1985: 243). Some quantitative data confirm that: in 1989 on average, one-third of the housing units had less than 4 square metres per person and two-thirds had less than 6 square metres per person (*Ket qua dieu tra mau nha o*, 1990).

At the start of the process of industrialisation, many young people migrating from their villages were still single; they lived in collective houses without private kitchens and sanitary facilities. Eventually they got married. According to the official policy, state employees were to be provided with state housing. They were allocated low-rent accommodation in accordance with their rank within the state apparatus. Nevertheless, the type of building where they lived was extremely uncomfortable. As Tran Hoai Anh (1993) has shown, a typical example of this were the collective houses in Doc Tho Lao, Nguyen Cong Tru street, and Kim Lien living quarter (Hanoi). There were no private kitchen, bathroom and toilet for each family. Instead, several families had to share sanitary facilities and a collective kitchen. That was something of a paradox: the family was no longer the production unit, it was supposed to be the consumption unit only; however it lacked the necessary spatial conditions for it to function effectively in that capacity. (In the eyes of the government, compared to production, consumption in general is underrated.) Needless to say, this created a lot of conflicts among families; people resisted this collective arrangement and eventually abandoned it. The families cooked in the corridor in front of their rooms.

Why had such an inappropriate building type been adopted for family life? According to the state building sector, the collective house reflected a misunderstanding of apartment building type in other (East European) countries, and an ignorance about the quality of housing (Tran Hoai Anh, 1993: 7–8). In my view, although this type of housing was imported from abroad, it corresponded well to the official ideology of collectivism of the new regime. Being ideologically oriented, it was considered to be suitable for the new generation with a new way of living, when the conditions for private ownership of land and construction of house were no longer permitted. The idea of collectivism and collective living was so strong that possession of a private house was considered to be morally reprehensible. In fact, it was regarded as the embodiment of individualistic behaviour, even though the house was for the whole family, not just a single individual. An exclusive devotion to one's family was identified with individualistic behaviour. In this sense, what is understood as 'individualistic' in Vietnam is not so in Western sense; in fact it means familistic.

Moreover, the neglected kitchen also meant there was no attempt made to improve working conditions of housewives, and no mechanisation of housework chores. In this sense, housework would continue to be manual and time-consuming for an indefinite period. It was only with the recent developments since the late 1980s that the idea of the collective kitchen and sanitary facilities was abandoned totally in favour of private ones for every household. Nevertheless the traces left by the early socialist concepts of family life can still be seen today and have adversely affected not only individual families, but also general public opinion regarding correct family values.

Distribution policy in the shortage economy

The central-planning economy also affected the family as a consumption unit in another way. Placing substantial emphasis on heavy industry meant neglecting, to some extent, the problem of consumption. Shortage was an inherent part of the economy.[6] The 'shortage economy' was accompanied by many serious problems in distribution. The state provided the state employees with a benefits system that was denied both to rural residents and to non-state employees in urban areas. However this system turned out to be, in many cases, a mixed blessing.

Each state employee's family received a food allocation based on the number of people in the family. They were given a food coupon, including a ration of rice, corn, wheat, and other low-priced foods. However, due to the shortage problem, the seller's 'market' predominated. Families had endless trouble in getting the rations to which they were entitled. Family members, especially women and children, had to spend hours queuing in different shops. According to the data about housing problems in Hanoi in the late 1970s and early 1980s, a working woman spent about three hours and fifteen minutes each day on household chores, mainly buying the rations for her family; whereas a man spent just one hour and fifty minutes (Khuat Thu Hong, 1991). The figures cannot be checked, but give us some approximate estimations. In such a situation consumption took a great deal of time and energy on the part of family members. Women with outside jobs were overloaded by both family commitments and job responsibilities; frequently a conflict of roles arose.

The reason for this state of affairs lay in the character of the central-planning economy. Because of the way the economy was managed, production units in industry had little interest in either the value of what they produced or consumers' demands. On the other hand, in the Marxist ideology an overemphasis on consumption was considered to be corrupt, and so the government tried to eliminate it. Much of the service sector that had fulfilled family consumer demands was downsized because it was seen as promoting capitalism; its consumers were labelled as following a bourgeois way of life. According to an American reporter's observation in Hanoi in 1984, there were very few restaurants left because of the heavy taxes on 'unwanted luxury establishments' (Shaplen, 1986: 79). This specific repercussion not only affected the family, but also undermined the Northern culinary tradition, which was famous for its originality as well as its excellent blending of Chinese and French cuisine. As a result, the family was left to itself in organising consumption.

As a consequence, the state employees kept their official jobs, but were present in workplaces only nominally. Because they were paid on the basis of the number of days they worked rather than on their production rates, people became alienated. On the one hand, family members were lazy when working in state factories. In fact, they invested a lot of their working time going to different shops and buying their rations. An official of the Hai Phong city committee said in 1971 that during the American bombings of 1965–68, the situation that emerged 'in a number of places' was one of:

> free work stoppages, of coming to work late and going home early, of disorderly and negligent performances, of profitlessly prolonged meetings, of rules and regulations of production not being respected, and of internal discipline rules being violated.

The number of days and hours of useful work was therefore very low, productivity declined, and output gradually diminished (Woodside, 1976: 264). Although this description is accurate, it did not do full justice to the real situation, which was far worse.

The other side of the coin was that people had to look for second jobs and extra business to get some additional income to feed their families as consumption units. The afore-mentioned American reporter described the difficulties of everyday life in Hanoi in 1984, and how people managed to make both ends meet. Even with a modest ration system for basic necessities, and with low, government-controlled rents, more income was needed by the majority. That was why 'just about everyone was moonlighting in one way or another, or buying and selling or bartering goods on the side' (Shaplen, 1986: 80).

Further undesirable side-effects of the shortage economy materialised, as evidenced by one Vietnamese official: 'A number of social evils developed, such as dishonest trading, smuggling, the stealing of state property, lives of immoral obsessions, the loss of hygiene ...' (Woodside, 1976: 264). Thus all this resistance to the imposed changes at last led to a deep socio-economic crisis that forced the communists to change their policies in the late 1980s, as we shall see in the section about renovation policy.

UNPLANNED SOCIAL CHANGES

During the last half century there have also been some changes that were not planned in the social steering programme of the government. These include wars that can be regarded as the hostile external and internal contexts of socialist steering, as Therborn (1995) puts it, and the so-called renovation and 'open door' policy.

Wars

Whereas the population of the Red River Delta did not have to participate in external wars from 1885 until 1940 (when Japanese troops invaded Vietnam), 'and had not been subjected to the heavy death tolls', as Gourou (1936/1955: 224) pointed out, it had withstood repeated foreign ravages throughout the last half century: first by the French, when the Delta was one of the principal battlefields of the country, then by the American air forces. Two other wars – one in Cambodia that lasted over ten years (1978–91); the other at the Chinese border in 1979 – caused heavy losses of life among the soldiers who came from the Delta. The effects of these wars on the family were incalculable.

Loss of family members. The most obvious consequence of the wars was the loss of life. The number of military and civilian deaths was not revealed in Vietnam for a long time; the government was afraid that the number might lead to a loss of morale during the wars. However, according to a first toll released by the Vietnamese government twenty years after the American war ended in 1975, more than one million North Vietnamese and Viet Cong soldiers had been killed; another 300,000 were listed as missing; 600,000 were wounded; and in addition, about two million civilians had lost their lives. These numbers do not include casualties of the South Vietnamese soldiers. The war left two million Vietnamese invalid, and nearly as many suffered from the effects of chemical defoliants used by US forces. This source also said that the numbers were incomplete (Agence France-Presse, 1995).

More cruel than any other war, the American one left, according to the above source, 50,000 children born with deformities as a result of the dioxin Agent Orange. Of course, statistics alone can never tell the whole truth about the human cost, in both physical and psychological terms, to the families of these deformed children. The numbers of deaths during the wars in Cambodia and at the Chinese border are unknown.

However big the numbers may be, they cannot convey the full horror of the terrible losses of Vietnam, nor their effects on the family. An unknown number of families, for example, split up because of the war. During the American war, many families in the Delta sent their husbands and sons to the South. Countless families lost fathers, sons, and brothers, but never learnt when or where their relatives had been killed or buried. From the Vietnamese perspective, this is a double loss because their families lack the means to pay proper homage to their dead. When a southerner visited many families in the North, he found that invariably there was an altar set up in the corner with photographs of a husband or children killed in the South. Very often, even the place of death or burial was unknown. This is 'a loss of unimaginable proportions for these people, who revered the dead and held their final resting places sacred' (Truong Nhu Tang *et al.*, 1985: 243–234).

Population imbalance between men and women. As a result of these losses, Vietnam faces a large population imbalance between men and women. The 1989 census revealed that females comprised 51.5 per cent of the population, but men made up only 48.5 per cent. Among marriageable adults, the gap was even greater: 58.2 per cent of those in the 20–39 years age group were women, while men made up only 47.2 per cent (Hiebert, 1994).

As a consequence, when polygamy is officially forbidden, many women have to stay single. Who are they? They may be war veterans. During the American war, it was not only men who were mobilised: young, single women were also recruited if they volunteered. They often joined the so-called volunteer youth brigades, whose tasks were to build, rebuild, and repair roads along the Ho Chi Minh Trail, and to be guides. Many were killed or wounded; others spent their youth in isolated and remote forestry areas, with little chance of finding a husband. When the war was over, they came back to their native villages. It was too late for them to marry in a country where the imbalance was exacerbated by the death of so many young men, and where a 30-year-old was regarded as a lost cause.

An unknown number of other women are war widows. Many of them never had the time to start to raise a family and after the war and the loss of their husbands, they had little chance of remarrying. Apart from them, a great many other women also face similar problems. One must bear in mind that the family is still the only institution in Vietnam that guarantees a social support in old age. This creates tremendous anxiety for these unmarried women: who will take care of them when they get old? The only solution is to have children out of wedlock. It is among this group of women that a new family type has appeared: families of single mothers.

In the traditional family, that was unacceptable. As mentioned in Chapter One about the double standard of conduct for men and women, custom often decreed that an unmarried mother had to pay a heavy fine to her village. Not long time ago, between the 1960s and the 1980s, unmarried women who dared to get pregnant were heavily accused. Those who were state employees were often ordered to write a letter admitting the fault of having a child outside marriage, or 'illicit sexual relationship' as officials usually put it. A special meeting was held during which they were forced to read the letter loud to others, who then criticised them. In the end they were given a warning (from their bosses) to desist from premarital sexual relationship (Hiebert, 1994).

Nevertheless, recently the official policy towards single mothers has changed dramatically. This is owing to, on the one hand, strong pressure exerted by many women who were victims of the wars, and on the other, to the government policy of recruiting mainly women forestry workers and state farmers, and concentrating them in remote enterprises where it was impossible for them to find husbands. (The female forestry workers symbolise the government conception of women's liberation: they are taken away from their parents' family to engage in areas of state production, where there are hardly any men. In fact, that is a continuation of gender separation, but on a much larger scale.)

Unmarried women are now allowed to have a child. The way they achieve this is to have a brief affair with a married man (no unmarried men are available), get pregnant, then to sever all contact with the child's father, even though he may be living and working in the same village (Le Nham, 1994). In such cases, because many men want to keep the affairs secret, and the women themselves finish the relationship, children bear the mother's family name. In other words, these families follow a matrilineal system. Compared to the patrilineal system prevalent in the traditional family, this is a marked change. However, it is still not easy to foresee the social problems that this type of family faces, as well as the ones it causes to the family institution and relationships between the two sexes. Many wives do not dare to criticise their husbands for having extramarital affairs; they are afraid that their marital status will be threatened if they reprimand their husbands.

Post-war economic difficulties and military men's identity crisis. The continuous wars created a special group in the Vietnamese society: professional military men and veterans who spent much, if not most of their lifetime in military service. Official statistics about them have never been revealed. According to an estimate, in a country of sixty-five million people, there are approximately eight million veterans (Ngo Vinh Long, 1993: 202). The wars affected them differently. After the American war, many of them were demobilised. Coming back from the armed services, they had to adjust to a totally new environment unfamiliar for them: civilian life, which often entailed readjusting to family life, too. That created a lot of problems which find their clearest expression in contemporary literature (written works as well as folk songs) more than anywhere else. Unfortunately, no sociological study has dealt with these problems so far. For that reason I have to rely entirely on literary works.

A number of post-war novels and short stories deal with the themes of readjustment to civilian life and family concerns faced by demobilised military men. According to Nguyen Khai, a well-known Vietnamese novelist, these new works 'make up for lack of style and imagination by being more matter of fact, more realistic in confronting everyday hardships and problems' than pre-war authors' works (quoted in Shaplen, 1986: 32). What sort of problems do these men have to face?

Some of them went home from the front-line to discover heartache because their lovers or wives had not waited for them for a number of unusual reasons created by the wars. So the war had paid them for all their suffering and losses in action with more suffering and loss at home; their life, after many destructive years of wars, had been punctured by the sharp thorns of love.

Another problems is that as these men had spent most of their lives fighting, they have neither qualifications nor a trade. As a hero in the award-winning novel *The Sorrow of War* by Bao Ninh (1991/1993: 39) puts it, 'right now my only skills are firing submachine-guns and collecting bodies'. After the country's reunification in 1976, when almost everybody's high expectations of peace and improved social welfare were left unfulfilled, the situation deteriorated for demobilised military men. The glorious, bright rays of victory, the grand, long-awaited return did not bring the anticipated high standard of living; on the contrary, their living conditions were poor. They did not know how to earn a living, nor how to support a family. Many who have been left disabled receive regular financial assistance from the government, but that is far from enough. In the above-mentioned novel by Bao Ninh, himself a war veteran, after the demobilisation the hero felt that

> he was at a stage when he had no idea how he would spend the rest of his life ... He had no idea of how he would earn his daily living. It was a time of utter isolation, of spiritual emptiness, of surrender.
>
> (Bao Ninh, 1991/1993: 67)

In other words, many veterans are in a deep crisis; the glorious military victory does not bring the expected decent standard of living, but poverty. Having contributed to the country's military success, they feel they have earned the respect of society; however, for being poor, they are often looked down on with disdain by some groups. An American reporter tells us that 'a distinguished general in his retirement must depend on his wife selling cigarettes in the street; she walks two miles a day so she won't have to lose face with the neighbours'; the famous general Vo Nguyen Giap confirmed that this is true (White, 1989). In other words, the veterans survive mainly thanks to their wives' capacity to earn a living and frugal measures to make both ends meet.

The problem facing demobilised men is learning to adapt to family life. A lot of them are unable to live up to their roles as husband and father in the family institution that is undergoing such marked changes. As professional military men, they were totally different from the rest of society; they were socialised into roles that were characterised by a rigid hierarchy, by discipline, specific values, norms, ways of dressing, and greeting. Above all, they were taught and trained to withstand the privations and hardships that are said to be an integral part of the life of a revolutionary military man. As a result of this, they accepted almost all the privations. In terms of the family, they were often away from home, and had little interaction with other family members apart from periods of leave. As the writer Ma Van Khang (1985) puts it in his best-seller novel *Mua la rung trong vuon* [Leafshedding season in the garden], they never had to feed the family and socialise the children. Leaving the military life, coming back to family life, they bring with them those values and norms that are, in their view, the best, revolutionary, and socialist ones.

However, the post-war social reality makes them disillusioned. Having once had faith in the Communist Party and its propaganda, they are disappointed to see so much nepotism and corruption among high-ranking officials, on the one hand, and unemployment, poverty, and rising criminality among the young, on the other hand. In their families, because of the need to overcome huge financial difficulties and earn a living while their men were away at war, many wives and children learnt the art of compromise and no longer accepted those ascetic, austere norms and values that the husbands, as veterans, still held dear. Consequently, a generation gap and marital conflict have arisen in their families. In response to his older brother's demand on the revolutionary moral principles, a hero in the above novel by Ma Van Khang says: 'I am afraid it is not suitable to emphasise morality at present. We have been poor for too long a time'. By contrast, a heroine – the wife of a retired military man – is quite renowned for her protest against the revolutionary moral values that emphasise only a materially simple way of life and which are applauded by her father-in-law and husband. This is confirmed by an older revolutionary leader:

> We know that young people have their own aspirations – that they want better clothes, some up-to-date fashions, a richer culture. These things should be welcome. That's progress, and we're not fighting it. But their minds and spirits are important. We must keep them Vietnamese, and their achievement will then be great.

A Western author comments that that seems like more hope than conviction (Shaplen, 1986: 65).

To put it another way, a great number of military men have experienced a fundamental crisis: everything they have achieved and of which they are so proud – like their medals – will not put food on the table. In addition they are often despised by certain segments of the population. They are men, yet they are not able to act as breadwinners. On the contrary, they are so poor that they cannot feed themselves, let alone their families. Many of them have no jobs, no qualifications, and no way of making money, and therefore have to rely on their wives for their survival. Their sense of self-worth and even self-identity are threatened. Lacking sociological research findings, we do not know how many families are in this crisis nor how well they are coping with it. In short, the wars' multifarious impacts on the family are quite enormous, but we do not have scientific proof to determine precisely the effect they have had on the family.

Renovation, the 'open door' policy, and economic reform

The declining productivity of the co-operative land and the state industrial enterprises led to a socio-economic crisis from the late 1970s. In December 1986, the government launched its economic reform programmes, known as *doi moi* [renovation], the aim of which is to move away from a central planning economy to a market-led one. They have also adopted a policy named *mo cua* [open door] towards the West in an effort to raise trade and encourage foreign investment.

This is a forced step for the government as the leaders of social steering. In fact, some changes in the same direction as renovation had taken place much earlier. The first attempt to encourage peasant families to farm more productively on the basis of a contract system had been made in Vinh Phu province as early as 1966, but the leaders regarded it as

> a decentralised management method that weakens the collective economy and incidentally enlarges the household economy sector. It is contrary to the principle of socialist management. It is a symptom of rightist thinking.
>
> (Luong Van Hy, 1992: 203)

So they stopped it forcibly: the provincial Party chief was said to have been placed under house arrest (Wurfel, 1993: 24).

The practice was secretly revived in Hai Phong province in 1977; although it had impressive results, it was regarded as *khoan chui* [dubious, or illegal contract system]. By the end of the 1970s, the threat of widespread famine as well as other socio-economic difficulties had forced the leaders to take note of the grass-roots pressure for change and to tolerate experiments that were not laid out in their plan. In 1979 they decided to try a 'contract system' in agriculture that would establish a direct link between peasant families and the state. The state-owned enterprises would be permitted to break some official regulations, and exchange or sell goods on the open market in order to raise cash and buy material or pay bonuses to workers. That was why this was called *pha rao* [fence-breaking] in the sense that individual factories made efforts to break through the constraints of the central planning system. In spite of that, these were just reactive adjustment measures, aimed at rescuing the long-term 'socialist project'.

Although the renovation was begun in December 1986, it was impossible then to achieve a drastic reform package. Three further years of deeper socio-economic crisis would be required before the Party gave up their old economic management system, and carried out more fundamental reforms in 1989. Peasant families had to wait until April 1988 to be recognised as the basic unit of agricultural production. All this tells us how reluctant the leaders have been in implementing renovation policy (for a summary, see Tria Kerkvliet, 1995). We shall now examine those reforms and their impact on agriculture, industry, and trade.

Agricultural reform. In 1981 the government authorised the household contract system, according to which the household, through a two-year contract with the co-operatives, was responsible for certain links of agricultural production: transplanting, tending and harvesting the rice crop, for which it received work-point credits. The co-operatives did the rest. Collectively owned land was allocated on the basis of the household's adult workforce. A production quota was fixed. Income of a contracting household depended not only on the value of each work-point in paddy and the number of work-points accumulated by the household, but also on the crop yield over and above the quota. Households which exceeded the quota were allowed to keep the surplus for themselves. This reform made an important contribution to increased production in the early 1980s.

However, it did not really change the responsibility of production from the collectives to the individual households. Therefore it could produce only a short-term effect. Fundamental changes were required. In 1988, the government issued the Directive 10 that guaranteed co-operative members long-term (fifteen-year) leases on the contracted land and at least 40 per cent of the production quota for their performing the tasks of transplanting, crop tending, and harvesting. Household contractors that exceed contract yields through increased investment in terms of labour and capital have the right to keep all the surplus for themselves. The co-operatives are responsible for tractor ploughing, irrigation, insecticide spraying, and crop protection. In other words, the co-operatives now play only supporting roles – such as helping the households with getting water, seeds, and fertilisers. So the peasants in the collective sector have greater control of the fruits of their labour. On the other hand, the existence of various economic sectors, including the household sector, is reaffirmed.

In addition, in 1993, the new land law was adopted. However, it does not recognise the land-ownership right of families. Instead it states that all land belongs to the whole people; 'long-term user right' of individual households means twenty years for short-term crops (rice), and fifty years for long-term crops (timber, rubber). When the term ends, the user rights can be withdrawn from a household only if it fails to exploit the land adequately. User rights are inheritable and can be transferred against payment of compensation (i.e., sale).

Although still limited in their scope, these reforms are said to herald a fresh wind of change in the Delta. The movement away from collectivised agriculture towards household production means that peasant households have become the principal production units in countryside. As a result of this, there has been a substantial increase in food production since 1989. This has also proved that the family is the most efficient unit in Vietnam's agricultural production so far. The co-operatives have almost stopped operating in a number of places.

Industrial reform. The replacement of the central planning by a new economic management system means a fundamental restructuring of the economy. That includes the reorganisation of the state sector on the one hand, and the recognition of the essential role of the non-state sectors on the other hand. The previously heavily subsidised enterprises have to rely on themselves and compete with others in production; to do that, they are forced to reorganise. That resulted in large-scale redundancies in the state sector. A great number of people lost their jobs; other state employees found their previously secure jobs in jeopardy. In addition, the return of hundreds of thousands of migrant workers from Eastern Europe and the former Soviet Union, and the demobilisation of soldiers have all served to accentuate the employment and income generation problem in urban areas. A survey in 1992 reveals that a majority of families in Hanoi that have recently become impoverished are the ones whose main providers lost their jobs in the state sector (Trinh Duy Luan, 1993). The number of families classified as poor is small (32 among the randomly chosen sample of 800 surveyed households), but it reveals a trend.

On the other hand, the recognition of the private sector means that private enterprises are allowed. The small private enterprises mushroom almost everywhere, resulting in the redistribution of labour on a wide scale. This means that state employment is no longer the only way to get a job; that has deep implications for marital and family relations, as we shall see in the next chapter.

One example of private enterprises is Nam Giang commune, Ha Nam Ninh province (Dang Canh Khanh, 1991). In the commune, Van Chang village was traditionally famous for its smithy, but it was not allowed to ply the trade. After getting permission to restore their trade in the late 1980s, families in the village opened more than 500 blacksmith outlets; other villages also followed them, or began to specialise in subsidiary trades, in food processing and food supply.

Trade reforms. From the family's viewpoint, the most marked change is the elimination of price subsidies through the coupon system. Family members no longer have to spend hours queuing in different shops. The state trade monopoly has been abolished and private traders are allowed to conduct their business. Traders, and vendors are not looked down upon any more; and shops and goods are available everywhere. With this new spate of competition, shop assistants in the state trade sector have had to adopt a friendlier, less condescending attitude towards customers. Before the market economy, shops were empty and shop assistants were authoritative.

Compared to the previous phase, when commerce was viewed by the communists as unworthy of respect, the current enthusiasm for free enterprise is a marked change. As a communist official in the well-known novel *Paradise of the Blind* by Duong Thu Huong (1988/1994: 50) puts it,

> in our society, there are only two respectable types of people: the proletariat ... and the peasantry ... The rest is nothing. The merchants, the petty tradespeople, they're only exploiters. You cannot remain with these parasites.

It could be said the beginning of the renovation was a commercial phase in the sense that a million families opened shops. Families have greater opportunities and seize these opportunities with unprecedented enthusiasm. Houses in the cities and towns, as well as along the main roads, have been turned into shops, restaurants, and workshops. The commercial phase has been followed by a construction phase: people began to renovate their houses or build new ones with modern, Westernised facilities and style, and to create better material conditions for family life.

Cultural reform. The economic reforms gave a great impetus to changes in the cultural field. However, these changes are going on in two directions.

First, *an intensification of rituals* has taken place. As households regained their roles as the primary production units and amassed more resources, collective resources of the co-operatives have been accordingly diminished. As a result of this, mutual assistance among relatives has resumed its traditional importance, and kinship ties have regained their essential role as a source of assistance, e.g. through the restoration of the reciprocal feasting system. In a number of places, the extended kinship network with its diversified activities (fund-raising, shared ancestor worship, etc.) has also become re-established and is helping its member families in different ways.

An active engagement in trading activities brings with it some uncertainly; there is often a risk of loss. Therefore people have begun to turn to religious rituals to gain a sense of psychological security. Also, the growing economic surplus permits consumption-oriented ritual activities, and in fact is channelled into them. All these have led to the restoration, intensification, and even increasing elaboration of the pre-1945 rituals and religious activities both inside and outside the household. Among those rituals, there are the ones that promote the separation of the sexes and the age hierarchy (Kleinen, 1993; Luong Van Hy, 1993). All the efforts made earlier by the government in this field did not achieve the desired goals.

Second, *Western influence has been increasing.* This is the result of a number of factors: students and guest-workers return with new ideas from Eastern Europe; there has been an expansion of economic relations and tourism with the capitalist countries; moreover, with the advent of new technology there has been an increased flow of information. One of the side effects of the reform programme and the increased prosperity has been the proliferation of video recorders, television sets, and radio cassette players. This has been accompanied by the increased availability of foreign films on video, which the government has had great difficulty in controlling. Accusing this influence of spreading violence and pornography, and of undermining all the traditional values, the government has been making enormous efforts to impose controls, but without much success.

How do these reforms affect the family? On the one hand, they have reduced poverty on a large scale across almost all social categories. A Western researcher (Tønnesson, 1993) even writes about the emergence of so-called 'family capitalism'. Although this may be an exaggeration, there is no doubt that life has become much easier for families that have managed to increase their income. This creates general satisfaction not only among the rich, but also in society at large.

On the other hand, social differentiation has taken place. Before the renovation, the overwhelming majority of population were equally poor; now there is a greater disparity between the rich and poor families, especially in cities and towns. As for the situation in the countryside, although there is no reliable data, we can refer to the empirical sources which the above Western researcher quotes. According to a report about living conditions in the countryside in 1993, peasants can be divided into three classes: 10–20 per cent rich; 50–60 per cent with an average income; and 20–30 per cent poor (5–10 per cent being very poor).

In addition, the co-operatives no longer have the resources to provide poor peasants with food and assistance. Meanwhile, public services like health care and education, especially rural child daycare centres, diminish in number and deteriorate owing to a lack of state funding. Losing its control of pricing, the government no longer has the resources to fund different agencies that used to share a number of the family's welfare functions. The quality of such services has declined and they are no longer free of charge. Thus charges have been instituted for health services and education; costs have risen and are well beyond the reach of most poor families. Families have to assume the burden of care for sick members and young children, which was previously shared by state-funded agencies.[7] In other words, the family may have regained its function as a production unit, but it has had to shoulder more social obligations which the outside society previously helped to provide. Society can no longer afford to share. Thus the well-known proposition about the loss of function of the family has been disproved in the case of Vietnam.

In all this transition, it is women who are likely to be most adversely affected. Although some women who are engaged in trade can earn more and improve their situation in the family, this is not the case for all women. Even for the fortunate ones, it is necessary to adopt a cautious interpretation of their economic role and family status. However, it is this degree of caution which the Norwegian researcher Tønnesson seems to lack. Taking a Western-centred view of a causal connection between women's economic power and their family role definition, he seems to overstate the case when he writes: 'In Vietnam the commercial revolution seems to have strengthened the general standing of women' (Tønnesson, 1993: 17). As Luong Van Hy (1989: 745) has pointed out, although women in the traditional family played a prominent economic role, especially in the marketplace, they did so not to replace their domestic-centred roles but to increase the financial resources of their families. It is not ruled out that many of them are now doing the same.

What about women in agriculture? During the collectivisation, while many women worked full time in the rice fields, their responsibilities at home did not change much. Since the economic reforms, families have often reorganised their division of labour. In addition, as the government's restrictions on rural–urban migration were relaxed, a great number of men (especially in areas close to cities and towns, where farming is less profitable than other businesses), have relocated and sought different occupations as hired labourers. Therefore, in those areas there is a likelihood of the feminisation of agriculture. Women have to work harder in both rice cultivation and household chores. As a result, their working hours are extremely long: 16–18 hours/day, compared to men's 12–14 hours (Dang Nguyen Anh, 1991). Those figures are just approximate. This means that women have no time for rest, recreation, for extending their knowledge, or for social communication.

How are they paid? Although women in the co-operative system did not earn the same as men, they received income paid as paddy and as cash according to the work-points they had accumulated as individual workers. In other words, their contribution to the family's income was calculable and visible. Now that the family has regained its role as productive unit, the family income is reckoned as the sum of the total household labour. For that reason, the individual contribution of each family member cannot be easily identified and women's contributions may become more invisible.

Moreover, women's contributions may be devalued for two reasons. First, compared to the non-farm jobs that many men look for in other places, the agricultural jobs in which most women are engaged are less prestigious: it is hard work, but low income generating. Second, in the market economy, cash is the barometer of economic success, so the fact that women are concentrated in less cash-generating activities does not improve their position.

There has been a worrying trend too in the educational sphere: children are increasingly dropping out of school. The demand for family labour and cash income, together with the burden of school fees, means that more children are being kept away from school. If a choice has to be made, daughters (rather than sons) are more likely to be kept away from school, or forced to leave school early to help the family economy. Thus women are losing the educational opportunities which had been hard-won only since 1945. This is really worrying; its implications for future generations cannot be underestimated.

While it cannot be denied that the women's liberation movement has secured some significant improvements for the position of women, yet in many respects gender relationships both inside and outside the family have taken a negative turn. In urban areas, family members tend to take their meals in restaurants wherever they like; the traditional importance of the family meal as a socially reinforcing ritual is becoming eroded. Similarly, parents are so busy making money and conducting business that they often have no time for the children or for each other. For those families the ties between members have become loosened. There are other alarming signs: the number of street children in some big cities is on the increase, and there are more reported cases of wife-beating (Le Thi Quy, 1996) – although this may not be a true increase as perhaps previously the wives were too frightened to come forward.

As incomes have risen, more and more husbands are having affairs, or even resorting to the modern equivalent of concubines. Polygyny has spread in different ways. Newly rich men think that if they have the money, they can buy everything. As a result, although prostitution is illegal, it is on the increase in cities, towns, and coastal holiday resorts, posing a threat to the cohesion of the family. Among the rural young people who migrate to the towns and cities to earn a living there have been a large number of young girls. Many of them are likely to become victims of prostitution. To make things worse, many women, particularly young girls, are falling prey to a modern slave trade which is being practised in some areas.

However, although the renovation policy has brought about some unintended and undesirable consequences, these cannot obscure the mass of positive changes that have occurred: many families have considerably improved their standard of living; enhanced their present and future life chances; and have managed to secure better prospects for their children. These people finally feel liberated from state employment and its restricting regulations. In general, there has been more freedom for people to make their own choices and this has had a dramatic effect on family relations.

CONCLUSION

For the purposes of our analysis we have so far dealt with each of the social changes separately, but of course they are connected and interwoven. By dividing the last half century into two stages – first, the implementation of the so-called socialist project and, second, the renovation and open door policy – we can see that initially the family changed from a unit of production to one of consumption. Social services were built up to share, to certain degree, different functions of the family. Family relations were democratised to some extent. These were the positive consequences of the social changes.

Nevertheless, the social changes also caused some negative and unintended consequences to the family as the results of the land reform and collectivisation: primarily the weakening of family ties and the overloading of working women. Since the late 1980s the family has not only regained its function as a productive unit, but has also been handed back the functions that the state social agencies used to share with it. While many families are improving their standards of living and gaining freedom, others are impoverished. In a number of respects, the pre-1945 family ties are tending to re-establish themselves.

It would be better to look at the social changes and their effects on the family in terms of the two crucial family relations: husband–wife and parent–child. In brief, the social changes tend to strengthen the husband–wife ties in some respects and weaken the parent–child ones. However, one should not ignore the wider context in which these changes have been taking place. The family is now the only caring institution for the elderly, and the gender issues have been obscured by the emphasis on class issues. As for the weakened parent–child bond, it is worrying when no social support institution offers any significant care for the elderly. The recent reforms may have improved life significantly for many families, but there have also been some negative repercussions, particularly in the husband–wife nexus.

By examining those changes in terms of social steering, we can say that the view of normative functionalism taken by the state leaders (i.e., that family members must bridge the gap between the family and society in order to work hard for socialist construction in the state-run enterprises and co-operatives; that they must teach their children to become good citizens; and that the family must contribute to the integration and harmony of the social system) is not adopted by a lot of families. During the central-planning economy, peasant families spent more and more time on their private garden plots rather than on the co-operative farms and made use of the state input (fertiliser) to improve their yields. Furthermore there was growing absenteeism among the state workers in a great many units as attention was diverted to the private economy. Families generally resisted the changes imposed on them by the leadership; consequently reform measures had to be taken.

If the reform measures of the late 1970s and early 1980s were not aimed at a change in the nature of the leadership's economic model, the late 1980s reform is of a different character. They are all 'bottom-up' reforms in the sense they are initiated by the families.

NOTES

1   The data in this section are secondary: they are quoted in Allen, S. 1990. 'Women in Vietnam'. Hanoi (unpublished manuscript).

2   The sample of Houtart and Lemercinier included both non-Catholics and Catholics, but those data were for the whole sample. From now on,

when this source is quoted, if no specification about the non-Catholics is made, the data are about the whole sample in general; the ones about the non-Catholics are not available.

3   My family suffered a lot from the household registration policy. In the summer of 1980, while working on the outskirts of Hanoi, my wife was sent to a new workplace, which was a new building site in Ha Nam Ninh province. She was about to give birth to our child at that time, but there was neither kindergarten, nor any kind of child daycare centre in her new workplace. Therefore my wife appealed to her bosses to change their minds, but her name had already been struck out in the former workplace's household registration book and transferred to that of the new workplace.

When the former workplace decided to re-admit her, her name could not be re-entered in the household registration book there. The reason was that on paper she was regarded as moving from a rural area (Ha Nam Ninh) to an urban one (Hanoi), although in practice her name had been transferred from Hanoi to Ha Nam Ninh province for only two months. As a consequence, my wife had no food rations and other necessities. My daughter was born in September 1980 and had neither a birth certificate nor food rations. In spite of being a state employee, I was unable to help my daughter in this matter for the reason that according to the state policy, children were considered to be the dependants of their mothers, not fathers.

Finding no other way to get out of this difficult situation, my wife had to apply for a job as a guest worker in the former Soviet Union in March 1982. Not until my wife left was I able to procure my daughter's birth certificate. Eventually, in June 1982 (almost two years after her birth), my daughter started to get her food rations.

4   Despite a limit on the total number of state employees, it was extended, but ineffective. This led to occasional demands for a reduction. In late 1991/early 1992 the country's national assembly set a 20-per-cent reduction target for state employees. Due to the vital importance of the state employee status, it was easy to manipulate it as a means of *thanh trung noi bo* [internal purge]. For instance, ostensibly to meet the objectives of this campaign, the director of a certain Hanoi academic institute drew up a list of twelve people who would have to leave the Institute (i.e., lose their state employee status). The crucial criterion for making the list was how one performed one's job, but in fact many people were put on the list not because their work was inadequate but because they did not get on with the director. Well aware that if they remained on this list, they would never again be able to get another state-sector job, a number of these blacklisted employees fought hard to get their names removed from the list.

5   Apart from anecdotal evidence, no other proof is available about this discrimination.

> According to an anecdote, an old woman was delighted to see some fish in a state-run shop, but the shop assistants had not yet officially started work. The old woman had to wait. However, she was the first person in the queue, and was almost sure that this time

she would have fish for her dinner. At last the shop assistants started to sell fish. When the old woman approached the counter, she was told that the fish would be sold only to those who had a coupon given to state employees. Unfortunately for her, she was neither state employee nor a relative of any state employee, therefore she could not buy fish. Furious, the old woman beat the private parts of her body very hard, and scolded them: 'Why didn't you give birth to state employees? Why did you give birth to only non-state employees?'

On the other hand, people who were given coupons for food and other necessities had their own worries, i.e. losing them. Because the coupons were so vital, losing them was a great danger. That was why there existed a popular saying *mat so gao* [to lose one's rice coupon] to describe a worry. If somebody looked worried, people might ask: 'What is the matter with you? Why do you look worried as if you have lost your rice coupon?' As people often joked, if a lower-ranking official dared to disagree with the boss, the boss may threaten to deprive the official of his rice coupon; the official would invariably back down. However, since the coupon system was eliminated in 1989, this saying has disappeared from the vernacular.

6   Due to the shortage, I was often hungry throughout my childhood and youth.

7   According to one source, the number of in-patients in a district hospital fell by 50 per cent after the introduction of fees (Allen, 1990: 41). The likelihood is that thereafter those who fell ill stayed at home; invariably it was the women who would have to take care of them.

CHAPTER THREE

The Husband–Wife Relationship

In the previous chapters we have examined the general characteristics of the traditional family, and given an overview of the social changes that have been affecting the family since 1945. We shall now explore in more detail the two ties that are often said to have made up the backbone of the family relationships: the one between marital partners, and the one between parents and children. We begin with the husband–wife relationship and follow the time order, or life course approach (understood differently from family life-cycle, as Morgan [1985: 177–180] has pointed out). The life course approach is vital for our understanding of a lot of problems and issues of family life. It serves not only as an organising framework for presenting our material, but also as a perspective.

The husband–wife relationship starts, naturally enough, from the initial encounter: whether they know each other before marriage or not, which is linked to the method of spouse selection. This then is our starting point. Then we shall deal with this relationship in terms of what each partner expects of the other; how they interact in different domains of family life; and how marital conflicts are resolved.

The large body of evidence about the marital ties in the traditional family comes from a few studies undertaken by historians, anthropologists, and ethnographers. The contemporary evidence is gleaned from different sociological surveys, most of which are not concentrated on our topic, but provide us with useful information. In addition to the scholarly evidence, literary works are also used to some extent.

THE HUSBAND–WIFE RELATIONSHIP IN THE TRADITIONAL FAMILY

SPOUSE SELECTION

Marital partner selection is not only the starting point of the family cycle, but also a burning issue in the traditional family. A number of family patterns depend on the way a couple is established. Moreover, as a family researcher has pointed out,

> by studying the way the conjugal couple is made up, we can also understand changes that have occurred in the family and that are linked to modifications arising from industrialisation and urbanisation.
>
> (Segalen, 1986: 107)

In the existing literature it is generally agreed that until the end of the first half of this century marital partner choice was not the prerogative of young people, but of their parents. In some cases parents might not arrange the marriage but instead allow the son or daughter to choose a marital partner for themselves; however, they still had to get parental approval. However, that was normally the custom only for extremely poor people and was often looked down upon by public opinion. In some ways the arrangements by parents were quite helpful for young people if they had little chance to meet suitable partners. Nevertheless, in other ways the arrangements were often made at the expense of the young people. This was reflected in the decisive power of parents, and the lack of young people's say in the selection of a spouse. The following narrative is revealing.

> A man from an upper-class family could not marry the girls whom he had truly loved and who wanted to marry him. One among them was very beautiful; she was called Lu. They first met while he was attending a village school at a communal meeting house, that is before he was 12 years of age. She wanted to marry him too and frequently teased him in those days. However, her family was poor: her father was a lowly soldier in the native guard and her uncle lived at a pagoda. She herself tended buffalo for his godfather. Because he did not dare to speak too often to his father, let alone to state his desire to marry Lu, his older sisters helped to tell his parents about his desire to marry her. On learning this, his father called him in immediately, and said that it

was a matter of matching wealth and status. Therefore the son's preference to marry a buffalo tender was unacceptable. Consequently, the son had to give up his marriage preference and marry someone else at the age of 14, while he was still at school. The marriage was arranged between two families of the same social standing, between the son of the presiding official of one village and the granddaughter of his counterpart in another village. This matching of social status was the primary consideration of the marriage.

His two half-brothers married even earlier, at the age of 13. In general,

> in our system it was the parents who expressed opinions and made the decisions ... All of us were married through parental arrangement with utmost concern for the social standing of the involved families.
>
> (Luong Van Hy, 1992: 75–76)

So, as usual, parents selected a bride for their son. It was not only the parents who had the power to decide upon a marriage partner for their offspring, they also had to consult other members of the lineage. The 'marriage consultants' often included grandparents, uncles, aunts, etc. The power of parents and other relatives of the older generations in the selection of a marriage partner was recognised by both the law (article 94, Gia Long Code of Law; quoted in Le Thi Nham Tuyet, 1975: 137) and public opinion. Those people decided when and with whom a young family member might marry, disregarding the opinion of the young person most directly involved. The young person had to obey the family's arrangement in accordance with the dictates of *hieu* [filial piety]. As a saying went, *cha me dat dau, con ngoi day* [a child is seated where its parents choose the place for it, whether it is willing or not]. According to Le Thi Nham Tuyet, the parents' arrangement depended on many different factors that were not totally related to the young people involved. However, the researcher does not give us concrete evidence; she just mentions some factors, for instance the parents' poverty and the desire to become rich, mutual debts, gratitude to the counterpart family, or even what she calls superstition. There were also cases where parents of two families had arranged their children's marriage well in advance, when one or both the wives were pregnant. The respective sets of parents made an agreement that their children would marry each other if they turned out to be of opposite sexes (Le Thi Nham Tuyet, 1975: 140).

Nevertheless, the most important criterion was the match in terms of wealth and status, particularly for upper-class families. The marital alliance then was to be class based. The ages of two sets of parents, particularly that of the two fathers, were also crucial: there should not be a considerable difference in age between them. The reason was simple: in a society where age was a determining criterion of social hierarchy, a significant difference in ages between two people demarcated a differentiation in rank: they could not become equal counterparts. After the marital alliance was established, the two respective families often kept in touch and had certain mutual ritual obligations. It was only when their children's marriage was in conflict that bad relations might develop (Phan Ke Binh, 1915/1992: 207). In some cases, the groom's family refused to accept the bride's behaviour after the marriage; they would bring her back to her parents and claim to have returned her to them (thus signifying a divorce).

To ensure the compatibility of the two respective families, a careful investigation into family backgrounds was deemed absolutely essential. Not only the living members of the two families (including parents, grandparents, siblings and other relatives), but also dead members of up to three previous generations were subject to investigation. As a popular proverb put it, *Lay vo ken tong, lay chong ken giong* [Choose a suitable breed and branch of the family when marrying]. A verse from *The Tale of Kieu* has become quite popular: *Tram nam tinh cuoc vuong tron, phai do cho tan ngon nguon lach song* [I have always planned for our lifelong union. So I must inquire about the source and sound the bottom of the river (i.e., inquire about your origin)].

In these circumstances, of course, poor, lower-class families had no choice but to look for counterparts of the same social standing. However, in some cases, parents of poor, lower-class families could marry their children (mainly daughters) to men of higher social standing, but often as concubines, or in the form of repayment of a debt.

Young people were investigated by parents only in terms of their age compatibility (it was believed that people born in certain years of the lunar calendar would not make a good match; so they had better not marry each other).

The novel *To Tam* by Hoang Ngoc Phach (1925) furnishes us with an illustration of an arranged marriage.

> To Tam and Dam Thuy were two young people, both from families rooted in the old traditions. The heroine, To Tam, was a beautiful, French-educated girl, a great reader and ardent student of literature. She developed a deep admiration for Dam Thuy, a fine young writer, through reading his

publications. By chance they happened to meet and fall in love, but To Tam's mother – the widow of a judge – had promised to marry her to someone else according to the prevailing custom. At the beginning To Tam resisted because she had fallen in love with one person, and she could never love another. And if she did not love, she would not marry.

However, her mother had fallen gravely ill and was anxious to secure her daughter's future. Of course the old woman wanted to marry her daughter to one who was 'worthy' of her. Painfully torn between love and filial piety to her dying mother, To Tam could not conceivably defy her mother's choice. One senior member of To Tam's lineage – her uncle – felt sympathetic to her plight and tried to intervene on her behalf, but in vain. Married according to her mother's wishes, To Tam fell into a depression. No sooner had the wedding taken place than she herself fell ill. A month later she died of a broken heart, leaving for her lover Dam Thuy a pathetic diary that she kept from the days of preparation for her wedding until the time of her death. In fact the young girl's death was a suicide. In a society that emphasised 'face', this 'solution' of young people brought about not only suffering, but also embarrassment to the whole family.

If we read a conversation between To Tam's mother and her uncle, we may say that the line of argument of the old woman ('In a respectable family, children owe obedience to their parents', etc.) seems not to be fictitious at all. On the contrary, it may be quite familiar to every Vietnamese in the sense that one can hear it in daily life. Two points from the old woman's words should be made clear. First, parents regarded the arrangements for marrying children to be not only their right, but also their duty. They could not have peace of mind if they grew old but had failed in their duty to their children. That was why the old dying woman was deeply anxious to fulfil her duty to the daughter before her last breath. As she put it,

> I am not in the best of health and when one's children have grown up it is very necessary to make sure of their future. If someone suitable comes and asks for her hand, I am very willing that he should have her. As for love or hate, this matter is for destiny to decide.
>
> (translated and quoted in Nguyen Khac Vien and Huu Ngoc, n.d.: 527).

This was the common concern of most parents. Second, parents always thought and said that they wanted their children to be happy. In the words of To Tam's mother, 'no one would wish unhappiness for a child' (ibid.: 527). However, parents made decisions according to their own criteria: they never thought that if one wanted one's children to be happy, it would be better to let them decide. They believed that as the children were young, inexperienced, and led by blind love, they were incapable of making decisions for themselves. To quote again the same mother:

> They are still very young and inexperienced. How can a girl of that age be expected to read people's hearts to see if she is making the right choice? You keep saying she should simply marry whom she loves but you know the saying 'To love too much is to lose one's head, then once awakened you see that people are mocking you'.
>
> (ibid.: 527)

It was only parents (who knew much better than children) who should decide. This novel is said to have brought tears to the eyes of an entire generation of students and intellectuals in urban areas at the time (ibid.: 523) because it reflected the tragic situation of many young people. In the words of Schafer and The Uyen (1993), it 'shocked some readers and entranced others, particularly young women'.

Many other novels shared a similar topic: the tragic love story, the conflict between romantic love and arranged marriage. As an inevitable result, most young heroes and heroines lived unhappily. 'Romantic love versus arranged marriage was a major plot element in many of the most important novels written during the 1930s' (Jamieson, 1993: 106–107). To mention just a few of them: *Nua chung xuan* [In the midst of spring] by Khai Hung (1933); *La ngoc canh vang* [Golden branches, leaves of jade] by Nguyen Cong Hoan (1934); and *Doan tuyet* [Breaking the ties] by Nhat Linh (1935).

A sceptical reader may well doubt the scientific value of those literary works from a sociological viewpoint, but the following fact is not insignificant. Although a never-ending stream of such novels appeared, their popularity continued unabated; in fact, their heroes and heroines attracted thousands of passionate supporters. For instance, 'Breaking the Ties' was the most celebrated novel of the decade, and republished many times during the four decades following its initial appearance. It was required reading for high school students in the South of Vietnam until 1975 (Jamieson, 1993: 146).

It should be pointed out that not all arranged marriages led to unhappiness for the partners: having become accustomed to each other, some developed shared interests, hobbies and outlook. For others, genuine affection or love may even have developed. However, this often did not happen and many young people had to put up with their loveless and unhappy marriages.

If young people did not agree with their parents' arrangement, they had only a couple of options: to run away from home or to commit suicide. However, any child doing such a thing was regarded as being 'filially impious' according to the traditional Confucian norm, and was renounced by the family (a very severe form of punishment). In most cases, parents did their best to persuade the child to accede to their decision. Generally the mother's soft powers of persuasion combined with the father's more dictatorial approach would have the desired effect. In some areas, a bride might make a token gesture to express her reluctance towards the groom. An elderly villager recalled that when married to somebody against her will, a bride asked for five (or seven) lavish trays for her friends on the eve of wedding as a way to incur unnecessary expenses on the groom's household, because the latter bore all the wedding expenses in those days (Luong Van Hy, 1993: 279). This measure was targeted at the groom's side (because of their active role in arranging the marriage), not at her parents who also had played their part in this matter. In literature and in life, some young people dared to oppose their parents' wishes, but in fact, they were quite rare. According to Jamieson, although young men and few women grumbled about their families' old-fashioned ideas, few of them would dare to challenge them or senior family members outright. By contrast, most continued to live with their parents and to fulfil the demands of *hieu* (1993: 134).

The reason was that even until the first half of this century in the family, filial piety was still the cornerstone of morality and it led logically to an absolute obedience to superiors (parents, seniors) and self-sacrifice. The most crucial implication of filial piety here is that children were forbidden to judge parents' behaviour; they should unconditionally accept that parents were always right. Even when parents were wrong, children were not allowed to argue. The only thing they could do was to let the parents know their opinion and hope the parents would take it into consideration; failing that, they had to stoically accept whatever decision was reached.

For several hundred years, Vietnamese youngsters were taught filial piety with exemples of children who 'knew *hieu*'. Nevertheless, the popular collection of tales *Nhi thap tu hieu* [Twenty-four excellent examples of filial piety], which was of Chinese origin and translated and rewritten in verse by a Hanoi scholar in the nineteenth century, was more accessible to the average reader thanks to the romanised script and modern printing technology during the first half of this century. It is difficult to estimate the collection's influence, but one could guess that it was rather widespread. The heroes and heroines in the above novels often mentioned the concept of filial piety, and followed its guidance. In other words, socialised this way in a heavily hierarchical family system, most children dared not oppose parents' arrangements of their marriages for a very good reason. As Jamieson (1993: 134) has put it, to stand up to parental authority 'was to invite disaster'.

As we have seen in the above story told by Luong Van Hy, the sons of an upper-class family married at the age of 13 or 14. That means parents often planned a marriage when the child was still quite young, too young to understand the importance of the event, let alone to resist. Probably this is the second reason why young people did not oppose their parents' arrangements: often they were too young to understand the significance of the marital bond. One of the young grooms from the story later recalled: he was still too young then to understand why his wife had moved into his family home after the wedding ceremony. He asked her after three days why she was still in his house, and had not returned to her own home (Luong Van Hy, 1992: 74). This is surely not an isolated case, but unfortunately, we have had no available data about that.

One interesting point can be made from the evidence given by the above researcher: just as his wife was 16, two years older than he was, at the time of their wedding, his two half-brothers married slightly older women so that the latter could help with household chores (Luong Van Hy, 1992: 76). In other words, in child couples, it was generally preferred for the girl to be some years older than boy so that the former could become a worker in the husband's family, at least in doing household chores. Therefore, their working ability was the first and foremost individual quality that was emphasised. Little wonder then that in child marriages, young couples lived as brothers and sisters and constantly quarrelled like two children.

On the other hand, poor men did not marry at a very early age. There is the interesting case of a man of the same lineage as the afore-mentioned child couple, who was born in 1921 and did not marry until the age of 27 because of a dramatic downturn in his family's fortunes. In the meantime his two cousins married at the age of 13 (Luong Van Hy, 1992: 76–77). The reason was that marriage was a great rite of passage. It required a lot of money, including the bride-price, which the groom's family had to deliver to the bride's family before the wedding, and expenses for the banquets. Lacking firm evidence about the average age for marriage, we cannot draw a conclusion about how prevalent such cases were. However the evidence available suggests that popular custom favoured early marriage, except where poverty proved to be a prohibitive factor.

To evaluate parents' rights in the sphere of marriage, we should note that in traditional Vietnamese society, no matter what class, no event even came close in importance to that of marriage; in fact, its primacy can scarcely be appreciated by most Westerners. Although Gourou (1936/1955: 219) noted that the 'bachelor by preference' was a social type completely unknown in the Delta, this was applicable to women as well. To live a single life was unacceptable, except for a small number of Buddhist monks or some people who were considered marginal unfortunates. Celibacy was regarded as an expression of personal difficulties.

The primacy of marriage took root from a reality imbued with universal religious practice for most of Vietnamese: the worship of ancestors and continuance of the line of descent. This had a profound effect on marriage and relations between the spouses. That was why there was a custom whereby a new bride was presented as the new member to the ancestors at the altar table. That was the indispensable climax of the wedding ceremony: the groom took the bride to the altar table and they prayed together. As Le Thi Que (1986: 20) points out, without this presentation, the young bride remained a stranger. However, the great significance of this act was to announce to the ancestors that there would be children to practise ancestor worship. That was why before arranging a marriage, parents often consulted other members of the lineage: grandparents, uncles, aunts, etc. The new bride had to be approved of by all these senior members to ensure her suitability to serve the lineage's interests. So marriage was not a personal matter for the young couple, but of general concern to the whole family and lineage.

WHAT WAS EXPECTED OF BRIDES?

We can gain some impression of what was expected of a bride by reversing the 'seven reasons for divorce' that were laid down in the Gia Long Code of Law. Divorce meant that the expectations of marital partner(s) had not been met, and the permissible reasons for divorce are revealing. According to this Code of Law, it was mainly the husband who had the right to initiate divorce. Based on the so-called 'seven outs' men could repudiate their wives on the following grounds (Phan Ke Binh 1915/1992:63):

- Infertility
- Adultery
- Neglect of parents-in-law
- Talkativeness
- Theft
- Jealousy
- Incurable diseases.

Of the seven reasons, there were only two that directly affected the husband–wife bond: adultery and jealousy. Let us though initially examine the first ground for divorce, namely infertility.

The basis of the first reason was that an infertile woman would fail to produce any children, especially sons. That meant she was guilty of not creating the next generation, threatening to lead to a discontinuity of the family sacrifices (since there would be nobody there to practise ancestor worship). A woman's infertility may have been caused by a variety of reasons, but in practice, it was inevitably the wife who incurred the blame. The first and foremost aim of marriage was to produce offspring, particularly male ones, to secure the continued worship of ancestors.

The third reason for divorce was if a wife disobeyed and lacked filial piety towards the previous generation (her parents-in-law); by so doing, she broke the continuum of descent. 'Neglect of parents-in-law' meant, among other things, that the wife did not submit to her mother-in-law. If a conflict happened between mother-in-law and daughter-in-law, the senior female must always come out on top; otherwise, the daughter-in-law was accused of neglecting her mother-in-law.

It is probably surprising for Westerners that the relationship between a wife and her husband's family was so emphasised. This becomes particularly apparent if one examines the prohibitions facing children during the three-year mourning period once their parents die: unmarried children were forbidden to marry; married women were forbidden to get pregnant; moreover women who got pregnant during the mourning period were punished (Dao Duy Anh, 1938/1992: 221). To avoid those prohibitions, there was a custom named *cuoi chay tang* [the hurried wedding to avoid the mourning period]. When one of the parents (or members of the senior generations) was dying, or had already died, but the death had not yet been announced, people hurried up the wedding that otherwise would have to be held three years later. In the marital ties established in such a way, newly-wed couples had neither the time nor the heart to enjoy their new relations, let alone to go on honeymoon. Instead, they had to participate in serving the dying person if (s)he were still alive, or in the funerals and mourning ceremonies, and to show their grief if (s)he were already dead. In this sense, the marital ties were subordinated to the relations to the previous generations.

Marital relations were secondary in comparison to intergenerational ones, as can be seen in the following proverb: *Lay vo vi con* [It is because a man wants to have children that he takes a wife] (Le Thi Nham Tuyet, 1975: 137). In other words, the motivation of marriage was to produce offspring, not to satisfy the need for marital happiness. Moreover, if a couple had no child, the husband was allowed by the official law to repudiate his wife (as mentioned above), or take one or more concubines. If he still had no child, the husband might realise that he was infertile. In that case, he would agree to his wife having sexual relations with another man in the hope of procuring a son. In such a case the husband would in effect be condoning adultery (the second ground for divorce). The usual arrangement was for the wife to travel far from home under the pretence of doing business; once pregnant with the other man's child, she would return home (Toan Anh, n.d.: 23). Of course, such cases were kept secret; therefore it is quite difficult to judge how common it was. No further details have been given by the source, but it is mentioned that in the Vietnamese language there was even an idiom denoting this custom (*tha co*).

The same source also mentions the cases where a sterile man took as his concubine a woman who was several weeks' pregnant. When born, her child was considered to be one of his own. We need to recall that women were regarded as belonging to men as their property; unfaithful wives received brutal punishment (see Chapter One) from society at large, not just legal repudiation by their husbands. Only when we put all those facts together can we understand how much the parent–child ties were emphasised at the expense of the husband–wife ones.

The seven grounds for divorce generally comprised perceived shortcomings on the part of the wife, but these were viewed as serious failings which damaged the husband's reputation, interests, health and his family's harmony. In brief, what was really at issue in most of them was the harmony and solidarity of the family and lineage through the intergenerational bonds.

The primary importance of the intergenerational relations compared to the husband–wife ties could be seen not only in stipulations of the official law, but also in daily life. The communal structure of the family and the emphasis on the intergenerational relations at the expense of conjugal ones were also expressed in the sleeping arrangements. To understand the significance of, on the one hand, the lack of marital intimacy and, on the other, the prevalence of gender separation, let us examine the following narrative of a man of upper-class background.

> After the wedding, he still slept with his male relatives in the living room, where the ancestral altar was located. His wife slept with his senior female cousin. It took quite a while for the marriage to be consummated. For intimate moments with each other, the couple had to wait until everybody fell asleep, whereupon they would spend time together discreetly in a corner of the house.
>
> (Luong Van Hy, 1992: 73)

In this narrative male and female household members were separated to the extent that the married couple slept apart from each other. We need to keep in mind that the narrative was about an upper-class family, that is, it may or may not be representative of a majority of population. However, according to Le Thi Que's (1986: 26) observation, grandparents may sleep in the same room with their grandchildren, while an aunt may sleep in the same bed as her niece. Privacy was deemed to be not very important, unlike in the West. However, given that about a third of one's life is spent in bed, just whom one spends this time with is no trivial matter.

Westerners might judge the Vietnamese sleeping arrangements as 'overcrowded' and attribute this to a lack of space in 'densely populated' Vietnam. Jamieson (1993: 27) takes this view when he writes about the relations between a bride and a groom: 'The house would often be very crowded, and she and her husband would have little privacy in which to build intimacy.' Nonetheless, that was not the case here: in such an upper-class family as the one cited above, surely there would physically have been enough room for the newly-wed couple if the conjugal ties were emphasised. There must be a social logic behind the sleeping arrangements.

From a sociological viewpoint, sleeping customs are consonant with major interpersonal and emotional patterns of family life within a culture. The overcrowding in the Vietnamese family bedroom was only partly a function of lack of space; it derived more directly from the strength of the intergenerational bonds. The sleeping arrangements tended to underplay conjugal intimacy between husbands and wives in sexual and other matters in favour of a more general familial cohesion. In lower-class families, it was accentuated through lack of space; it was not uncommon to see married couples sleeping in the same room, even the same bed as their young children. If they had several children, the husband might sleep with the older ones in one bed, and the wife with the younger ones in another bed.

Thus there was no room for emotional relations between husband and wife. The husband–wife bond was less one of affection and more one of duty. A married couple, although they might lack affection for each other (they may even have made their first acquaintance at the wedding ceremony) felt it their duty to continue the husband's lineage. It did not matter whether they felt love for each other. To Tam's mother described it in the above-mentioned novel like this:

> ... as for love or hate, this matter is for destiny to decide ... There may be disagreement [of her daughter on the arranged marriage] now, but once they start living together they will just have to get on, won't they?
>
> (Nguyen Khac Vien and Huu Ngoc, n.d.: 527).

It would be wrong to say there was no love in the traditional society, but this was not the emotion that most of the couples felt towards each other. For many couples, love might develop between them after marriage or it might never come. That explains in part why few Vietnamese brides could refrain from crying on their wedding day (Le Thi Que, 1986: 37): an uncertain future was awaiting them.

Love was regarded by society as undesirable in marriage for two reasons. First, love with its vagaries and uncertainties sometimes ran counter to the interests of the family and lineage. It was outside the parameters of the lineage's concern with social standing when choosing marital partners. Second, love might lead the husband to pay too much attention to his wife and to be swayed by her whims. He would tend then to pander to her demands, and place conjugal relations higher in his estimation than relations between generations and ages in the consanguinal family. In fact, for a man to 'do everything that his wife tells him' (*nghe vo*), was considered to be a very bad character trait, a serious deviancy from the norms of behaviour expected of a husband. As a matter of fact, his mother, sisters, and other female relatives would try to exert their own influence, thus building a 'front-line' against his wife.

The vernacular embodies these attitudes. As Jamieson (1993: 25–26) has noted, in Vietnamese the wedding ceremony was commonly called *ruoc dau*. *Ruoc* means 'to welcome', 'to greet', or 'to escort'. *Dau* means both 'bride' and 'daughter-in-law'. The Vietnamese never speak of the wedding procession as 'welcoming a wife'. It is always called 'welcoming a daughter-in-law'. In the researcher's words, 'the bride's role as daughter-in-law is given social and cultural emphasis, linguistically expressed, equal to or greater than her new role as wife'. He linguistically interprets it well, but does not seem to succeed in capturing the essence of the bride's role expectations. In fact, her role as daughter-in-law and mother were given greater (not equal) emphasis than her role as wife.

In other words, a woman through her marriage was regarded first of all as daughter-in-law, then mother, and last as a wife. She was expected to be a submissive daughter-in-law, to be a good worker, and to produce many children, especially male ones. A peasant's expectations of his wife tallied in most respects with those of his parents: to take care of his parents, to bear children, to carry the burden of household chores, to take part in rice cultivation, and in many cases, to be the subject of sexual exploitation. As for the wife's role, the ideal was total devotion to her husband. She was 'bad' if she so much as looked at another man (Jamieson, 1993: 27). In her role as wife, a woman was expected first and foremost to observe strictly the double standard inherent in the society (see Chapter One). As Jamieson (1993:27) noted, '[the] Vietnamese were second to none in having a double standard for judging the sexual conduct of men and women.' To put it another way, a wife was expected to be absolutely faithful to her husband throughout her married life, indeed even after his death. As a famous verse from *The Tale of Kieu* puts it: 'Chastity is worth a thousand gold coins.' That was why there were so many customs to punish sexually impure brides.

Although Confucianism was declining, its marriage manual still taught the wife of a wealthy man to treat her husband as if he were her king or her father (Eisen, 1984: 15). The same source also mentions that to conclude the traditional ceremony, the bride prostrated herself twice before her husband, who remained standing over her, nodding his approval. We need to add that this ceremony was required only for those who were of an inferior rank in the hierarchy. In the novel *Breaking the Ties*, the writer Nhat Linh described the ceremony that was performed twice during a few years when Than, the hero, took two wives. The wives both had to bow down on the mat in ritual prostration to the ancestors, the husband's parents and the husband himself. The concubine had to kow-tow not only to them, but also to the wife (Jamieson, 1993: 139). In this hierarchical relation, even though a couple slept in the same bed, there was no intimacy between them.

It is understandable that sexuality was viewed as simply the means to produce children. That was why many people disapproved of couples who slept together once their children had grown up, or if they had a new-born child of their own at the same time as a grandchild: in the eyes of the society at large, this was shameful. A woman of middle-age was supposed to be taking care of her grandchildren, not a child of her own. Talking about sexuality was a taboo. Unfortunately research on sexuality in marital life has been non-existent until now. We can only speculate that men took the sexual initiative. Because of ignorance about sexual matters, particularly widespread male ignorance of female sexuality, and also because of the patriarchal legacy, sexuality served only men's pleasure. The woman's role was just to give pleasure, not to receive it.

The relationship between middle-class spouses was different. Compared to the peasant family, the wife's role was accorded more importance. However, that does not mean there was equality or intimacy between husband and wife. On the contrary, the relation was highly contractual in the sense that both partners had certain fixed and non-negotiable obligations. A great majority of bourgeois women willingly let their men become officials. Middle-class men expected their wives to manage enterprises and properties (landed estates, commercial and industrial enterprises) while they themselves took care of 'French business' (*viec Tay*). Wives were also expected to provide a comfortable home for husbands to return to after a hard day at work, and to utilise the money in an appropriate way, and even to make a profit (Vietnam Resource Centre, 1974: 15–16). On the other hand, the roles of the daughter-in-law and mother roles were rather similar to those in the peasant family. The middle-class wife was also expected to participate in the care of her old parents-in-law as well as her children, although her family may be able to afford to hire servants and nursemaids.

To quote Nhat Linh in the novel *Breaking the Ties*, one may sum up the demands made upon women in marriage as the 'role of being baby-making machines, of being little servant girls without any wages' (Jamieson, 1993: 139). Those demands were intense, and it was difficult to meet all role expectations, to satisfy everybody in their husband's family. No wonder many daughters-in-law could not endure their role, and were forced into conflict with their husbands' relatives (especially younger sisters). In such an eventuality, the mother-in-law always sided with her own children, which inevitably led to an exacerbation of the conflict. When a wife failed to do what was expected of her, divorce was sought. The Gia Long Code even stipulated that once a wife had committed one of the 'seven outs', if her husband did not throw her out, he himself would be liable to a cane-beating of eighty strokes (Le Thi Nham Tuyet, 1975: 140). Of course that was what the law stipulated; we do not know the extent to which that was put into effect.

Nevertheless, a husband could not always do whatever he pleased. First, he had to consult others: parents, grandparents, siblings, and other relatives. However, in a society where blood ties were emphasised, those people often created a blood alliance against the wife, who was considered to be an outsider. Second, the husband had some legal constraints to his right to throw his wife out. He must not repudiate the wife if she had fulfilled the mourning duty to at least one of his parents (i.e., the duty to the previous generations), or if she had contributed to enriching his family, or if she had no living relative left in her natal family. The last constraint is worth commenting. It was not designed to be supportive to the women themselves; rather it reflected the idea that someone without a family was not recognised in the Vietnamese society.

Even after taking into account the three legal constraints to the husband's right, one can come to conclude that the institution of marriage aimed mainly to serve the interests of the husband and his side of the family. What about the aims of marriage for women? What can we say about women's expectations?

WOMEN'S EXPECTATIONS

As stated earlier, celibacy was unacceptable. For women, spinsterhood was a misfortune. The importance and permanence of the family as an institution, and the insecurities of unmarried life were emphasised repeatedly for centuries in proverbs, and folk-songs. One folk-song went:

> An unmarried woman cannot help but run around worried and insecure
> Sisters, it is miserable not to have a husband
>
> (Eisen, 1984: 180)

Another folk-song ran:

> A conical hat without a strap is in danger of disappearing with the wind
> A boat without a steering rudder settles into violent roll
> A woman without husband is in the same situation.

In the words of a female teacher in the first half of this century, for a woman, being a wife was 'as natural as eating food' (quoted in Marr, 1981: 207). Unmarried women were identified as *e* [unsold, left on the shelf] in Vietnamese. They experienced feelings of inferiority, like the shoddy goods that no customer wants to buy. They often lived with their parents while the latter were alive. Not only the spinsters themselves, but also their parents and siblings felt ashamed about the situation. There was another cause of concern: a young woman who had lived at home too long might escape the control of her natal family, meet somebody of the opposite sex, then get pregnant, which would prove a disaster in the eyes of her family. That was why parents who had a young unmarried daughter regarded her as something of a time-bomb: they were really relieved if someone wanted to take her off their hands.

There was another reason for concern. In many areas, a spinster in the family might deter suitors for other unmarried family members. Counterpart families investigating the background of potential marriage partners would wonder at the reasons for her unmarried status. They would doubt not only her behaviour, but also that of her whole family. This meant that the spinster was a considerable burden and worry for the entire lineage.

Moreover, compared to married life, women's position in their family of origin had many disadvantages. The Gia Long Code of Law stated that daughters had no right to inheritance. Although officials may follow tradition and, except for rare cases, let the sons and daughters have equal shares, in fact, daughters often receive smaller amounts than their brothers. Even among the middle class, young women were frequently said to have committed suicide over the division of inheritance (Vietnam Resource Centre, 1974: 8–9). The attitude taken towards daughters as temporary members of their family of origin acted as a incitement to get married. Once married, a woman might suffer from mistreatment at the hands of her mother-in-law; however, she enjoyed some rights that were denied her in her parents' family. If she worked hard, she could enjoy the results of her labour. If she bore children, she could rely on them while she was alive, and be worshipped by them after her death. If she wanted, she could get even with the way she had been mistreated at the hands of her mother-in-law by ill-treating her daughter-in-law! With the passage of time she could improve her status in her family.

So the first aim for a great many women was to avoid the undesirable status of spinsterhood. The second motivation was to have children, within the framework of the marriage, in order to secure the old age. Therefore women were taught not to expect romance or happiness out of marriage; they expected little from it. A peasant woman getting married to a student might expect him to become an official or civil servant so that she could share her husband's honour and reputation, and have the title 'Mrs Clerk', 'Mrs Judge', etc. An urban woman whose husband was a French civil servant expected him to support the family. A poor woman marrying someone rich would expect him to provide her with some material security. A poor peasant woman who married within her class would only expect her husband to be hard-working, a workmate in family rice cultivation, to be good from a general moral point of view (not a drinker or a gambler for instance), and to set a moral example to her children.

In this context young, French-educated women in urban areas may have been atypical of the female population in general. If we turn to a fictional case, Loan, a new woman in the novel 'Breaking the Ties' by Nhat Linh strongly opposed all the old role expectations of her as an obedient daughter-in-law, a baby-making machine, and a submissive wife. She expected her husband's family to treat her with respect. She felt that she was a person equal to the other members of the family, that she had the right to be happy, and to choose what she wanted. However, everybody around her regarded her behaviour as too shocking and daring; it was unacceptable even for a French prosecutor (Filimonova, 1992).

Nonetheless, a woman's expectations depended on not only her social background, but also the marital status of her partner: whether she was the only wife, or the first/second wife, or the concubine. If she played a concubine's role, her expectations must have been very minimal. That in turn depended a lot upon the fortune of each woman. Although from time immemorial women had opposed polygamy by using folk-songs like this to warn their sisters: 'If you get hungry, eat brined fish and bitter figs, but don't ever get married to a common husband', concubinage was at its height during the first half of this century and it became increasingly difficult to oppose it (Vietnam Resource Centre, 1974: 37–38).

The reason was that the colonial economic policies hit peasant women extremely hard: the same source (ibid.: 35) tells us that almost every traditional craft and occupation of women was destroyed by the French economic policies and monopolies. Becoming landless together with their families, and what was much worse, having no access rights to common land, women also had great difficulty finding agricultural work. Even if some of them were lucky enough to find it, they were underpaid. To survive, women had to rely on men.

So the position of peasant women relative to men deteriorated seriously. Vietnamese newspapers during this period (ibid.:35) were full of stories about women being mistreated and committing suicide, and of course, about men abusing their wives. If young women did not want to become concubines of landlords and better-off peasants, they had to work for them as servants, or escape to cities and become workers, servants, and prostitutes. That was why in folksongs women often compared their fortune to raindrops: some went to a palace, others to a marshy field. The lucky ones married men of high social status and were freed from manual hard work and poverty; others married bad and lowly men. They had no choice.

Although some middle-class women may have had comparatively high expectations of their husbands, the majority of women learnt to expect very little. Compared to men's expectations of their marital partners, women's were minimal. That was revealed in the following folk-song: *Chang oi gian thiep lam chi, thiep nhu com nguoi do khi doi long* [Do not get angry with me, my darling! I am just like the cooked rice left from the previous meal for you to snack on when you get hungry].

MARITAL ENDINGS

Very little is known about one of the ways in which marriages ended, *viz.* widowhood. We know only one form of marital ending – divorce – but have no data about the frequency. There has been so far only one study dealing with divorce long before our century. In this research, Yu (1990) makes a distinction between three types of divorce:

- a husband repudiating his wife;
- a divorce imposed by the authorities; and
- a divorce by mutual agreement.

However, he presents no data either. Instead, based on his impressions about the relatively high position of Vietnamese women in the seventeenth and eighteenth centuries in comparison to their Chinese counterparts, he overstates that women in Vietnam seemed not to hesitate to get a divorce when they felt their rights and interests were infringed by their husbands.

In fact, at least during the period under discussion, according to Phan Ke Binh (1915/1992: 173) divorce was difficult, particularly for women. A husband could get a divorce on any of the seven grounds outlined previously, whereas a wife's only ground was that her husband had abandoned her. Moreover the juridical formalities and customs were complicated for women, but not for men. A woman who sought to divorce had to offer some betel leaves and areca fruits to her village head and representatives, and only when they agreed could she remarry. It was not easy for her to get their agreement in a society that was strongly biased towards men. This meant that divorce was not only expensive, but also complicated for women; however, it was not so for men. The only thing a husband had to do was to write a document stating that he repudiated the wife. She then had to report this and show the document to the district mandarin before getting permission to remarry.

Due to the priority given to the continuum of the lineage (rather than the interests of its individual members) and the establishment of alliances between kin-groups, people paid particular attention to the stability and harmony of the family, which was considered a sacred institution. They strongly opposed divorce and considered it immoral. When divorce did occur it reflected badly on the reputation of both marriage partners, but especially the woman. Among the three types of divorce, the first type, (where the husband renounced the wife) was probably the most common, and it was the wife who incurred the blame. Every woman thrown out of her husband's family attracted heavy public censure; she was believed to be completely at fault. A folk-song went: 'Nobody has the heart to cut the ears of a nice cat; a woman thrown by her husband has no words of her pride'. The song implies that if the wife had been a good one, she would not have been thrown out of the family. Divorce caused an enormous stigma to a woman. For that reason it was extremely difficult for them to remarry, although sometimes they remarried as concubines to old men or widowers. Consequently women hardly ever initiated divorce; instead, they often put up with unhappy marriages.

However, some women could not bear their marriages; and they could do nothing but leave their husbands' families for their natal ones. In that case, they were subject to the punishment of both the official law and customs. The article 108 of the Gia Long Code stipulated that if a first wife left her husband's house, she would be beaten a hundred times with a cane and the husband would be permitted to sell her to whomever he liked. Should a concubine run away from her husband's family, she would be beaten eighty times; if she remarried another man after she had run away, she would be beaten 100 times, then brought back to her legal husband. The new man whom she had illegally married, would be considered to be her fellow-criminal; and his property would be confiscated (Le Thi Nham Tuyet, 1975: 140).

The official law may frequently have been ignored, but traditional customs on this issue persisted. In Phuong Bang village (Ha Son Binh province), on the 15th of the eighth month, native guards suddenly broke into a villager's house, where there was a woman who had left her husband and returned to her parents' family. They brought the woman back to her husband's house; on the way, they clawed, punched, and insulted her. In Sai Son village (the same province), there was even a custom that women who were not satisfied with their husbands were brought to a communal house (the public place in every village), tied up there, beaten, interrogated, and questioned about their 'sins', then brought back to their husband's house. This custom lasted for several days in the eighth month of every year (Le Thi Nham Tuyet, 1975: 144). How common that was outside those villages may be open to question, but there is no doubt that divorce was very difficult for women.

It could be said that marriage was a trap for many women. They had no choice but to marry; once married, they were like a bird in a cage, a fish caught by the fishing rod (as a folk-song put it). They had no way to escape from an unbearable marriage. The external pressure played a massive part in sustaining a marriage. That explained in part why divorce was infrequent. If a husband was not satisfied with his marriage, he could take a concubine or get a divorce. Perhaps the first solution was preferable to the second one for different reasons. If the husband renounced his wife, he would first have to divide his property according to the official law and customs. That meant he lost a part of his property. Second, it might be expensive for him to remarry. Third, if his wife was from an upper-class background, her natal family would resist the divorce and the social stigma that would accompany it. It would create all sorts of problems for him.

At any rate, he had various options open to him in order to resolve the problem of dissatisfaction with his marriage. As for the wife, if she was not satisfied with her marriage, the only people to whom she could turn and discuss her problems were her parents' family. Sometimes they might try to advise her, even to intervene, but often in vain. Moreover, the two involved families came into conflict. The only useful advice she could get from her parents, who were believed to have been more experienced in marital matters than she was, was to put up with the unhappy marriage forever. Otherwise, she had only one way out: to commit suicide. Right before 1945, the number of young women committing suicide was abnormally high, and according to Le Thi Que (1986: 7), the cause of that was the passive struggle between daughters-in-law and mothers-in-law (not the husband–wife conflict). The author also explains that when the old morality imperiously commanded the young brides to submit to their mothers-in-law, they accommodated themselves to that. However, when some of the young wives in big cities came into contact with European culture, they discovered the new idea of individual freedom and became discontented with their lot. Unable to resolve the conflict, they chose the tragic way out of the dilemma.

In brief, everything that has been discussed so far can be understood and explained in terms of marriage's significance: marriage served the kin-group interests, not the individual's. This was revealed in two respects: first, marriage was an institution designed to produce children as well as to take care of old members for the kin-group; second, it was aimed at the establishment of alliances between kin-groups. Therefore the ideology that subordinated individual well-being to the benefit of the group was promoted; there were many people with a vested interest in a marriage's continuance, and a lot of pressure was brought to bear on the couple.

Women in particular were taught not to expect too much of marriage. Men were more demanding, but for their families in general, not so much for themselves as individuals. Such limited expectations acted as an internal mechanism preventing marriage from breaking down. In addition, the external pressure also forced people to put up with their marriages even if the marital bonds were not satisfactory. That was why divorce was rare. In a patriarchal society, where children belonged to their father's group, a groom's group would not accept the idea that a bride, for whom they had paid a substantial bride-price, might fail to produce a child for them, or fail to take care of her parents-in-law in their old age, or that she might wish to leave her husband. In this sense, this group's aim was to take and secure the rights over the bride's reproductive as well as productive powers.

I have argued that if parents had simply introduced their children to suitable partners, as well as dissuaded them from unsuitable ones, and had stopped there, let children decide themselves, they would have played a helpful role. But parents often felt they knew best, children knew nothing, and so they made the decision, regardless of their children's emotions. This situation, together with the difficulty in obtaining a divorce, led to a total lack of freedom in marriage.

If the lack of freedom in the choice of marital partner was the most acute contradiction of the traditional family, how has this feature changed under the impacts of the social transformations during the last half century? This will be examined in the next section.

CONJUGAL BONDS IN THE PRESENT FAMILY

In the modern family there is particular emphasis on a conjugal bond based on free choice and romantic love. So, has marriage in the Delta become increasingly free due to the effects of the recent social changes? Has there been an improvement in the closeness and intimacy of the conjugal relationship? Both the 1960 and 1987 Laws on Marriage and Family stressed the importance of freedom and the voluntary nature of marriage, but how is this put into effect? Have the conjugal relationships become equal? We shall try to find some answers to those questions.

MARITAL PARTNER SELECTION

Young people are now enjoying some freedoms that previous generations never had. This is especially the case for those living in urban areas who are educated and from educated family background or those who live far away from their family of origin, and who got married during the last few years. One of the few studies to examine this issue is that of Belanger and Khuat Thu Hong (1995). As a qualitative study based on group interviews, it reveals some interesting findings related to marital partner selection in Hanoi since 1965. Among their respondents were some people who put great emphasis on love: 'Love [in marriage] is important, love must come from oneself' (ibid.). There were also those who made all the decisions for themselves when it came to choice of marriage partner, and then informed their parents afterwards.

> For one man, consulting his parents was a matter of finding out their reaction, not to get their permission. Of course he

had to present the woman to his parents, but his parents were easy going, they did not oppose his choice at all. The man married in Hanoi, the capital city, after the renovation policy and has received a secondary education.[1]

Another man, born in Vinh Phu province but living in Hanoi, married at about the same time and expressed similar sentiments about his freedom to choose a spouse. He did respect his parents but they were living in the countryside, and he had been living independently since he was young. Therefore, asking for their opinion had only a ritual meaning.

(Belanger and Khuat Thu Hong 1995)

The following story of a woman is no less persuasive.

> She married at the age of 26. Initially her family objected to the proposed marriage because the young people's ages were not compatible. She told her family that if they did not agree, she would not marry anyone else but would remain a spinster, so they reluctantly had to acquiesce.

(ibid.)

In this case, the parents still exerted some power over their daughter, but the daughter fought against them, and in the end, she won.

How were these children able to gain this freedom in their choice of partners? The first man said his parents were easy-going; the second said his parents lived far away. Neither seems to recognise that over and above those personal factors, times are changing. A woman from the above study, who is much older than the two men, acknowledges this reality when talking about her daughter: in her view, the young people have more freedom than before. No doubt a revolutionary change has occurred in this matter. Children no longer wait for their parents' arrangements; instead, they take the initiative in looking for a mate, and decide themselves. Some do not even have to consult their parents. For them, consultation with the parents is just a gesture of symbolic significance. However symbolic the gesture is, the two men have one thing in common: they still had to present their fiancées for parental approval. That means that the old pattern, or traces of it, have persisted.

The above study, qualitatively oriented, cannot tell us how widespread this new freedom is. Freedom in marital partner selection reaches its apex, so to speak, only when young people choose for themselves without having to get the older generation's approval. Nonetheless, this is quite rare, as we shall see. Most of the examples of free choice that were previously cited occurred in Hanoi. In the countryside, existing evidence gives rather a different picture.

According to a quantitative study, conducted in 1990 in two communes in Ha Bac and Ha Nam Ninh provinces, asked about who decided children's marriages, only 4 per cent and 3 per cent of respondents respectively said that the children made decisions themselves. By contrast, 92 per cent and 96 per cent respectively reported that the children made decisions with parents' consultation and approval (Binh Minh, 1991). If these data are reliable, one has to say that freedom of marriage as a legal stipulation has up to now remained a far cry from reality. Backed up by traditions, parents have not given up their authority without a fight. Parental power can still be seen on two levels: arrangement for marrying a son (or a daughter) to a certain person, or let the child choose, but approve or disapprove of his (her) choice. The former practice can still be found, particularly in the countryside, but the latter is more widespread in both rural and urban areas.[2]

Newspapers every now and then report the cases in which parents arrange marriages for their children, or reject their children's choice. For instance, in one issue of *Phu nu Viet Nam* (6 April 1992), a weekly newspaper for female readers, under the rubric 'Readers' letters' there are letters from three different young girls complaining about their parents' disapproval of their love. One can hear even in Hanoi a story about how a dying mother told her daughter that her last wish was for her to marry a rich man, instead of choosing her poor current lover. The following press report is worth noting.

> Yen, a beautiful girl, already has a boyfriend who was a former classmate and is in military service now. However, a rich, respectable family in the village asks a go-between to approach her parents, and negotiate about an arranged marriage between Yen and their only son. As a result, Yen's parents suggest she should marry the son. As they put it,
>
>> a girl's youth is short-lived, she cannot wait for her boyfriend indefinitely; moreover, what would her boyfriend bring her materially? Love cannot guarantee any good standard of living. Meanwhile the family that wants to have her is rich and respectable ...
>
> However, Yen shows no interest in the match. Having failed to persuade her, the parents take a stronger measure. Their argument is that parents can never let their child tell them what to do; once they have reached an agreement with the

counterpart family on the marriage, she has to obey. Although she cries, and asks for the marriage not to go ahead, the date for it is set. Yen is forced to go through with the wedding ceremony. However, on the night of the wedding, she suddenly disappears, leaving only a brief message which says that she has to come to terms with the label 'filially impious child': she runs away to protect her love, and asks for her parents' forgiveness.

(Nguyen Tuan Minh, 1992)

Scholarly research also reveals similar cases. The group interview in the study of Belanger and Khuat Thu Hong (1995) reveals that parents still exert strong power over their children.

> A man with a university education, who got married in 1981, says he is the oldest child in his family. When he was 28 and still single, his parents were very worried. Since his parents were not healthy, they needed him to marry. Moreover, they wanted to have grandchildren. In their view, if they had not forced him, he might have delayed indefinitely.
>
> (Belanger and Khuat Thu Hong, 1995)

The parents in this story remind us of To Tam's mother and her worry about her deteriorated health when the daughter was still single. In a way, after about a half century, the sense of responsibility towards grown-up children on the part of parents remains unchanged.

Parents may take even stronger measures to impose their power on children.

> A man who had studied in Russia and met his girlfriend there said that his parents did not agree with his choice because the two families were not compatible. Although he had loved the girlfriend for five years, his mother still opposed their marriage. The mother even went to Russia and stayed there for a year in an attempt to stop the relationship.
>
> (Belanger and Khuat Thu Hong, 1995)

If the story is true (and it does stretch credulity somewhat), it shows that parental power in the choice of marital partner knows no geographical boundaries!

What about the young people's reactions to the parents' arrangements or disapproval? Again, there is a lack of hard evidence but some general conclusions may be drawn. Some young people give their parents a free hand to decide everything, especially those living in the countryside. Others may choose marital partners themselves and then present them to the parents. Even young people who enjoy relative freedom still have to get parental approval of their choice, as the above cases have shown. Should the parents disapprove of their choice, what would the young people do?

The above qualitative study by Belanger and Khuat Thu Hong also mentions that there are three solutions. The first option is one of resistance: they have to oppose their parents either by persuading them gradually, or by maintaining their position (the Russian-trained man from the same study says that he was convinced he was going to live with the girlfriend for the rest of his life, not with his parents, so he decided to marry her) (Belanger and Khuat Thu Hong, 1995). Those who adopt this confrontational approach must be very sure of their love and very strong-willed; moreover they must be capable of living independently of their parents. Whereas men seem determined to go ahead with their choice in spite of all parental opposition, women tend to be more conciliatory and try to talk their parents round to their way of thinking.

The second option is for the children to give up their choice if the parents do not approve. For example, a female respondent who was born in Hanoi and had a vocational education, says that if the parents did not accept the children's choice, perhaps the young couple would have to part. The third and final option is for the children to run away from home with their lovers, as did the girl in the above press report! What the percentage split is for each option is open to empirical investigation, but one can guess from everyday experience that the most extreme option (i.e. a complete break with the parents) is rarely taken. It is not easy to battle against one's family of origin when opportunities to lead an independent life outside of it are so limited.

It may be surprising to learn that a large number of young people recognise their parents' power. In the study of Belanger and Khuat Thu Hong (1995) a woman explains that parents always perceive things more clearly than children. This view that age brings wisdom might be construed as typical of someone with only a vocational education. However, the view of another woman with a university education living in Hanoi may surprise us. This woman claims that when one is in love, one often does not see things clearly, so it is easy to make a mistake. So when one is about to marry, one has to pay attention to the opinion of the family (Belanger and Khuat Thu Hong, 1995). Here it is love, not the inexperience of youth, that is blamed for the likelihood of making a mistake. Clearly in the eyes of these two women the characteristics of youth (having no experience and being blinded by love), and love itself are distinctly negative attributes.

Why do parents disapprove of their children's choice? What is their motivation? The above story about the Russian-trained man tells us that the reason is the incompatibility of the two involved families. How is incompatibility defined? Is it the same as the traditional meanings of those concepts (matching wealth and status)? How do the recent social changes (particularly the relative equality between people in terms of wealth, and property that existed until very recently as a result of the social steering programmes) affect these concepts? According to a survey in two communes, 26 per cent of respondents (the sample's size is unknown) suppose that the criterion of compatibility between two involved families should be maintained. The author adds that it no longer means the matching of wealth and property, as it did in the traditional family, but the matching of ages and good behaviour in terms of moral order and discipline of the two families (Binh Minh, 1991).

The study by Belanger and Khuat Thu Hong (1995) confirms one of these meanings: compatibility is viewed, among other things, in terms of age. It may mean the age of the two sets of parents as well as that of the two young people. In one woman's words,

> the ages of the parents of both sides must be the same so the relationship can be good. I am the eldest child of my family, and if I want to marry someone who is the youngest in his family, my parents would not agree.
>
> (Belanger and Khuat Thu Hong, 1995)

Thus, it is not only the comparative ages of two young people, but also the order of birth in the respective families that matter. This is shown in the story of another woman who threatened to remain a spinster if her family did not agree with her choice simply because the ages were not compatible. However, we cannot be sure that the consideration of birth order is common. Moreover, the study does not specify how age compatibility is calculated; perhaps the age investigation is carried out according to the Chinese horoscope, but a further discussion later will reveal a new sense of age compatibility.

Apart from the age issue, the study also throws some new light on the whole concept of compatibility. The Russian-trained man explains that the parents opposed his choice because they thought the two families were not compatible. His parents thought that because he was from Hanoi and had studied abroad, they had to select his future wife very carefully. His parents wanted him to marry someone with a high-level educational background (Belanger and Khuat Thu Hong, 1995). Here, then, education and the urban–rural distinction are considered as factors of compatibility. A middle-aged woman recalls how her husband initially opposed their daughter's choice: although the young man involved had studied with their daughter in Russia, his family was not compatible with theirs: they were not from Hanoi, nor were they as intellectual as theirs. It took a long time for her to convince him, but finally he accepted (ibid.). Thus the concept of compatibility means the matching in terms of education and social location (the urban–rural distinction).

Obviously these meanings of the term 'compatibility' would not have concerned the traditional family. One may say they are the products of the recent social changes: the increased opportunities for education, and the distinction made between the urban population and the rural one during the period of socialist reconstruction. Such considerations, if they existed in the pre-1945 period, were deemed to be of far less importance than the post-1945 one. Nonetheless, the concept of compatibility means even more, as will be revealed in the three following case histories, also from the same study.

> The first case is of a Hanoi woman who was in love with a man from a capitalist family. Her family told her that it was impossible to marry him. At that time, family background was considered to be very important. Later she met another man and married, and realised that a similar story had happened to her husband's older brother. First, he loved a very beautiful girl but she was from a capitalist family so his family opposed the match. Then someone introduced him to a very ugly girl but her family had an excellent revolutionary history. His family agreed immediately. If one was a state employee, the potential spouse's family background was very important.
>
> (Belanger and Khuat Thu Hong, 1995)

> The second case relates to another Hanoi woman who was in love with a soldier for four years. However, they could not marry because her family believed his family was not compatible with theirs. In her family both her father and mother worked for the government, whereas his father was a professor and his mother just a housewife. Her family strongly objected

to the match since the two young people did not share the same family background.

(Ibid.)

In the third case, again of a Hanoi woman in the same study, the ideal husband at the time would be one from a similar family background to hers, so the two families could become close to each other. Second he should have a stable job. Third, he had to be a state employee; in his family no one should be in private business. All the members of his family must work for the government. If just one person in his family was involved in private business, the family was disliked because these people 'had one foot in the public sector and one foot in the private one'. The woman's family and many others could only accept a marital partner whose family met these rigid criteria.

(Ibid.)

We need to specify here that all these people married during the period 1965–85. Given the class approach and the official discrimination against the families labelled as landlords in rural areas (see Chapter Two), or as capitalists in urban ones, it is understandable that in the first case, the woman's family opposed the young man from a bourgeois background. As she explains, because of his family background, access to university was very difficult for him. If he could study, it was only in certain fields such as forestry or agriculture, which did not have much social prestige (ibid.). Here it was not only the pragmatic analysis of the pros and cons in terms of material interests of such a marriage, but also the consideration of social values and prestige that played a role in the family's stance towards the match. This case reminds us of how Chinese women base their choice of spouse on the criterion of a 'good' (i.e. politically correct) class background (Wolf, 1985).

What about the second and third cases? In the second story, the family disapproved of their daughter's choice not for the reason that her lover's family was bourgeois, but because his mother was just a housewife. In other words, the mother was not a state employee. Unlike a bourgeois, a housewife was not a class enemy, of course. So what was the objection? That can be accounted for only in the light of the sharp discrimination against non-state employees in urban areas. As we saw in Chapter Two, the official policy trusted and granted privileges only to the state employees and discriminated against the non-state employees as second-class citizens. The discrimination was so severe that in the woman's opinion (from the second story), if she married him it would hinder her upward social mobility. So the concept of compatibility had a political meaning: it meant the two involved families had to share the same social standing, they both had to be state employees.

According to the authors, this criterion is mentioned by all the participants who discussed criteria for marital partners. As a respondent says, at the time 'everyone' looked for 'a government cadre with a permanent position' (ibid.). Obviously this is an exaggeration because the non-state employees could not do so: in fact, they were left with far fewer choices. Unfortunately the authors of the study do not specify whether any non-state employees were included in their survey, and if so, how they reacted to this criterion. In other words, the study focuses on how 'the family, the State and the individual interplay to satisfy their desires and fulfil their requirements in the marriage process' , but it totally ignores the distinction between the state employees and the non-state ones. That is its biggest failing. Nor have the authors specified the social standing of their respondents' families, but it seems (at least from the quoted case studies) that all the respondents are from a state employee background. One cannot suppose that most of the urban residents at the time were state employees if one has no quantitative data on which to base that assumption. Even if it was correct that most urban residents were state employees, one would still have to include some non-state employees in one's sample in order to hear their voice. Furthermore in the shortage economy the state could hardly afford to extend to everybody the scarce privileges that the state employees enjoyed. In other words, the number of the state employees must have not been unlimited. That means there might be some bias in the study's sampling. Therefore we have to guess that the non-state employees often had no other option but to select a marriage partner from among their own ranks. As for state employees, we must now turn our attention to the state's role in their choice.

THE STATE'S ROLE IN YOUNG PEOPLE'S CHOICE OF MARITAL PARTNER

What were the advantages of marrying a state employee? Why did some people have to select marital partners among the state employees? Belanger and Khuat Thu Hong (1995) mention the following benefits: the *co quan* (work unit in the state sector) distributed housing units and coupons for food and clothes. Through the *co quan* one had access to public services such as health care. We need to add that the *co quan* was also an important source for the procurement of certain socio-political services (obtaining official travel permits, work permits, or even interventions with the courts and police, etc.), and certain consumer goods (e.g. bicycles, cigarettes). In this respect the *co quan* in Vietnam and the 'unit' (workplace) in China (Wolf, 1985; Walder, 1986) played a similar role. So due to certain privileges to which non-state employees were not entitled, and which were given by the government, state employees were very much in demand on the marriage market. By contrast, non-state employees were undesirable as marriage partners, at least in the eyes of the state employees.

Working for the government not only guaranteed economic stability by providing housing and food through the *co quan*, but also meant having a 'good' family background (*ly lich*) since this family background had been accepted by the workplace. As the researchers put it, 'it was thus a guarantee of family compatibility' (Belanger and Khuat Thu Hong, 1995). Thus the work unit in the state sector not only offered essential material benefits, but also facilitated the selection of a suitable spouse. This was owing to fact that to get a job in the state sector, the candidate had to undergo a careful screening process, one crucial part of which was to have a 'good' family background (*ly lich trong sach*) from the class viewpoint.

This is confirmed by an account of how a forestry worker (viewed as a state employee) is recruited: the applicants should have enthusiasm, and should be politically reliable and not involved in any illegal business. That is the standard for the state employees. Their parents and grandparents must be the ones who did not collaborate with the enemy. If the parents are Communist Party members, it is easier for their children. Their behaviour in the commune, and how they implement government regulations is also very important. They should be models and examples for others. 'The chairman of the commune writes a recommendation in the applicant's CV and adds a stamp. If they do not want to recommend someone, they do not write anything' (Liljeström *et al.*, 1988: 78). Every state employee has a file of his (her) family background that is kept by the personnel department of every work unit.

Nonetheless, the state's role in marriage expressed through work unit in the state sector did not stop there. Many young people had to obtain the *co quan*'s approval of their choice; otherwise, they could not marry. The opposition of the *co quan* might take different forms, for instance a refusal to sign the document needed for registration of marriage. Here are some examples.

📁 According to a woman, who was born in Hanoi in 1939 and married at the age of 33, she and her boyfriend loved each other, and wished to marry. Her family agreed but they had to delay their marriage. The reason was that at the time the *co quan* played the most important role in the final decision; if the two *co quan* did not grant permission yet, they could not marry. The boy was from the South so the *co quan* had to investigate his past to make sure he did not already have a family down there. It took four years before they could marry. As she puts it, 'overall it was very complicated'. Everyone who wanted to start dating had to go through the *co quan*. 'If the *ly lich* had anything unclear then it was difficult'.

(Belanger and Khuat Thu Hong, 1995)

📁 Another woman, born in Thai Binh province in 1959 and married at the age of 23, says that her *co quan* was very strict. If somebody wanted to start dating, they had to inform the personnel department of the *co quan*. It was only when the *co quan* gave permission that they could start dating and marry.

(Ibid.)

On what basis does the workplace approve or disapprove of an employee's choice? The study shows that the workplace, after having been informed about its member's prospective spouse, conducts some investigation into his (her) family background and marital status. The meaning of the workplace's intervention and investigation is not just to avoid polygamy as the first respondent mentions, but also to make sure about the desired class endogamy: marriage to a class enemy is considered to be a dangerous distraction from the class struggle and therefore is not allowed (see Chapter Two). To quote the communist poet To Huu in his well-known poem *Bai ca xuan 61* [The spring poem of 1961], a couple consists not just of a man and a woman, but also *hai nguoi dong chi* [two comrades]. As the poet puts it, he shares his heart between the Communist Party, his poetry, and his wife. In spite of this comradely solidarity with his wife, however, it is the Communist Party (not the wife) that gets the biggest share of his heart, then poetry, and last his wife. We need to make it clear that *dong chi* [comrade] as a noun and a term of address has been in use only since the communists appeared, and mainly among themselves (Luong Van Hy, 1990: 142–143).

However, the study does not specify to which *co quan* those respondents belonged. In fact it is impossible to impose rigidly the regulation according to which everybody had to report to his (her) workplace on the prospective spouse. As mentioned in Chapter Two, the regulation has been applicable only to Communist Party members, high-ranking army officers, and people in such important domains as the security forces. From the evidence presented in the quoted study it is also clear that the workplace played a major role mostly among people of rural origin 'since their families often lived far away in the countryside' (Belanger and Khuat Thu Hong, 1995). At any rate, the regulation has affected the marriage plans of a great many people. For them, parental power has been replaced or perhaps overtaken by the power of the state through the workplace.

Why does the workplace play such an influential role? Why do people submit to the power of the workplace? The study explains that the workplace is more than a guarantee of economic stability; it is also a bridge for social mobility. When one is employed by the government, one's prospective spouse needs to be approved of by one's *co quan*. The reason is that

> selecting a mate without respecting the political boundaries could influence one's aspirations for political involvement in the Party. In some cases it may affect one's opportunities for professional promotion.
>
> (Ibid.)

Nevertheless, it is by no means certain that the class criterion in marital issues will guarantee marital satisfaction. A woman working in the security forces relates the following story.

> When she was young, she dreamt of having a husband who was one or two years older than her, equal in physical attractiveness, and with the same or higher educational level. More importantly, in her dream, she should be his one and only love. Later, she worked in the Ministry of Interior Affairs where a high social position and morality were the norm. If people there loved someone, they had to report it to the *co quan* for approval. If a person from outside wished to marry someone in her Ministry, the *co quan* had to investigate his family background (*ly lich*).
>
> Her future husband came to her family to introduce himself, and his *co quan* talked to her *co quan*. However, his *co quan* showed that he was a Party member, even a leader of a Party unit, so it was not necessary to investigate his past.

Moreover, a member of her *co quan* was from the same village as her future husband, and wanted to help him to marry. Supposing that she was old for a single woman, her *co quan* also wanted to match them together, and they simply agreed. As for herself, trusting her *co quan* and her friend who had introduced her to him, and believing that he was a Party member and ten years older than she, she accepted the arrangement.

On the day that they registered their marriage, she found out with some dismay that in fact he was twenty years older than her, not ten. However, she thought that she was getting too old to find a husband, and her family had already agreed. Therefore she decided to go ahead with the marriage; it was only afterwards that she discovered that he was already married to another woman. She realised that she had made a big mistake:

> I believed in my *co quan*. I thought he was a Party member and that his family background was good [*ly lich trong sach*]. I did not suspect him, but it was no guarantee at all, there was no happiness, nothing.

After this unhappy event, she became suspicious and mistrustful of everyone. Having changed from a very romantic girl of Hanoi to an unhappy and disillusioned woman, she could do only one thing: to wish for her daughter's happiness and for her not to suffer as she had done.

(Belanger and Khuat Thu Hong, 1995)

If the story is true, it is not only the woman but also the two workplaces that were deceived by a polygamist disguised as a communist. We do not know how many other people have suffered from similar unhappy marriages, so it would be rash to draw any general conclusion. We can state that in this case at least, class endogamy did not bring marital satisfaction!

When discussing the role of the workplace, it would be wrong to neglect the other side of the picture. Sometimes they play a supportive role in helping their employees to find spouses, and to celebrate wedding ceremonies in inexpensive ways. That may be very significant, especially for those who want to marry but have certain difficulties in getting to know people of the opposite sex (as we have seen in the story of the above woman), or who have limited resources to spend on the wedding celebrations. Generally speaking, if the workplaces had known when to stop, and had not intervened in their employees' choice of marriage partner, their role would have been very supportive.

Belanger and Khuat Thu Hong (1995) divide the period of their study (1965–92) into two stages: namely 1965–85 and 1987–92. They believe that since the renovation in the late 1980s, a radical change has taken place in Hanoi. In the first stage (1965–85) the parents introduced the potential spouse to the young adult. In the second stage (1987–92) the young adult introduces a potential spouse to the parents; all the people from the younger groups select their spouses themselves. Nevertheless, parental approval is still central to the process.

However, as previously noted, it seems that their sample consists of only the state employees whose parents played an active role in selecting marital partners based on the criterion of a state employee background. The authors do not say anything about people who were non-state employees; it is unclear what their mate selection was like. For this bias, the authors' characterisation of the 1965–85 stage (as the one in which parents introduced the potential spouse to the young adult) may somehow overstate the case. It may have been applicable only to state employees in urban areas. It is not excluded that during the period, there were already some young people who chose their spouses themselves, then presented them for parental approval. That may be true of non-state employees in urban areas, as well as of people in rural areas.

So it could be said that during the first stage, apart from parental power, a great deal of control was also exercised by the state through the workplace. The state's role was both direct and indirect. From a literary source – for instance the novel *Ly than* [Separation] by Tran Manh Hao (1989/1990) – we learn that the authorities might intervene directly in marital issues by arranging marriages between people of the same class background. However, that needs to be confirmed by hard scholarly evidence which is not yet available. A more common practice for young state employees in urban areas was to be instructed by their parents to choose another state employee as a marriage partner. Another frequent practice was for people to choose their marital partner themselves, then report to their workplace, which would approve or disapprove of their choice on the ground of class endogamy. As a respondent in the study puts it, 'in our time, when we wished to build a family we had many dreams but the limitations were numerous because of the circumstances of that period.' Free choice in marital issues was not only recognised by law, but is also considered to be its core. However, at least for those people, it was not a reality. The free choice was given with one hand, but taken away with the other, so to speak.

As for the stage from 1987 to now, it is still difficult to identify the tendency. However, it is clear that after the renovation, the political involvement in the choice of a marital partner diminished. From a woman's perspective, nowadays the society has changed considerably: there is much more freedom in marriage and fewer constraints. Political and the family background criteria are of lesser importance than previously (Belanger and Khuat Thu Hong, 1995). The reason is that the private sector of the economy has been recognised and opened up. People no longer regard the state sector as the sole guarantor of economic security and upward social mobility; therefore the workplace's role has been reduced considerably. Nonetheless, as long as the workplace in the state sector still monopolises the special benefits that are not available elsewhere (permission to travel abroad, for instance), it will continue to act as a magnet to many people.

Parental power, too, is to some extent on the wane because young people are finding it easier to make friends outside the family with the mushrooming of dance halls, clubs, etc. In spite of this as well as the decreased role of the state, for a vast majority of people, as we have seen, free choice means that children choose spouses for themselves, but they must still get parental approval. As for the non-state employees, and people in countryside in general, due to the limitations of the study by Belanger and Khuat Thu Hong (1995), and due to the lack of other studies, we can just extrapolate the findings from the study by Binh Minh (1991) that in both stages, parents still have a very important say in children's marriage. In other words, to draw a conclusion about how spouse selection is carried out during the period since 1945, we need more convincing evidence about the say of family members, including young people both before and after the renovation, in rural and urban areas, for both the state employees and the non-state employees.

So if a twofold division is needed, it would be better to divide the period 1945–95 into the stages 1945–86 and 1987–95 and to characterise them as, first, the one in which the workplace played a crucial role in choosing a spouse and, second, the one in which the workplace's role has been reduced. In both stages, parents still exert power over spouse selection, but there have been some signs that in the second stage, parental power has been reduced to some extent in urban areas. Young people may choose their marital partners themselves, but they must get their parents' approval. That is a compromise between the arranged marriage of the traditional family and modern marriage.

CRITERIA FOR SPOUSE SELECTION

Who is chosen as a marital partner of a man and woman? The answer to this question tells us something about the marital relationship; whether or not the husband–wife nexus is more equitable today than it was in the traditional family.

First we will take a look at urban areas. A study by Mai Kim Chau among young single people in Hanoi reveals some interesting results. Listing fourteen qualities that are supposed to be necessary for a good husband/good wife, the researcher asked his respondents to choose the most important one. The number one quality for both wife and husband was to have a stable job. Next came the qualities necessary for family life: the wife should take care of children and do the household chores well, and behave politely to her parents-in-law. The husband should be gentle to his wife and children, and should show concern for his spouse. High level of education was ranked in third place (quoted in Khuat Thu Hong, 1991).

Ambivalent in some cases, the listed qualities may be understood differently by the respondents, and are therefore hard to interpret. However, the criterion 'having a stable job' was considered to be paramount by almost all the respondents. This is understandable in such a poor society where earning capacity is a guarantee of, or at least closely related to, the economic well-being of a family. Again this is similar to one of the criteria of Chinese people (Wolf, 1985). Nevertheless, we should not lose sight of an important difference: whereas a number of Chinese women in 1980–81 emphasised 'no intellectuals' when choosing spouses (Wolf, 1985), education has always been held in high regard in Vietnam. If the researcher Mai Kim Chau had specified more concretely what 'having a stable job' meant (did it mean working in the state sector, for example?), his study would have been more interesting: we would have had something to compare to the findings of the above-mentioned study of Belanger and Khuat Thu Hong (1995).

Belanger and Khuat Thu Hong confirm some findings of the former and throw new light on the issues that are not clear in the study by Mai Kim Chau. Like the respondents in the study by Mai Kim Chau, a man married at the age of 32 in 1977 said that at the time it was essential to choose someone who had a stable job to maintain the family (Belanger and Khuat Thu Hong, 1995). The authors state that the achievement of professional stability in the government is a *sine qua non* for marriage stability for both spouses. As a woman in their study puts it, the couples must have stable jobs, it is only then that they can build a happy family. This is especially required for men: we have already quoted the woman who said that the ideal husband 'should have a stable job' (ibid.).

The above quotations come from people married before the renovation policy, but still hold good even for people who married since 1987, particularly women. Whereas some men say that for an ideal wife, the most important thing is to have some beauty, not a job, i.e. that they emphasise physical appearance as a prime criterion, the women continue to insist that the ideal husband should have a good education and a stable job with a good revenue (ibid.). This may remind us of the pre-1945 pattern in which the man was the bread-winner in the middle-class family.

There have been some major changes. Before the renovation policy, both spouses had to work in the state sector to earn enough income for their family, but this is no longer the case. A revival of traditional gender roles is becoming evident, as one woman in the Belanger–Khuat Thu Hong study pointed out. She said that as the bread-winner, the man must be mature enough to support his family economically. The most important criterion for a women is to be ready to take care of the family and to be able to assume the responsibility of being a mother. According to one male respondent, it is better if a woman has a job, but if she does not, it is OK because the man must be the leader, so it is not necessary that his wife has a revenue (ibid.). Both these respondents married at the same age (21), in the same year (1990). They must have been well-off in economic terms to think this way. However, the Belanger–Khuat Thu Hong study also reveals that some women insist that the wives should work not just because of economic necessity, but also for sexual equality.

We have so far dealt with only the economic considerations of choosing an ideal spouse. As for the personal qualities, it is more apparent that the traditional pattern prevails. This can be seen in the ideal qualities of each gender separately as well as in 'ideal' age difference between husband and wife, which many still consider to be desirable. For people married before 1987, as the Belanger–Khuat Thu Hong study shows,

> one condition for a good match is that the wife should be a few years younger than her husband ... This condition is

widely mentioned by people no matter what their educational level or their rural or urban origin.

(Belanger and Khuat Thu Hong, 1995)

The age difference is not perceived as a threat to the family's harmony and stability; on the contrary, it is considered to be a factor guaranteeing the balance in marital life. As the authors put it, 'it is believed that women age faster than men, so the age difference will maintain a balance in the couple' (ibid.). In other words, the couple should not be of the same age; there must be an age difference between them. The authors give some examples: according to a woman who was born in Hanoi in 1960, and had finished college education, a husband must be four to five years older than his wife. 'This way he is more mature and the woman will respect him as an older brother.' A husband must be older than his wife, so she will respect him more and he will pamper her – that is also the desire of another woman, who also has finished college education. In her words, 'if we are the same age, it is not convenient' (ibid.). The third woman states that the best age difference is between five and six years, because the husband is supposed to play a role like 'a big brother' who takes care of the family. 'If we marry someone of the same age, so according to the saying *ca me mot lua*, we cannot stand each other and will quarrel all the time' (ibid.).

These examples presented by Belanger and Khuat Thu Hong leave a lot to be desired. First, they do not clarify whether the age difference stipulated by these people is a reality in their own marriages or simply their voiced preference. Second, they are given from a woman's perspective; no male opinion is included. However, the examples demonstrate that women in this period were given a choice which the older generations were never offered (they could, to some extent, look for the man of their dreams), moreover they wanted the man to be 'the leader and the protector of the wife and children' (ibid.). So a slight difference in the ages is preferred: the age pattern of 'older brother, little sister' is the ideal. Thus women themselves wanted to be weak, small, and vulnerable, and in need of a strong protector and guide. Compared to the traditional pattern 'older sister, little brother' in which the wife was often some years older than her husband (Luong Van Hy, 1992: 76), this is a reversed preference. It is uncertain when people started to believe that women age more quickly than men.

From the empirical evidence presented by Belanger and Khuat Thu Hong, I would like to emphasise here a point that seems to have escaped these researchers. The new pattern is highly unequal and male-oriented, because in the cultural context that emphasises age as one of the three determinant factors of hierarchical status (see Chapter One), this gives a great advantage to the spouse who is older, the man. In other words, it is taken for granted that the conjugal relationship is of a hierarchical, not equal, character. More significantly, the inequality is regarded as necessary for the marital balance.

This finds expression not only in the age difference, but also in the ways marital couples address each other. To make that clear, Belanger and Khuat Thu Hong analyse the Vietnamese system of address. In their view (it would have been more convincing if they had some quantitative data to confirm this), in Hanoi, instead of using the united (and equal, we need to add) term of address *minh* (Luong Van Hy, 1990: 64), the kinship terms are widely used. The husband refers to himself, and the wife addresses him, as *anh* [older brother]. By the same token, the wife refers to herself, and the husband addresses her, as *em* [little sister]. This is confirmed by O'Harrow (1995: 178). As we saw in Chapter One, the relationships between siblings have always been hierarchical. Belanger and Khuat Thu Hong also clarify the meaning of the saying *ca me mot lua* (that means disapprovingly that if there is no hierarchy like fishes of the same age, it is unacceptable) which the third woman in those examples uses as a justification of her preference for the hierarchy between the couple (Belanger and Khuat Thu Hong, 1995).

If Phan Ke Binh (1915/1992: 61) is correct, at the beginning of this century, couples used a different form of address. The current form used in Hanoi may derive from Quang Nam, a province in the central part of Vietnam. We do not know how and when it has changed, but we are certain that it has put the couple into a hierarchical, not equal, relationship. This is not just a question of semantics; it really influences people's social behaviour.[3]

Available data for rural areas and for the whole country in general reveal the ages of couples when they first married, and confirm that this age difference is common. In Hai Van commune (Ha Nam Ninh, 1979), 18 years is the normal marriage age for girls (Houtart and Lemercinier, 1984: 100); the husband is generally somewhat older, but the variations are never very significant. According to a survey among 206 women in two communes of Thai Binh province, the mean age of first marriage is about 20.4; there is no significant difference in this respect between three age groups (20–29; 30–39; and 40–49) (Johansson *et al.*, 1996). Most wives are two to three years younger than their husbands (Le Thi Nham Tuyet *et al.*, 1994a).

The 1988 demographic survey gave some estimates of the average age at first marriage for women over time. Women who married in the late 1950s and the 1960s had an average marriage age of 19.9 years; for women aged from 25–44, it was about 21.2; for the younger cohorts of women (20–24), a small postponement seems to be taking place. Recently, urban women seem to be marrying two to years later than their rural counterparts (Banister, 1993: 21). The same source also tells us that the mean age at marriage was 23.2 years for women and 24.5 for men (for the whole country), so the pattern 'older brother, little sister' is prevailing.

The age difference, and more importantly, the unequal pattern of 'older brother, younger sister' as the model for the conjugal bond say a lot about the hierarchical character of this family tie. That is also a vivid reminiscence of a classic literary reference which compares the man to the bamboo and pine trees (*tung quan*), and the wife to the mistletoe (*cat dang*). The bamboo and pine with their evergreen foliage can endure hardships and protect the weak parasitic mistletoe against natural disasters.

Belanger and Khuat Thu Hong (1995) suppose that most people married after 1987 still mention the age difference, but that it is no longer a paramount consideration. However, the authors have given no evidence to prove that. Moreover, the desired personal qualities of an ideal husband and wife for this group have demonstrated convincingly that, although some people prefer a more egalitarian conjugal union, the traditional role division still prevails. To cite three cases of their study:

- A woman born in Hanoi in 1968 supposes that an ideal husband should first of all be upright and honest, then knowledgeable. Being knowledgeable does not mean that he should have completed a certain educational level, but rather that he should have a broad and general culture. On the other hand, he must have a stable job to support his family.

- A man born in 1954 and married at 33 considers that an ideal wife should know a lot about family matters (taking care of her husband and children). She should pay attention to his work, his health, and his feelings. Moreover, in everything she should be 'a friend', not just a cook.

- Another educated man born in 1967 states that in choosing a wife, the main criterion is femininity expressed in her gentleness, her care for the family, the husband, and children. The second one is her beauty. In brief, she mainly has to know how to take care of the family, so the husband can concentrate on his work. It is not necessary for her to have reached a high educational level. If she has it, it is welcomed, 'but it is not necessary'. As for her profession, she can have a job to contribute to the family income 'but it may be any job, like sewing'.

(Belanger and Khuat Thu Hong 1995)

The authors try to demonstrate that there has been a marked change in attitude among those who married after 1987: some still prefer the traditional role division; others hope for a more egalitarian conjugal union. However, even in the first case cited above, where the young woman breaks with tradition by declaring that education is not simply a matter of formal diplomas, she still holds the view that the man must have a job and be the bread-winner. Moreover, it is the man, not the woman, who is supposed to acquire knowledge – this is reminiscent of a gender differentiation in the traditional family. The fact that moral uprightness is ranked as the first and foremost criterion clearly reflects the traditional outlook which finds expression in many folk-songs, popular sayings, and proverbs.

In the second case, the wife is expected to share in everything happening in her husband's life, this is a new addition to her traditional caring responsibility. For the third case study, the woman's caring function is ranked as the first criterion; her education does not matter. Her earning power is not necessary; if she has a job, it may be low-paid, and of low prestige, of secondary importance compared to his. On the other hand, in both the second and third cases, the man has a job which is considered to be of great importance, and the wife must respect it and support her husband in his performance of it.

There is no doubt from the group interview notes that the criterion 'having a stable job' comes up over and over again as the prime requisite of both ideal husband and wife. However, people prefer the traditional pattern in which the man is the bread-winner, and the woman adopts the caring role. The authors do not mention anything about a change in the mode of address between couples since 1987, but it seems that hierarchical terms are still being used. It seems that Vietnamese couples do not need to confirm, reconfirm, and strengthen their relationships by using equal, 'saccharine terms' like the English ones 'darling', 'honey', and 'sweetheart'.

What about the criteria for selecting a marital partner in rural areas? This issue is documented by the aforementioned study of

Binh Minh (1991) in the two communes of Trung Xa and Hai Trung. The author asked the respondents to mark what qualities they appreciated in their prospective spouses. The listed qualities were similar for both sexes (good-looking, hard-working, virtuous, high-earning, and having some non-farming occupational skills), except for an additional quality for men: they should have non-agricultural jobs outside their native villages (*thoat ly*). The survey results are set out in the following two tables.

Table 1: Men's criteria for selecting a wife, Trung Xa and Hai Trung communes, 1991

	Per cent of male respondents	
Female quality stressed	**Trung Xa**	**Hai Trung**
beauty	66.0	67.0
hard-working	91.5	69.0
virtuous	91.0	92.0
high-earning	4.5	24.0
non-farming occupational skills	0.0	51.0

Source: Binh Minh, 1991

Table 2: Women's criteria for selecting a husband, Trung Xa and Hai Trung communes, 1991

	Per cent of female respondents	
Male quality stressed	**Trung Xa**	**Hai Trung**
handsome	19.5	28
hard-working	83.0	75.0
virtuous	92.5	90.0
high-earning	9.5	20.0
non-agricultural job	7.5	20.0
non-farming occupational skills	0.0	53.0

Source: Binh Minh, 1991

There remains a degree of ambiguity in the terms (for example, what does the adjective 'virtuous' mean? How can the researcher be sure that all the respondents understand it in the same way?). Some differences in the data between the two communes may be attributed to the local socio-economic conditions. However, there is one thing which both communes clearly have in common: virtuous (*dao duc* in Vietnamese) people of both sexes are preferred by the overwhelming majority of the respondents.

CONJUGAL INTERACTION

After seeing how men and women choose their marital partners, let us examine how they interact with each other in marital life. Having a degree of freedom in the choice of a spouse, they are supposed to establish marital ties on an equal, close, and intimate basis. What are those ties like in fact? There is a significant lack of evidence upon which to base a firm conclusion, but there are clear trends. We shall take a look at the ways couples interact: first at work, then in free time, and in other domains of family life.

Interaction at work

In rural areas between 1960 and 1986, the collectivisation of agriculture had the effect of a possible separation of marital couples while in co-operative production. They might belong to the same work group, but participate in different subgroups. In order to survive or to supplement their incomes, families would often involve themselves in domestic production activities (farming and animal rearing, etc.). In this respect, as the study of Houtart and Lemercinier (1984: 109–111) in Hai Van shows, women generally had a larger share of the work than men, especially those women who were under 40, whose husbands were non-cultivators. According to another survey in Tam Son commune, Ha Bac province in 1983, 74 per cent of respondents said that in rice production, women did more work than men; 19 per cent estimated an equal contribution; only 7 per cent supposed that men did more work than women (Vu Manh Loi, 1991).

As for the distribution of household chores, in 39.4 per cent of the families questioned by Houtart and Lemercinier (1984: 114), the traditional pattern persists, according to which women undertake all the household tasks. The men shared on average only 20 per cent of the domestic chores (including heavy ones such as drawing water from the well and transportation of materials) with their wives and children (Luong Van Hy, 1989: 752). We need to add that the sharpest division that has been made is not between heavy and light work, but between male and female spheres of work. Everybody is expected to do his (her) work, no exchange is desirable. Gender identity is closely bound up with this gendered division of labour.

The situation does not seem to have improved after the renovation policy. In a survey conducted in Quang Bi and Dai Yen communes (1989), women carry out most of work for both main (agricultural) and sideline occupations; men's role seems limited to assisting in all kinds of work, except for land preparation. The usual working time put in by men is about two-thirds that of women (Vu Manh Loi, 1991).

In urban areas, a survey carried out among Hanoi's residents in 1983 by Trinh Duy Luan (quoted in Khuat Thu Hong, 1991) leads to a similar conclusion: women do most of the household chores. However, the shift to the market economy has put severe strains on gender relations: the women are really under pressure from different family members to follow the traditional gender roles (to assume the financial and caring responsibilities in the family) and to observe the traditional moral norms.

To get an insight into this question, let us look at the well-known short story *Tuong ve huu* [The Retired General] by Nguyen Huy Thiep (1988). In this story, though the husband and wife are modern in the sense that they are both well-educated, have jobs, love and respect each other, they also have a very traditional division of labour. The wife takes full responsibility for both childcare and earning money to supplement their limited salaries. The husband is free to study, relax and enjoy himself. In the male narrator's words,

> Thuy [i.e., his wife] knew a lot about running a household and raising children. As for me, I saw myself as rather conservative, unpredictable, and maladroit.
>
> (translated and quoted in Pelzer, 1993)

It is only thanks to the wife's enterprise that the family is well-off, but that is in conflict with the view of the husband's father, a retired general. Being puritanical, egalitarian, and embodying both the strengths and weaknesses of the socialist system, the general does not accept the way his daughter-in-law runs the household. (She takes in some people as servants and puts them to work on money-making activities that he considers immoral, as well as household chores; she abandons her distraught mother-in-law; and thinks of everything, including social obligations, in monetary terms). As a result, there is a growing tension between the general and his daughter-in-law. He feels absolutely lonely although he lives among his close relatives, and in the end he has to leave the family. The daughter-in-law also seeks to relieve the tension to some extent by asking the husband to cut down on smoking expensive cigarettes, but it seems from the story that there is no easy solution to her dilemma.

Pelzer concludes that, in this story by one of Vietnam's most popular and controversial writers, 'the pattern of the dependable, financially astute wife and unpredictable husband is an old Vietnamese and Southeast Asian stereotype' (Pelzer, 1993). To put it another way, market liberalisation does not change many of the gender relations within the family, but just increases the burden that women have been carrying in accordance with the traditional gender roles. So with regard to husband/wife interaction, the rigidly demarcated roles still exist.

Interaction in free time

What about the interaction of the husband and wife in their free time? The study of Houtart and Lemercinier (1984:115) already warned about the overburdening of women in rural areas before the renovation policy. The researchers pointed out the negative consequences of this state of affairs and the difficulties women faced in broadening their social horizons, and in caring for and educating their children. What concerns us here is 'the risk of effecting inequality between the sexes, particularly, in the cultural sphere, and at the political level, even if the political intentions are the very opposite of these effects' (ibid.).

Since 1987, according to a survey, a man has had about 5.5 hours of leisure time per day; whereas a woman has only had one hour (Vu Manh Loi, 1991). No wonder couples spend leisure time separately, even if some of them may prefer to spend it together. According to Mai Kim Chau, there are far fewer women than men going to film or theatre shows (usually in the open) (quoted in Khuat Thu Hong, 1991). In other words, husbands continue to enjoy themselves without their wives. In urban areas, newly-wed couples may continue to go out together some time after the wedding, but often stop when the first baby is born. No study about baby-sitting arrangements for the sake of parental entertainment has been carried out, but we may guess that they are inadequate or non-existent.

Do people who married more or less freely, and who are imbued with a sense of romantic love, feel strongly about companionship? Are they still being kept apart because of the gender separation? In rural areas, for instance Viet Hung commune, Vinh Phu province, whereas in the past the newly-wed husband and wife slept separately, the newly-wed couple in an extended family now normally shares a bed in one of the two side rooms (usually the storage room of the house that belongs to the husband's parents). As a researcher comments, this shift results from greater importance being assigned to the conjugal ties (Luong Van Hy, 1989: 751).

However, the same author also relates the story of a female artist. When paying a visit to her husband's parents, she and her husband were accustomed to being apart. During the meal, male and female members ate separately: her 4-year-old son shared the food with his father and grandfather in the main room while all the women (her mother-in-law, sisters-in-law and she herself) ate together in the kitchen (ibid.: 752). We do not know how common that is, but the story *Bai hoc nong thon* [A lesson from the countryside] by Nguyen Huy Thiep (1988) also gives a vivid description of a similar meal. It is difficult to assess what the local residents' reactions would have been had she gone out with her husband. Would they have reacted in a way similar to the Chinese people in such a situation?

In her book Lang (1946: 201) recounted how Chinese people strongly disapproved of a couple who were walking hand in hand. Finding the couple's conduct immoral, people poured a bucket of excrement over their heads. While the Vietnamese custom is certainly less extreme than in China, it is a fact that married couples in rural Vietnam traditionally did not go out together; this is mentioned by Phan Ke Binh (1915/1992: 66) at the very beginning of this century. This custom then seems to have persisted, as witnessed by the female artist's account.

Little is mentioned in the existing literature about the situation in cities, but one may say without fearing of overstatement that although a couple can enjoy going out together, kissing and embracing are still regarded by many people as inappropriate behaviour in public places, in the presence of children. Whereas an educated man in the study of Belanger and Khuat Thu Hong (1995) may expect a great deal from his wife, in terms of being his friend, his companion, and sharer of all his emotions, others may not think this way. The marital ties that are based on gender separation rather than companionship are still preferred by some.[4]

Interaction in family decision-making

Having examined how husbands and wives interact in work and leisure, we now move to a major issue in married life: decision-making in the family. It is difficult to compare the present family to the traditional one because of the lack of hard evidence about the past patterns. We are told, on the one hand, that women had little to say in the important decisions in upper-class families, but that they played a greater part in making decisions affecting the whole family among the lower classes on the other hand.

The women's liberation movement and the socialist ideology as well as the Laws on Marriage and the Family have sought to destroy the old pattern that favoured men, and to promote gender equality in all spheres. The study by Houtart and Lemercinier (1984) showed that in almost half of all rural marriages, the couple discusses and reaches a mutual agreement, but the percentage is lower in the case of young wives, and higher in the case of middle-aged ones. In 29 per cent of the cases the wives decide alone, but the percentage is far higher for older wives. Among the listed activities (food; clothing; purchase of a bicycle, radio and so on; savings; internal management of the house; and type of production in domestic economy), the matters in which the wives act on their own are the bread-and-butter issues of daily life: e.g. purchase of food and clothing. The husbands make decisions alone in only 14 per cent of the cases.

However, men still have a decisive say in one issue: the internal management of the house (how to arrange and protect the ancestors' altars and so on); this has traditionally been considered to be a male preserve (Houtart and Lemercinier, 1984: 116–122). From the data furnished by the study, when the wife is younger than 40 years of age, the men also take sole responsibility for decisions relating to the type of production in the domestic economy. That means that contrary to Dang Nguyen Anh's (1991: 167) affirmation that there is no differential by age in the roles and positions of women in family decision-making, the older a wife gets, the more say she has. However, her sphere of influence is mainly at the basic level, referring to bread-and-butter issues. Nor does she have much say in the domestic production, which has a long-term effect on family life, even though she may contribute more to it financially than her husband. Moreover, she cannot involve herself in the symbolically charged activities related to ancestor worship, which are an exclusively male domain.

Another study also provided us with some information about household decision making in a village of Ha Bac province in 1983. Chu Khac reports that the joint conjugal decision making is evident in 34.2 per cent in household chore allocation, 42.4 per cent in work allocation, 47.6 per cent in major budget items, 42.3 per cent

Table 3: Household decision-making in Ha Bac province, 1983

	Per cent of cases where sole decision made by	
Area of family life	Husband	Wife
Household chores	16.7	39.0
Work allocation	20.8	28.2
Major budgetry items	17.8	20.8
Child's marriage	7.8	9.6
Child's education	18.6	12.2

Source: Chu Khac, 1986

in child's marriage, and 41.2 per cent in child's education. For decisions taken solely by one partner only, see Table 3 above.

The author comes to the conclusion that rural women are aware of being equal with men, in fact they have long been on equal footing with men (Chu Khac, 1986). Nevertheless, his data and analysis as well as conclusion should be interpreted with some care for both methodological and conceptual reasons. The readers are not told anything about the percentages of male and female respondents in the sample; no distinction has been made between different types of households: whether the husband is present or absent at home, what occupation and age group a couple belongs to and so on. In conceptual terms, if the fact that the wife has more to say in such matters as household chore allocation, work allocation, and major budget items is perceived as equality, it also means that she has to do more, her responsibilities and burdens increase. In other words, what is understood by the author as equality in fact means inequality.

As for her children's marriages, if she has a little more to say than her husband, it does not indicate any departure from the traditional gender role, as we have seen in Chapter One. Similarly, it is still the husband, not the wife, who has more to say in the issue of a child's education: the traditional gender demarcation persists. Last, but not least, there has been no word about whether the wife has more influence over the marriage of her sons or daughters; neither have we been told whether the husband is interested in the education of his sons or daughters.

The other data about decision-making in Dong Duong commune, Thai Binh province (1983) are provided by Vu Manh Loi. Fifty-one per cent of a sample of 256 people affirmed that it is the husband who decides the family division of labour; 11 per cent thought it was the wife; and 27 per cent said it was both of them. The same source says that in Hai Van commune in 1990, it was the husband who had the greater say in decisions concerning a child's marriage and occupation. As for the use of family income, on this issue both the men and women agree that they both have nearly equal say. Nonetheless, in-depth interviews show that the wife acts on her own when deciding the everyday expenses; when deciding on larger purchases the husband takes responsibility in consultation with the wife (Vu Manh Loi, 1991).

No data are available about the educated modern wife in urban areas. Empirical observation suggests that she is demanding and gaining more authority in the home. Educated, more competent, and independent, she tends to marry someone from the same social group, who accepts the concepts of gender equality and has more confidence in his wife's capabilities. Therefore she is more likely to run the home, or at least be consulted, and considered by the husband. Nevertheless we need to keep in mind that in a society where sharply distinguished gender roles prevail, strong and aggressive women are often viewed as highly undesirable. 'Those women do not want husbands, they want to be husbands' – that is the way they are seen and evaluated. As O'Harrow (1995) has noted, such women are often described disapprovingly as *du* [fierce] and called *su tu Ha Dong* [Ha Dong lioness].[5] Men who do whatever their wives tell them to do are 'the subject of hundreds of Vietnamese jokes' (ibid.) and humorous anecdotes in which the disapproval is quite strong.

In brief, if the suppositions about the decision-making process in the traditional family hold water, it is obvious that the present status of women has improved significantly. Moreover, unlike the suppositions about the traditional family that differentiated only between different social groups, the data about the present family suggest strongly that one should talk separately about each gender's sphere of influence, since this is the wellspring of female power. For example, in the family it is the woman who takes the responsibility of financial management (in Hai Van commune for instance in 1979, that was the case for 87 per cent of families [Houtart and Lemercinier, 1984: 108]). As the authors pointed out correctly, 'this endows [the woman] with a very real power since she controls the consumption habits of the members of the family' (ibid.: 108). In the words of Nguyen Tu Chi (1991: 66), the woman does not keep the money for herself; it is spent 'for the whole family, for her husband, her children and sometimes for maintaining the fame of the family (in preparing a feast to entertain her husband's friends)', but the woman has the right to comment about this.

Women have often exerted power in the family by claiming that they have a secret stash of money that their husbands do not know about. O'Harrow (1995: 165) discovered that Vietnamese daughters are taught by their mothers, if not explicitly, then by example, that they should always have some money of their own, that they cannot depend on men. On the other hand, it is commonly the wife who handles the family finances, collects her husband's wages, and puts him on a sort of allowance. Often a 'special struggle' develops between the couple. The husband tries to hide to some extent the true amount of his earnings; otherwise, he would not have enough money for cigarettes, tea, and going out with his friends. Similarly, the wife deceives or secretly invests the earnings from her embroidery and selling cakes, 'so her husband will not think her rich and take advantage of her to spend his money on *les petites amies*' (O'Harrow, 1995). Thanks to this economic survival strategy, the woman retains her power and often takes the upper hand.

However, it would be misleading if one were to rely heavily on quantitative data about decision-making, because they do not cover one of the acute problems of the present family: the decision on the number of children. If a family wants to break up the two-child limit, who makes the decision about that? The qualitative study by Gammeltoft (1997a: 201) argues that because a woman's sphere of influence is often narrowed down by the husband and in-laws, when it comes to the issues that are closest to the body (sexuality and fertility) some women insist on their right to decide for themselves. In their reasoning, it is the women who get pregnant and give birth; therefore they should have authority in this sphere. Nevertheless, the study also presents evidence about women who have to follow what their husbands and in-laws decide (Gammeltoft, 1997a: 121). No quantitative data are available to confirm or reject the above observation.

Available quantitative data are also absent on other broad questions: for instance, how a couple would reach agreement (in a joint decision area) if one holds an opposing view. Whose say has more weight? If there is an argument, is a woman's opinion heard? The qualitative evidence reveals that in cases of disagreement, it is the husbands who decide, regardless of the strength of their wives' opposition (Gammeltoft, 1997a: 182).

Decision-making requires, among other things, a certain degree of intellectual capacity. In the traditional family, the opinion of women was often looked down simply because they were women. It was taken for granted that women did not know much outside their world – the kitchen. Proverbs and folk-songs have repeated for centuries: *Dan ong nong noi gieng khoi, dan ba sau sac nhu coi dung trau* [However superficial a man is, his intelligence is like a deep well; however profound a woman is, her intelligence is shallow like a betel-tray]. Here women's intelligence and wisdom are supposed always to be inferior to men's. Moreover, in the following proverb: *Khon ngoan cung the dan ba, dau rang vung dai van la dan ong* [However wise a woman is, she is still a woman; however foolish a man is, he is a man], the gender hierarchy is even more blatant: not only are women's intelligence, cleverness, capability, and wisdom berated, but women in general are always considered to be inferior to men. It is believed that they never can become equal to men. The available data do not confirm or reject the persistence of this blatant sexism, which was used to justify men's ascendancy over women, and to keep women in their place. On the other hand, as Goode (1982) points out, like other dominant groups, men often 'view small losses of deference, or advantages, or opportunities as large threats'; they do not readily allow their wives to share power.

Violence and wife-battering are said to have been the ways some men demonstrate their power if their dominance is challenged. To what extent this is true is uncertain. Family violence is often viewed as a social stigma, damaging the reputation of not only the involved couples, but also their close relatives; therefore the relatives usually try to intervene when it occurs. Owing to this social climate, violence is usually eschewed. On the other hand, it is also regarded as the family's internal affair, and not the business of outside people. Many female victims only reluctantly report about it, as they are afraid of damaging the whole family's reputation. A speech made by Xuan Thuy, a high-level official in the Communist Party in 1980 reveals that it is not rare for husbands to mistreat their wives, but that these husbands do not recognise their behaviour as unlawful. As he put it, although socialism has reserved for women their rightful positions as workers and citizens equal to men, a great many women do not dare to struggle against injustice and oppression because they are trapped in backward ideologies, and are subject to feelings of inferiority, passivity, and timidity.

> Although the feudalists have been overthrown ... these deep-rooted ideologies and practices have not been totally eradicated. These backward ideas have acted as a brake on the progress of women.
>
> (Quoted in Eisen, 1984: 19–20, 12)

Obviously, in the eyes of the ruling party, which believes itself to be the firm upholder of emancipation for women, the blame for domestic violence is laid squarely at the door of the class enemy (feudalists), not men and patriarchy.

On the other hand, it is also said that whether a woman is dominated by her husband or dominates him greatly depends on her socio-economic conditions, the social group she belongs to, on her husband (if he is not very competent, of course the wife is in superior position), and on the woman herself. In the traditional family, though women were totally absent in organisations outside the family,

> many men in these organisations, even at high levels, were under the influence of their wives when they expressed their opinions. Often they were assisted with advice by their wives before speaking publicly.
>
> (Nguyen Tu Chi, 1991: 67)

Le Thi Que even affirms this at a higher level. If you could not get through the front gate (i.e., the husband), go to the back gate (i.e., the wife or mistress). With the right woman's support you can get everything, from a passport to a position in the state ministry (quoted in Jamieson, 1993: 316). How women could exert such an influence on their husbands is still mysterious and the question now requires some empirical investigations. As for the present family, with the heralding in of the modern marriage (in which both partners are educated, experienced, and love each other), one might expect the wife to have a powerful place in the home, for her to be treated considerately by the husband, and for all the family decisions to be decided jointly by husband and wife. However, this is not made clear by the quantitative data.

Sexuality

What about the marital relationships in terms of sexuality? Again research has tended to neglect this issue; we know of no research on what happens in the bedrooms of marital couples. Outside the home we know there have been a lot of changes. It could be said that the renovation policy marks a watershed: before that, as Pelzer (1993) has pointed out, the socialist image of woman was that of a worker, fighter, and mother. The image of woman as sex object was roundly condemned. The disapproval reached the extent that it rejected not only the Western image of woman as sex object (beauty contests in socialist Vietnam were formerly considered to be bourgeois decadent Western institutions, and were banned), but also the native traditional village festivals which are reported to be rooted in pre-Chinese traditions and contain sexual licence. Pelzer also quotes a Vietnamese ethnographer who explained that the native traditional village festivals had been banned for many years 'because they were fertility rites', implying official disapproval of the sexual licence of those festivals. Here, the socialist ideology in fact does not deny the Confucian traditions, which viewed sexuality as unworthy, but continues them. What it rejects is the cultural survival of ancient times (Pelzer, 1993).

The absence of any cult of sex is, in Eisen's view, attributed to the fact that on the one hand, there is little public concern for sexuality, sexual relations, or sexiness (Eisen,1984: 196). When Westerners raise the issue of sexual freedom, Vietnamese women invariably respond by recalling their sexual victimisation at the hands of landlords or foreign soldiers and polygamists. For this reason monogamy is considered a cornerstone of women's liberation in Vietnam, not a source of repression (ibid.). In other words, monogamy seems to be understood as an end in itself; it does not include any problem in terms of sexuality. We shall see later whether or not this simplified conception corresponds with the reality even only in sexual terms.

On the other hand, the lack of concern with sexuality results from the fact that the socialist morality rewards people not for immediate personal gratification, but for devotion to work for the benefit of the whole society. No wonder the issues of sexuality and sexual relations appear to be obscured (ibid.). As a result, all the media concentrated on mobilising people to meet the demands of national defence and construction. Even *Tam su* [A heart-to-heart talk], the most popular feature of the Women's Union weekly magazine to which readers turned and asked for advice about love, marriage, the family and so on, just encouraged people to follow the socialist moral principles (ibid.: 197) as if there were no such thing as sexuality, and couples were asexual.

There were also in practice many obstacles to harmonious sexual relations between husband and wife. For one thing, as in the past, peasant families were living in one-room huts, and could not mystify sexual relations (ibid.: 196). In this context, the data provided by Houtart and Lemercinier (1984) are significant. According to this source, when questioned about the present form of the rural habitation (one- or two-room houses), 66.7 per cent of the non-Catholics in Hai Van commune, Ha Nam Ninh province, in 1979 were in favour of maintaining the present layout of the home

(Houtart and Lemercinier, 1984: 134). Only those under 35, who had pursued their studies up to secondary school level and were members of youth organisations, were more open to change. The proposal to transform the present home by increasing (extending) the number of rooms was rejected by 48.1 per cent (ibid.: 137). By looking at the reasons for rejection, one discovers that 58.5 per cent were satisfied with the present arrangement, 35.8 per cent said they respected the traditions, and only 13.2 per cent gave lack of financial means as a ground. Even people who were in favour of the extension, had only hospitality in mind: the separation of the house into rooms would permit them to offer more hospitality to their passing guests. Nothing was mentioned about the space for marital couples. The others reject this type of construction because they want to have at their disposal a large room in which all the members of the family can gather together on the occasion of a feast or reunion (ibid.: 137–138). That means that for the majority of marital couples, there is no room for intimacy.

For another thing, the double standard continued to exist. Many people still insisted on the traditional requirement that women be a virgin on the wedding night.[6] Of course that put a lot of pressure on young girls who faced different, even opposite expectations: their lovers insisted on premarital sex, while the future grooms demanded their virginity at the time of marriage. The double standard was applicable not only until the wedding night, but also for the whole of family life. Married men might be forgiven if they had an affair, but wives never enjoyed the same *laissez-faire* attitude (Eisen, 1984: 196). The double standard also meant that women's sexuality was supposed to serve men; men continued to take the initiative in sexuality for their own pleasure only. Of course the mere fact that the double standard continued to exist did not preclude the possibility that some women were no longer tolerant of the view, but we do not know about them.

A lot of things have changed since 1987. Newspapers are full of pictures of women wearing swimsuits. Manuals and handbooks on sex are published in huge numbers. In spite of debate and criticism initially, female beauty contests have been promoted everywhere. It is noteworthy that the beauty contests are organised to uphold the old value of chastity: for instance all the contestants have to be examined by medical doctors to make sure that they are virgins (Pelzer, 1993). Sponsoring foreign companies have been trying to promote their products, create a new market, and therefore help to form a new image of Vietnam's women.

The Husband–Wife Relationship

All this change is happening outside the home. Unfortunately, no study has ever been conducted to identify how those changes affect husband–wife relationships. To fill in the gap, we must turn to literary works. In the award-winning novel *Manh dat lam nguoi, nhieu ma* [The piece of land with many people and a lot of ghosts], Nguyen Khac Truong (1991) reveals some secrets about sexuality in a peasant family.

 The couple, Mr Ham and Mrs Son, have by tacit agreement not slept together for long time, since the children grew up: the husband sleeps alone, the wife – with a teenage daughter. Every time she feels a hand touching and shaking her leg during her sleep, she wakes up and understands who the dim shadow behind her bed is, and what that person wants from her. She gets up quietly, tries not to wake up her daughter, then goes to the husband's bed. No sooner has she lain down than he penetrates without any tender word. She silently fulfils her duty to the husband. One night when she is sleeping, he wakes her up to discuss some family issues. Being authoritarian, he scolds and insults her severely. After quarrelling, she goes back to her bed. Again during her sleep, he comes in, touches her leg, and shakes it. Still angry and sad, she is in no mood to have sex, but for the sake of duty, she reluctantly goes to his bed and satisfies his desire. Again there is no word uttered between them, as if they were both dumb: no kissing, caressing or physical affection usually associated with sex. While he is taking his pleasure, she is in tears.

(Nguyen Khac Truong, 1991: 262–266)

The description shows nothing other than a marital rape viewed in the eyes of some Westerners. A sceptical reader may doubt the story's validity and whether it is representative of society at large, but one thing is certain: Vietnamese people take it for granted that it is a wife's duty to satisfy her husband's sexual need whenever he wants, no matter whether she is willing or not. They consider it absolutely normal for a husband to make such demands. This act may be defined as 'normal' male behaviour that women simply have to endure, and a wife has to supply her husband with sexual services. If she does not do that, it is she who will be blamed. The concept of marital rape, or of monogamy as a source of repression in terms of sexuality, is unthinkable for the Vietnamese.

Indeed, when asked about husbands forcing their wives to submit to sexual advances against their will, one Vietnamese scholar gave a terse but clear response, 'Everywhere'.

(Goodstein, 1996)

An overwhelming majority of Vietnamese women are not aware of women's rights in general, let alone their own right to say 'no' when their husbands insist on sex if they are not willing to have it. For many of them sex is very often carried out dutifully. That is why those women perceive of sexuality as simply another burden in their daily life, especially if one keeps in mind that most rural women are often overburdened with rice production and household chores from early morning until late at night. Having sex is termed *lam viec* [to work] by many of them; they cannot bear having a lot of sex (Gammeltoft, 1997a: 34, 180).

Understandably, such a sexuality serves mainly, if not solely, men's gratification. This is shown in one woman's experience:

> If one does not want to but has to please one's husband, one gets angry, but he insists, he forces one, and afterwards one only feels anger, one does not feel any pleasure at all.
>
> (ibid.: 180)

In other words, sexuality does not become constituted as 'a prime means, as well as an expression, of intimacy' (Giddens, 1991: 164) as happened in modern Western societies. In many cases, in spite of becoming separated from procreation due to limited birth, sexuality still remains a means of repression. Again we do not exclude the possibility that educated and independent-minded women in big cities may expect not only to provide, but also receive sexual pleasure within marriage. With the changes in the family, romantic love has become a basis of marital ties, and for those women, sexuality may be connected with love and pleasure. However, no evidence about them is available at the moment.

Divorce

While great importance is still attached to marriage – this can be seen in the high marriage numbers (Banister, 1993: 19–21) – divorce is consistently viewed as highly undesirable. The ideal of a lasting marriage 'till death do us part' is still the dream for many people. This also finds expression in the popular argument which people use to justify the expense of the wedding ceremony: it is a once-in-a-lifetime experience. However, when marital conflicts erupt, and cannot be resolved, divorce is an option which many couples pursue.

Like marriage, divorce has changed, and one of the marked changes of divorce is that it has become widespread, and women are increasingly taking the initiative in seeking divorce. However, the study of divorce has been almost non-existent, or as Khuat Thu Hong (1991) puts it, it is 'in very beginning'. Data are quite hard to come by, and where statistics have been collected by a few government offices, the method has been somewhat haphazard and unscientific. Neither the number of divorces per 1,000 citizens, nor the number of divorces per 1,000 married couples, nor the number of divorces per 100 marriages have been systematically gathered. Instead, we are only provided with court figures about the total number of divorces in different years (not systematically) for the whole large region (North Vietnam until 1975, or the country as a whole since then, not the area under our study), and we have no way to ascertain how accurate they are. In general, we are told by a source (Khuat Thu Hong, 1991) that one can divide the time frame (1945 up to 1991) into three main periods:

1. 1945–65 (until the start of the American war) when divorce was high;
2. 1965–75, when the number of divorces decreased because of enlistment of men into the army and their absence from home;
3. 1975–91, when the number of divorces rose again, but substantially higher than before.

The first period is regarded as representing the breakdown of the so-called 'feudalistic marriage and family system' (Khuat Thu Hong, 1991). Probably the author means arranged and child marriages, or marriages based on economic considerations. In 1964, there were 16,000 cases of divorce in the North, and most of the applicants were women. For the third period, some data are available: in the whole country from early 1977 to 1982, there were 28,359 cases of divorce; in 1979, one out of fourteen marriages ended in divorce; in 1980 the rate was one in nine; and in 1981, it was one in eleven (ibid.). Another source gives us the following data: in 1978 there were 17,834 divorces; in 1991: 22,634; and in 1992: 29,225 (Le Thi Quy, 1996). At the commune level, out of more than 6,000 people in 1979 there were only seven divorces (Eisen, 1984: 193). Though the author Khuat Thu Hong does not characterise this period, divorce at this moment seems to be taking a different form. The grounds for divorce appear to be moving away from the way a family (in the kinship sense) is established to the marital relationship itself.

There is no doubt that divorce is increasing, especially in urban areas, though the rate is insignificant compared to that in many Western societies. One can associate the recent increase with factors such as the relative liberalisation of divorce laws and public opinion, and the improved status of women: their education, increasing economic independence (this all has been dealt with in Chapter Two), and the mounting expectations of an emotional bond between husband and wife.

It is difficult to make full sense of those changes if we stop at the quantitative data. Let us take a look at a divorce trial in Hanoi.

> The wife, named Nguyet, wanted a divorce because the husband, Hung, had been harassing her for a long time. The divorce had been granted by a lower court, but Hung was appealing against it. In the higher court, there were three judges, two of whom were women: the defence attorney for the wife was a woman, as was the investigator responsible to the judges for researching the case (that was almost unthinkable before 1945). The husband and wife spoke for themselves: they each gave their own version of the story, and responded to the other's testimony.
>
> (Eisen, 1984: 185)

In this case, it is not only the strength of the Women's Union but also the advantages women gain from living within a legal system committed to women's liberation that strike the American observer. The case happened in 1974, but certain aspects reflect pre-1945 behaviour on the part of the husband: like his male forerunners, he still beats his wife, accuses her of adultery, etc. On the other hand, the woman goes to school, affirms her right to have friends, and in reply to his repudiations, she accuses him; moreover, she initiates the divorce – all things that are unprecedented. That there are no mutual feelings left is considered to be the basic ground for divorce – this is also completely new.

There is another shift: the judges rule in favour of the wife (Eisen, 1984: 186). The wife gets the custody of the children and full legal responsibility for them. Compared to the pre-1945 divorce practice, in which women often had to leave the children in the husband's house, the right to take care of the children after divorce is a milestone achievement (of course it could also prove to be a burden if the woman is impoverished). In the words of the American observer, this divorce trial is really 'a dramatic struggle between "feudal hangovers" and women's rights' (ibid.: 185). When the scientific evidence is non-existent, perhaps nowhere have the improved status of women and their significantly rising expectations of marital partners been demonstrated more convincingly than in literary works of recent years. The different groups' diversified expectations have made themselves felt in the novel *Ben kia bo ao vong* [Beyond Illusions] by Duong Thu Huong (1987), a female writer.

> A boatwoman in this novel has to come to terms with a coarse and rude man. Nguyen, the hero from a big city, feels sorry for her (perhaps all she wants are some tender words, and a handkerchief as a gift from her husband). By contrast, Phuong Linh, the heroine, a modern woman in urban area, has made growing demands on her husband to the extent that Nguyen, the ideal husband seen from many points of view, has to say:
>
>> What do you want from me? ... You have a faithful, and dutiful husband who knows how to improve himself and how to behave correctly to other people. What more do you want?

Nevertheless, for some women, even a coarse and rude man may still be the man of their dreams. Mrs Tuyet in the novel *Thoi xa vang* [Echoes of Time Past] by Le Luu (1986) continually longs for a husband, even if he is rude to her, because at least she would have a husband; that is far better than being a spinster.

Ly, a heroine in the novel *Mua la rung trong vuon* [Leafshedding season in the garden] by Ma Van Khang (1985), demands that her husband give her something extraordinary so that she can be proud of him. Chau, an educated urban girl in the above novel by Le Luu, expects her husband to understand perfectly, through her non-verbal behaviour, what she wants, so that there is no need for her to say it. To satisfy her, he must guess what she wants! These novels could not have appeared even a few decades ago. These heroines with their inflated expectations would be inconceivable during the first half of this century. Generally speaking, in all those literary works, the wives who have high expectations of their husbands are living in urban areas, while rural women still have more modest hopes, but this is without doubt a remarkable change.

Interestingly enough, in the traditional family, if a man was viewed as virtuous in the eyes of many people, particularly the significant eyes of a woman, he definitely would be the man of her dreams. In the present family, such a man may win the sympathy of a lot of people, but that is no guarantee that he can conquer the heart of the woman he desires. This means the the image of ideal husband or wife is no longer generally agreed upon, as it was in the past; it now means different things to different people. In fact, even for one person, the image of the ideal husband or wife may vary according to the passage of time. Before, when a man was hard-working, filially pious to his parents, and good to his children, he was the perfect man; no one else could have been better. That is not enough now: he must necessarily be a good husband and compatible to his wife in many respects. This serves to explain the many divorce cases in which women are not satisfied with men, even though the latter seem to be perfect husbands in the eyes of overwhelming majority of people (Ngan Tam and Tran Thi Lien, 1985).

However, it would be an oversimplification to think that it is only women who have considerably higher expectations from marriage. Men too have growing demands on their marital partners. One of the crucial reasons is that in the traditional family, if a man was not satisfied with his wife, he could take as many wives as he could afford. That is no longer possible, at least not as a legal option. Therefore men demand and expect more from their wives. As the gender role has not changed accordingly, women are placed in a difficult situation *vis-à-vis* conflicting expectations. The remarkable increase in adulterous affairs in general, and those of men in particular, should be viewed in this context.

With the government's recent renovation policy, and the relaxation of control over people's personal life by the government, *nouveau riche* men think that having an affair is the way to satisfy their demands on women, and to show off their wealth. While pursuing an affair, some of them still want to keep their family. To them, family life is one thing, an extramarital affair is another; the latter is like a necessary change in the daily diet. As they put it in Vietnamese, the family life (the wife) is considered *com* [rice] whereas the affair is compared to *pho* (elaborate food made of rice, but well-processed, therefore more delicious); they are both necessary for a man and complement one another. Of course a lot of women today no longer accept this view; this probably accounts for the growing number of divorces.

Some men turn to prostitutes for sexual satisfaction. Asked about his respective opinion of wife, lover and prostitute, a man said that the three kinds of people are completely different from one another. There is a husband-and-wife relationship between him and his wife; love with his lovers (in the sense that there is responsibility for his wife and with his lovers); but fun with prostitutes. In his words, 'with the latter, we pay for fun, for all the love-making games that we prefer'. Another man said:

> I think it's quite different to sleep with my wife and prostitutes. With prostitutes, it's like eating the cake we have paid for. So we can do whatever we like, provided that we are satisfied. But with the wife, we must give happiness.
>
> (Barry, 1996)

This seems to reveal that in the Vietnamese marriages today the sense of responsibility is strong, probably even embodying the kind of sexuality in which men force themselves on their wives. In those marriages, men are not satisfied either; they turn to extramarital affairs and even prostitutes to compensate for the perceived deficiencies in their marital life (the sense of being carefree, sexually playful and fun-loving).

Meanwhile, the agents that once actively opposed divorce (government officials at workplaces, representatives of trade unions, members of the neighbourhood reconciliation teams; the Women's Union and so on) now more or less regard it as an acceptable alternative to an unhappy marriage. If both sides agree on a divorce, it no longer takes years to get approval. So if the traditional family was kept intact because of the low expectations from within as well as societal pressure, many families today rely principally on a continuing attraction between the spouses for their existence.

Previously the family was stable, but the marital life was poor. Now the quality of the marital ties has been improved gradually, and the internal expectations have been raised significantly, while the external social pressures to keep people from separating have diminished. Consequently the family unit has become fragile. However, it is still mainly women who encounter difficulties after divorce, not least in facing public opinion. Though more and more women initiate divorce, a divorced woman is still seen in the eyes of many people as immoral, even though a divorced man is acceptable (Gammeltoft, 1997a: 195). This means that the double standard here also works in favour of men. Divorced women even have to face difficulties in remarriage.

One of the reasons (or grounds) for divorce is 'conflicts concerning either the wife or the husband with the family on both sides, especially conflicts between the wife and her mother-in-law', as Khuat Thu Hong (1991) puts it. Another reason, no less important, is if a couple has no children. In addition, when doing everything possible to effect a reconciliation, divorce courts often justify their actions by mentioning the children's happiness (Eisen, 1984: 184). This requires us to contextualise the marital ties again in relation to intergenerational links within the family. Hopefully this may throw light on the changed and unchanged features of the marital ties.

First we shall look at the marital ties in relation to the previous generations, i.e., parents-in-law. Because of the prevailing pattern of the patrilocal family and its variations, we concentrate mainly on this type of in-law relations. Then we shall examine the connections between marital bonds and the next generations, i.e., marital ties in relation to the parent–child bonds.

MARITAL TIES IN RELATION TO HUSBAND'S PARENTS

Wedding for whom: young couples or their parents?

Until 1986, when the ceremony reform campaign was well under way, weddings were still expensive, but have become more so since 1987, when the intensification of rituals took hold (Luong Van Hy, 1993). The source does not specify who in the family carries the main financial burden of the wedding ceremony, but it is doubtless that very few young people, particularly in rural areas, can afford the expense. Most of them have only a small income, probably insufficient to cover the expenses; instead, they have to rely on their parents.

That is one of the reasons why parents still have a decisive say in their children's marriage. So parents play here a double role: as significant others, and as crucial payers of the wedding expenses. If they disapprove of a child's marriage, they will refuse one or both roles. The child is unlikely to manage without parents playing this double role; his (her) marriage may be lawful, but a failure in the eyes of public opinion. Before the renovation policy, some young people married in spite of their parents' opposition; they relied on the Youth Organisation, Trade Union or workplace to arrange simplified weddings which the government encouraged, but such marriages without parents in the double role were an exception.

As the above research reveals, if parents themselves cannot afford the wedding, they seek financial assistance from different sources; and it is not the young people's social network, but mainly relatives that lend a hand (Luong Van Hy, 1993). In such cases, the young people's opinions are insignificant compared to that of their parents. Everything is said to be done for the sake of the children, but it also, if not crucially, serves the parents' interests.

From an economic point of view, the expenses are a horrendous waste of money, but that is the price not just of the wedding itself, but also the involved families' status and prestige. As we have seen, rural families are often eager to demonstrate rank and status; a wedding has traditionally been a way of doing so. The larger the number of invited guests the bigger the show, the more status the involved families are ascribed. In rural areas, young people's social network is not as large as that of middle-aged and old people, and not yet fully established. Therefore the number of their guests is far less than their parents' guests. According to Vuong Xuan Tinh (1990), among several tens of *trays* (hundreds of guests) in a wedding banquet, there are only five *trays* (about thirty) of the groom's friends. Furthermore, those young people are served last (the first to be served are close relatives of senior generations, local officials, etc.). In the villagers' eyes, the young are the least important. So the wedding ceremony is mainly an occasion for the parents' social network, not that of young people.

In many localities, a vast amount of money is spent on the wedding banquet, while very little is given to the bride and groom directly. At his wedding, the groom sometimes even wears the same old, torn dress that he would on a normal day.[7] Hosts and guests attending the wedding pay attention to certain aspects only: how the hosts welcome the guests; where they are made to sit; with whom they are supposed to share the food. A conflict arises because of a hierarchy violation: a villager is put on the wrong mat. Nobody pays attention to the groom (Vuong Xuan Tinh, 1990). That is to say, the social hierarchy ritualised through the codified seating order and food arrangements is the crucial concern of most guests. Due to their position in the social hierarchy based on age, generation and sex, instead of being the central figures of the wedding, the young couple is of secondary significance! In this sense, the wedding is first of all an occasion of reciprocity for parents, and only last a rite of passage for the young couple. However, it should be said that in other places, particularly urban areas, one can also see brides and grooms beautifully dressed for their special day.

In-law relations

Until the present time the pattern of the patrilocal family and its variant has still prevailed. Consequently, the relationship of the wife to the in-laws is still quite important. How has it changed?

On the one hand, mother-in-law/daughter-in-law relations have improved significantly. Asked about this, an old woman in Thai Binh province in 1992 affirmed that mothers-in-law and daughters-in-law no longer quarrel as they did in the past; they often coexist peacefully with each other. If a daughter-in-law does something wrong, her mother-in-law would tell her with soft-spoken words. Many other female interviewees say that in the traditional family, if a daughter-in-law sat on a higher seat than her mother-in-law, she would be scolded immediately (because she violated the spatial hierarchy), but that no longer applies. In the past, intimacy existed only between mothers and daughters (due to the importance attached to blood relations). Now things have so changed that in many cases, as an interviewed mother-in-law in Dong Minh commune, Thai Binh province in 1992 said, hardly has a visitor been able to distinguish who is the daughter and who is the daughter-in-law in relation to the mother (Mai Huy Bich, 1993: 90). In the past, if a daughter-in-law did not suffer from her mother's-in-law ill-treatment she was said to have been lucky; at present young women seem to suffer far less than their forerunners. This change is acknowledged by mothers-in-law themselves, though some of them do so with anger because in their eyes the old hierarchy has been turned upside down (Gammeltoft, 1997a: 190).

On the other hand, there are still mothers-in-law who are too tolerant to their daughters, but too intolerant to their daughters-in-law (ibid.: 184). There is a good deal of evidence that some mothers-in-law and daughters-in-law are not on good terms with each other, and that can undermine the stability of a marriage. For instance, the above-mentioned mother-in-law, 55 years old, treats her daughters and daughters-in-law on equal terms because she herself had been mistreated by her mother-in-law; she wants to prevent conflict in this tie. She tells her own story.

 After marriage at the age of 19, she lived under the same roof with her parents-in-law. Eight months later the young couple built a house of their own on a separate plot of land. The mother-in-law disliked and scolded her often. Moreover she took full control of the young couple's income from fishing by demanding that the son bring all the fish to his mother, not to his wife. The mother-in-law even encouraged her son to abandon his wife, and finally forced him and his three children to leave their house and live with his parents, without the wife. Though the husband felt a strong attachment to his wife, he was scared of his mother and did whatever she told him. However, every now and then he secretly went back to his house to meet his wife. It was only thanks to a close relative's intervention that the young couple was given permission to be reunited.

(Mai Huy Bich, 1993: 89)

The episode in this story took place about three decades ago and there are still similar cases at present. In one particular family, the conflict resulted in a murder: the daughter-in-law made several attempts to kill her mother-in-law, and succeeded in the seventh one (Mai Huy Bich, 1993). Divorce is a more usual ending to the conflict. Let us examine a typical scenario. A daughter-in-law often speaks disrespectfully to her mother-in-law and so the latter encourages her son to divorce. As a result, a divorce is granted, and the husband gets custody of a little child. Later he remarries, but the new wife so ill-treats the child that the mother-in-law feels quite sorry for it. The old woman regrets her intervention leading to the previous marriage's break-up and the unhappiness of the grandchild, but it is too late now (Mai Huy Bich, 1993). Scholarly evidence confirms that in Hanoi in 1978, 30 per cent of marital tension resulted from in-law conflicts. (Le Phuong, 1986)

In many cases, when the conflict is irreconcilable, the husbands are on the horns of a dilemma: '*Ben tinh ben hieu ben nao nang hon?*' [Between the love for my mate and the filial piety to my parents, which one outweighs the other?] – to borrow a verse from *The Tale of Kieu*. If a son takes his wife's side, he would be accused of filial impiety by his parents; if on the other hand he takes his parents' side, he alienates and risks losing his wife. Such cases, in which divorce is sought or granted as a solution to the in-law conflict, even though the marital ties between the spouses are not bad, reveal that less emphasis is placed on marital ties than on intergenerational ones.

MARITAL BONDS IN RELATION TO CHILDREN (THE NEXT GENERATION)

With the widespread knowledge of contraceptive practices, and particularly with the imposed birth limit policy, for the first time in this century couples are able to delay or avoid parenthood, to concentrate on and enjoy the marital union, and to make their bonds really conjugal in the full sense of the word. These changes are profound not only in Vietnam, but on a world-wide scale, and they have far-reaching effects on family relationships. In some Western countries (for example in the USA), this has prompted some people to opt for the so-called voluntary childlessness (Sharon, 1986). What about the couples in our area of study?

In this regard, the parent–child ties still remain paramount, and the marital ones themselves cannot be on equal terms. This finds expression first in the fact that young couples seem to rush to have their first child almost straight after the wedding, as we shall see in the next chapter. In theory, the period between the wedding and the first birth should be one of the high points of a marriage, particularly for young people who love each other but have not had much chance (if any) for premarital sex or intimacy. We need to bear in mind that virginity is still traditionally required from a girl right up until her wedding night. In those circumstances, if the primary emphasis were placed on marital ties, one might expect those couples who had abstained from sexual intimacy previously, to take advantage of contraception to delay parenthood, at least temporarily, and to enjoy being together. Even those young people who may have enjoyed limited sexual relations before marriage would have gained far greater sexual freedom afterwards. Surely they too would prefer to delay parenthood to make the most of their newly-found freedom as a couple?

However, in practice, as we have seen, that is not the case. The period devoted exclusively to the marital bonds is quite short, and the period for childbearing and childraising comes very soon. In this sense, scarcely have the young people been released from the consanguine ties of their parents (they may in fact still be co-habiting with them) that they enter a new consanguine relationship by having children. It would be misleading, then, to describe the family as transforming from a consanguine one into a conjugal one.

The fact that the intergenerational link takes priority over the marital one can also be seen in the sleeping arrangements. We have already examined these arrangements in the traditional family, and how they derived not only from limited space within the home, but also from the emphasis on the intergenerational link. While no scientific evidence about the present situation is available, we can take a look at some press accounts.

Whether a baby should sleep together with its mother or separately is a topic of heated argument in an extended Vietnamese family living in the USA. Following the traditional sleeping arrangements, half of the members of the family insist that the baby should sleep together with its mother not only because of a lack of space, but also for the baby's sake and more importantly, to promote a closer mother–child relationship. They suppose that if the lack of space restricts the sleeping arrangements, it is the baby who should be given priority and put in the same bed as its mother, and it is the father who should be excluded from the bed. The other half of the family members insist that the baby should sleep separately from its mother, and that the husband should sleep with the wife. Unable to reach an agreement, the family consult the editor of a bimonthly magazine. According to the editor's unconfirmed estimate, 95 per cent of Vietnamese families have the baby sleeping with its mother (in many cases that means with both mother and father); this arrangement may continue until the child is 9–10 years old (Thuan Thao, 1994). It seems that in Vietnam the traditional sleeping arrangements still do not favour marital bonds.

Furthermore, having no children is still one of the grounds for divorce, as mentioned by Eisen (1984: 187), although we do not have data to substantiate this. Meanwhile, the novel *Ben khong chong* [The river watering place of unmarried women] by Duong Huong (1991) tells a moving love story in which we can see the significance of the marital bonds in comparison to the parent–child ones. In spite of the transgenerational hostile relations recorded in their lineage annals between the Nguyen and the Vu lineages, Nghia and Hanh – two young members of the two lineages – loved each other. Their families and relatives strongly opposed their love, but like many young people in the same situation, they broke away from their parents' control by marrying. They sought the help of local authorities and the Youth Organisation, which often competed with relatives in exerting control over young people. Their wedding was celebrated by those organisations, and no relative attended the ceremony.

Although they had to overcome many difficulties (no house to live in after the marriage; and Nghia's enlistment into the army; then his battlefield experiences and injuries) their love and marriage endured the fierce resistance of their relatives, and the hardships of the American war. Unfortunately, their marriage came to a tragic end simply because the couple was unable to produce the child that was badly needed for the continuation of the Nguyen lineage. The tragedy does not end there; there are much more tears that are still to come, but what concerns us here is that although the young couple successfully severed the ties with the previous generations, yet they were unable to manage without the generation to come. The marital bond cannot replace the parent–child one in Vietnam. However happy a couple is, their happiness is never complete without at least one child.

It is for the children's sake that many women come to terms and even put up with their unhappy marriages. If the ability to 'endure hardship' is a central element in the stereotype of Vietnamese women, and women have special talents for endurance (Gammeltoft, 1997a: 194), one of the reasons for this is their concern for children. It is widely known that family conflicts and divorce are extremely harmful to children; if a marriage breaks up, it is the children who suffer most. Therefore many women often stay even in violent marriages out of pity for their children, citing the popular saying: *Ca chuoi dam duoi vi con.* The meaning of this is that mothers should do the same as the *chuoi* fish that plays dead and gives itself to fishermen to save its young (ibid.: 233). Clearly, the children's interests are paramount.

In the life course, there is another stage when Western couples are once again totally on their own: when their children have grown up and are leading independent lives. This period is termed as the 'empty nest' in Western societies. In theory, up until this period, couples have been busy achieving most, if not all, of their life goals: children, properties, wealth, and careers, etc. Now they are free to spend the rest of their lives being together, living for each other, and enjoying marital life. One might expect this period to strengthen marital ties because with the passage of time, mutual understanding of spouses is increasing, though sexual attractiveness may be decreasing. What about Vietnamese couples in the autumn of their years?

In a study in Dong Minh and Dong Hoang communes, Thai Binh province (1992), one of the findings is not only that the women are having fewer children, but also that the childbearing and childraising periods have been shortened considerably. Based on a survey of 206 women of childbearing age (15–49) as well as the information those women provided about their mothers, the sample was divided into four age groups. The following findings came to light:

Table 4: Average number of children for women according to age

Present age group of women	Average number of children
Mothers of respondents	6.3
Respondents 40–49 years old	4.5
Respondents 30–39 years old	2.8
Respondents 20–29 years old	1.5

Source: Vo Phuong Lan, 1994

The childbearing period for mothers of respondents lasted for twenty-four years (Vo Phuong Lan, 1994), compared to about ten years for women aged 40–49 (Mai Huy Bich, 1993: 94). The figures may be of only relative significance, but a clear trend for fewer children is evident and a concentration of childbearing in early married life, rather than a more diffuse birth pattern spread throughout the fertile period.

One might suppose that if a couple has a strong emotional bond, but has given priority to the more important activity (procreation and continuation of the lineage), then the end of the childbearing period would be welcomed as an opportunity to reaffirm their own conjugal ties. However, the following interview with a 75-year-old peasant in Thai Binh province in 1991 tells quite a different story. His wife resides with his second son, looks after the grandchildren, and visits her husband only when she wants something. The interview is conducted along the following lines (Mai Huy Bich, 1993):

Interviewer: 'So you do not live together, do you?'

Old man: 'She lives quite nearby.'

Interviewer: '"However good the children are in taking care of the old father, they are never as good as the old mother", as the saying goes. Why don't you two old spouses live together? The grandchildren will be looked after by their parents.'

Old man: 'My wife does not like to stay here ... not for economic difficulties here, but because the grandchildren there are too young.'

The interview reveals that for some Vietnamese women, the care of young grandchildren succeeds caring for their own children, and dominates the marital relations even during what should be the 'empty nest' period, when both husband and wife ought to be free of direct childrearing responsibilities. In urban areas, there is a saying among old men: *Vi con mat nha, vi chau mat vo* [Due to one's married sons, one has to give up one's room to them; due to grandchildren, one has to lose one's wife] (Mai Huy Bich, 1993: 96). The meaning is that because housing conditions are cramped, one's married sons should be given priority; and one's wife looks after the grandchildren, instead of taking care of oneself.

How much truth is contained in this half-joking maxim may be open to question, but obviously the 'empty nest' concept is quite alien to many Vietnamese families, in spite of a recognisable period of old age due to increased life expectancy. When children grow up, old couples naturally long for them to get married, as well as the arrival of grandchildren. It is taken for granted that they will look after the grandchildren, at least in case of emergency. Until 1987, even in areas where child daycare centres were available, due to the high incidence of sickness contracted there, working parents often preferred grandparents to look after the grandchildren. In areas where such centres were not available, of course grandparents and older siblings were the main carers. After 1987, when daycare centres started to close down, grandparents have taken over more of the caring responsibilities. Thus, the intergenerational link is continuous, and the nest is never empty. That also means there is less time for marital bonds, even in the last stages of life course.

THE VISITING MARRIAGE

There is a special Vietnamese family type: the families in which spouses live separately for a long time for occupational reasons. The most common one is when a husband has a job away from his native village where his parents, wife and children reside. In a sense this is a visiting marriage: the married couple does not live together, but pays visits to each other. The frequency of their brief reunions depends on the distance between the husband's workplace and the home; it therefore varies from case to case, ranging from every weekend to several times per year. Very often the separation of such married couples lasts for years, decades, or the better part of a lifetime. In the latter case, the couple is reunited only when the absent spouse retires.

The percentage rate of this family type varies over time (it may go up in wartime), as well as from place to place. In Dong Minh and Dong Hoang communes, Thai Binh province, the rate was 14 per cent in 1992 (Le Thi Nham Tuyet *et al.*, 1994a). Once this was misunderstood by some Westerners. In their view, in some areas 'many workers were uprooted from their native communes and involuntarily separated from their families' at the hands of outside forces (quoted in Liljeström *et al.*, 1988: 1). In fact this phenomenon is not new: it has its roots in the remote past and became a way of life for people of different groups for centuries: peasants men joined the army of corvée-bound labourers, or in military service, and officials took their offices far away from home, and left their families in their natal villages. However, it is undeniable that the household registration policy has made it difficult for a state employee's family to unite or reunite if one of the spouses does not have a state sector job close to the other.

It is difficult to understand this seemingly incomprehensible marriage without looking closely at historical traditions and people's living conditions. (In many urban areas, because of the household registration policy as well as the crises in housing and employment, couples are prevented from reuniting.) Nevertheless, many of them seem to accept this state of affairs with equanimity. How do those spouses endure this lifelong separation? Here is an observation which may shed some light on the matter: in Vietnam, married women were accustomed to being separated from their husbands for long periods of time, but could not conceive of being unmarried. They rarely expressed a preoccupation with their husbands (Eisen, 1984: 195). The interviews with people whose spouses were often away from home for long periods are very revealing.

> In 1962, a married man left his family in Dong Hung district, Thai Binh province, for a mountainous area in Ha Tuyen province. He worked there and went home once or twice a year; the wife never visited him in the forest. Here is a fragment from the interview with the wife. When the interviewer asked: 'Have you ever considered going to the forest yourself?', the wife said: 'I want to remain and support my mother. She is 79 years old and I am the only daughter ... My husband returned home last year after having been away for 25–26 years. I did not want him home earlier'.
>
> (Liljeström et al., 1988: 88)

It may be surprising for some that the wife did not want to move to her husband's workplace, although there was no problem for her in obtaining a house (the source also reveals that her eldest son was there and stayed for two months). Instead, she preferred to stay in her native village to support her mother. The need for marital togetherness seems not to exist or to be neglected.

> Another man named Mr Bon was away from home for 30–40 years. He said that he missed his family, but he voluntarily accepted the spatial separation because he gained in other ways.
>
>> Mr Bon, for example, was liberated from heavy work in agriculture. Not having to break his back in the rice fields, he could expand the network of opportunities and open new paths of social mobility for his family. That is why many families 'sacrifice'. (ibid.: 76)
>
> That means his energy was turned not to his wife, but to his children.

Thus some couples feel the need for togetherness, but sacrifice it for the sake of the previous generations (old parents) as well as the next ones (children). In other words, the intergenerational links take precedence over the marital satisfaction. Nonetheless, this traditional type of family persists now partly because the present government has added something new to it, as shown in the following story.

> A collective wedding ceremony for four couples was held in the liberated zones during the French war. A leader of the group pronounced the couples married and congratulated them, then reminded them to maintain their dedication to the revolution. Three days later, the political assignments sent the husbands and wives in different directions.
>
> (Eisen, 1984: 195)

In fact, a great many wedding ceremonies, especially those for state employees in urban areas, are celebrated principally by their workmates. The master of ceremonies is most likely to be the head of the work unit. As an indispensable part of the new wedding ceremony, the master of ceremonies makes a speech to congratulate the newly weds and remind them not to neglect their revolutionary tasks. Apart from the speech made by the master of ceremonies, there are often slogans like *Vui duyen moi khong quen nhiem vu* [Do not neglect your revolutionary duty while enjoying your new union] prominently displayed in wedding halls – this practice is widespread not only in the Delta, but also in the South since 1975, as described by the overseas writer Dieu Tan (1991).

When assigning married couples to work, it is not unusual for the bosses to send them to different places; they show complete disregard for conjugal unity. However, couples may apply for transfer in an attempt to be reunited, but their applications may very well be rejected in the name of revolutionary priorities: they are required to put their work before their personal happiness. We also should not forget the fact that in this family pattern, equal sharing of housework and parenting is impossible; the wife has to perform all the roles, since the husband is almost a visitor. So the segregated gender roles continue indefinitely.

CONCLUSION

To sum up, the most remarkable change is that emotions and opinions of young people today have been more or less recognised in the selection of a marriage partner. However, marriage still serves mainly the interests of groups, not individuals. In the traditional family, that was first of all the kin group of patrilineage. Consequently, free choice was unacceptable in the past and divorce was difficult to obtain. Both men and women fell into the trap of arranged marriages but men often had their ways to get out of unsatisfactory marriages, while women did not. The external pressure that kin groups put on married couples played an enormous role in keeping marriages intact. Moreover, people did not expect much from marriage. Marital ties were just a bridge in the intergenerational links.

The two Laws on Marriage and the Family emphasise, first, freedom in mate selection by two involved individuals and, second, the egalitarian nature of the relationship between them. Nonetheless, those norms are not easily transposed to a larger population where the traditional forms still persist. The opposite of arranged marriage – the entirely free choice of young people – has been rejected in the majority of cases. The preferred option is a compromise between the two: young people choose a marital partner for themselves and then get parental approval.

The state intervenes, but mainly by imposing the class endogamy on the state employees in some domains and by encouraging it among people working in other domains. These strategies were largely successful: by granting the state employees certain privileges that the non-state employees did not have, the state helped them to be in great demand on the marriage market. If we bear in mind how the state employees are recruited (they must have a 'good' family background from the class viewpoint, and have implemented well all the state's regulations) and how they were treated (they were entitled to receive housing, food coupons, and coupons for other necessities as well as different disciplinary measures), we can understand how the state succeeded in getting citizens' conformity and loyalty in family issues.

However, the state's success is by and large limited to urban areas, and its heyday came during the period of the central-planning economy. Since the renovation policy, most people have ignored the political factors that the state promoted in the selection of a spouse. To quote Walder (1986: 248),

> the extraordinary job security and benefits, the goods and services distributed directly by the state enterprise in a situation of scarcity that affects other sectors of the workforce more severely, is an important source of acceptance of the system.

Nevertheless, the fact that the state interferes in the union of the two sexes creates some unforeseen consequences, and ironically has the deepest impact on marital ties. First, the emphasis on class endogamy has led to a new control over young people's choice. In addition to the parental control, the state employees in certain domains have to obey the requirements of the workplaces that act on behalf of the state. In cities the only ones who can consider themselves free are those who live far away from parents, or have liberal parents, or do not depend heavily on workplaces, or have tolerant bosses at workplaces, etc. The rest have little, if any, freedom. After the renovation policy, when state employment is no longer the only way to get jobs, and private employment is opened up, state influence in marital issues begins to wane. However, as long as some privileges are maintained exclusively for state employees, and if the state continues its demand for class endogamy, there will still be some state control.

Second, love based on class solidarity between married people is welcomed by the state, providing that it does not distract them from their duties and tasks. In this sense, companionship and intimacy between married couples are not encouraged by the state if they go beyond the allowed limits.

Third, the emphasis on class has obscured the gender issues and the strictly demarcated gender roles. In other words it has not improved the husband–wife relationship, nor has it established gender equality between them in reality. In many cases, marriage based on shared labour, mutual support, and comradely solidarity does not create a stable and happy family. The male domination and sharp gender separation in the family continue to exist.

On the other hand, the legal requirement of free choice and egalitarian relations have led to a redefinition of marriage as a consensual union that should bring some measure of personal fulfilment and which can be terminated if either partner so desires. More emphasis has been put by some groups, especially in cities, on the emotional gratification (and sexual one as well) of marriage. These people generally have higher expectations of marital partners, and demand more. Those with expectations of companionship and romance, satisfactory domestic arrangements, and personal fulfilment through marriage abandon an unsatisfactory marriage that fails to meet all these criteria and look for fulfilment with another partner. The absence of pressure from the kin groups, and the loosened control by the workplaces have made the stability of a marriage far more dependent on the emotions of the couple. Thus the marital ties have in some ways become fragile.

However, if we bear in mind that the urban population is still small in proportion to the whole population, then it must be concluded that generally speaking, marital ties have not become the central ones in the family; nor has the family transformed into the conjugal form yet, as in some Western societies. The other ties, that is, those between parents and children, remain paramount, as we shall see in the next chapter.

NOTES

1   Before the educational reforms of the late 1970s and early 1980s, the educational system in North Vietnam included the following levels.
- first phase (four classes)
- second phase (seven classes)
- third phase (ten classes)
- higher (university) education (Chaliand, 1969: 47).

After the second phase, those who did not wish to go further could choose vocational schools. In fact, this educational system was named a little differently by some other sources (i.e., primary school, secondary one, high one and university).

2   I myself experienced a difficult two-year period before my marriage. As a student at Hanoi University I met my wife in 1975. Although she was a university student born and bred in Hanoi, my future wife was unable to get her parents' approval of her choice. In fact, her father strongly opposed the relationship between his daughter and myself. Consequently, for two years we often had to meet secretly. At last, her father changed his mind.

3   A lot of people who are peers (classmates, for instance) do not want to marry each other simply because they have addressed as equals within the peer groups. They argue that if married to each other, they would feel it difficult, and uncomfortable to shift away from this form of address to the hierarchical one prevalent among married couples. A friend of mine, a female sociologist, does not address her husband according to custom; instead, she refers to herself and addresses her husband by names. That is considered by almost everybody as strange.

4   In February 1996, I had a talk to four intellectuals who went to Stockholm for a training course. A 35-year-old female researcher among them told me that she strongly disapproved of her friend who had intended to bring his wife to work in the same workplace. I asked her why she disapproved of that. She explained that a couple should be apart from each other for some time each day; therefore they should not be in the same workplace. Otherwise they would be together too much, they would have to see and hear everything together (a criticism of one of them made by a colleague, for instance). That was not good for them. When I asked: 'What about the people who work together and then fall in love?', all the four intellectuals said: 'Love before marriage is one thing; marital life

after that is another thing.' They did not think that working together as companions in a single work-team created a good basis for closer marital ties. On the contrary, they thought that marital ties should be related closely to gender separation.

5 I would like to correct here a misunderstanding made by O'Harrow (1995: 172). *Su tu Ha Dong* is a classic reference deriving from China – according to Le Van Hoe. See: Nguyen Du. *Truyen Kieu* [The tale of Kieu)]. Van Hac Le Van Hoe chu giai, hieu dinh, binh luan. Zieleks Co. Houston, 1976, p. 291. Another researcher, Nguyen Thach Giang, also holds a similar opinion in his notes for *Truyen Kieu*, Nha xuat ban dai hoc va trung hoc chuyen nghiep, Hanoi, 1972.

Therefore the geographical name Ha Dong refers to a place in China, not a Vietnamese region, which is a part of Ha Son Binh province in the Delta, as O'Harrow has misunderstood. The reference has become so popular that people suppose incorrectly that it refers to Ha Dong in Vietnam.

Also O'Harrow has misunderstood the so-called *Hoi so vo* [Society of men who fear their wives]. In fact, such a club has never existed. It is made up as an ironic way to criticise men who are scared of their wives. If people have told O'Harrow that this club now has branches in most countries of the world, that just means wherever there are Vietnamese men, some of them may very well be scared of their wives! Somebody among them may also be nicknamed *Chu tich hoi so vo* [President of the society of men who fear their wives]: this only means that he is pre-eminent in this respect.

6 Sometime around the late 1980s, *Tien phong*, a weekly magazine of the Youth Organisation, opened a discussion on the topic of chastity under the title: 'Chastity is worth a thousand gold coins'. Quite a few people still urge women to place their chastity above everything. One can take any issue of this magazine, as well as the magazine *Phu nu Viet Nam* of the Women's Union, and inevitably find articles about young brides thrown out of the groom's house on the nuptial night for the reason that they are not virgins.

7 A female journalist told me that in 1983–84 she saw many wedding banquets in rural areas where the bride had no time for herself. Instead she had to participate in the cooking and in serving guests, and so wore normal everyday attire. It is only when the representatives of the groom's family arrive, and the bride has to follow them to the groom's house that she puts on new clothes.

CHAPTER FOUR

Reproduction and Its Socio-cultural Meanings

This chapter is about the parent–child bond, but from a specific perspective. When analysing this bond, the focus is generally on parenthood and childhood; gender and child-rearing; the ideals of being a good father (mother, son, and daughter)'; the child's emotional attachments to the parent of the opposite gender (son–mother, daughter–father); to the one of the same gender (son–father, daughter–mother); the relations between authority and intimacy between parents and children; etc. Here the bond is dealt with mainly within the framework of reproduction, i.e., the process and its social dimensions by which new members are born into the family. There are other aspects of the bond but these are not considered in this study owing to a lack of research material. If, as Harris claims (1983: 171) 'parent–child relations are in one sense a curiously neglected area of sociology and history', then this is particularly true of Vietnam.

At present, in many parts of the world, people tend to take a rather narrow view of reproduction as a strictly physical process (from insemination to birth). As such, they do not normally associate the reproductive process with old people who are assumed to have neither the physical capacity nor the interest in having more children at their time in life. This misconception applies not just to laypeople, but also to some researchers: they often proceed from a standpoint that takes for granted the inevitability of children. As Macintyre puts it,'sociologists have taken normal reproduction and the problems attached to it, for granted as part of the natural order' (quoted in Harris, 1983: 172).

However, that is the case only in modern Western society. In Vietnam, as we shall see later in this chapter, people do not regard having children as the inevitable result of their marriage. Instead, they deliberately seek parenthood, often as a result of long-term considerations. Therefore reproduction means not just the process of birth, but also the lifelong relations of two generations at the very least. So dealing with the parent–child bond in terms of reproduction in Vietnam necessarily entails the question that 'remains largely unanswered' (Harris, 1983: 172): 'Why do people have children?' In other words, the bond is looked at here only in terms of the significance of children to parents. Since Vietnamese families often prefer sons, we shall focus mainly on the socio-cultural meaning of male children to parents, leaving aside that of the female ones.

In this chapter I shall first deal briefly with the situation in the traditional family. Then I look at the changed and unchanged traits in reproduction of the present family. The government's birth control policy is considered as one of the important factors of change, which has contributed to the creation of the smaller family. I shall also examine one of the obstacles to this, that is the preference for sons. To explain this preference, I shall deal with the concern about security in old age as well as a characteristic of Vietnamese culture that seems at first to be unrelated to reproduction – ancestor worship. In a way, this means that I have to deal with the opposite of birth, i.e., death (of parents) and, to some extent, the concern with life after death. This is a time-consuming but essential task, if we are to grasp the meaning of reproduction to Vietnamese people, and to understand its changed as well as unchanged traits.

In modern Western societies, industrialisation has distanced the basic relations of reproduction from the organisation of production. Reproduction tends to be viewed from a narrow perspective, as an individual's concern about giving birth, etc. (Robertson, 1991: 36–37). However, reproduction is viewed by people in relation to their whole life course – in the case of Vietnam, even to the afterlife. In other words, having children during the childbearing years is put into the framework of later life; therefore a researcher should examine reproduction in relation to their concerns about old age and death.

REPRODUCTION IN THE TRADITIONAL FAMILY

In the traditional family, to produce children was the first and foremost desire of married couples. A large family may have been the inevitable result of having no contraception, but it was also considered a social value. Having many children was widely viewed as a happiness, a dream, and a social value because the large family really met the vital demands of one's life. The first value among three traditional ones was to have many children. A popular saying that summed up the three values went: *Phuc, Loc, Tho.* It meant to have (1) many children, (2) a great many gifts and benefits from gods, and (3) longevity. On the lunar New Year festivals, according to a prevailing custom, people wished one another many children, among other things. In a similar vein, wedding guests would wish the newly-weds many children.

When it came to the question of how to feed many children, it was believed that 'if nature creates an elephant, it certainly would create grass [to feed it]', as a saying put it. That is a vivid illustration of an act of faith in the capacity of the economy to provide for the rising generation, and the rising generation's capacity to sustain and develop that economy (Robertson, 1991: 72).

During the last half century, reproduction, in the widest sense of the term, has undergone unprecedented changes; at the same time there has been some resistance to these changes. It is difficult to ascertain the trend of change in reproduction over the past half-century by using the birth rate because data are not available. Before 1945 birth was a concern of the family, not of the state. That was why to get accurate information about reproduction in the Delta, Gourou (1936/1955: 224) had to turn to the Catholic missions who kept birth and death registries more exact than the official ones. However, we cannot use this source for the reason that our subject (the non-Catholics) differs totally from the Catholics in the matter of birth control.

In spite of having no data, it is necessary to make one thing clear. It would be wrong to say that in the traditional Vietnamese family, women had as many children as they could because they married young (often before the age of 20), and gave birth right up to their menopause. That may be a hypothesis from a demographic point of view. In fact, there were some limits to their fertility. Many poor men and women had to delay marriage for years. Soon after giving birth, many women had to get up and return immediately to work, which damaged their health. On the other hand, the death rate considerably reduced the number of children who survived their parents and went on to produce offspring themselves.

An unknown but large number of men were often absent from their families for different reasons: they engaged in activities requiring regular and long travel (working as hired labourers, building dikes, and in military service). In the Vietnamese view it was considered improper for husbands and wives to sleep together once their children reached adulthood (see Chapter Three), especially when their children married (for the reason that sexuality was supposed to serve mainly the need for reproduction; after their children had achieved maturity, couples were expected to limit their sexual activities). All those factors would have kept the fertility rates below the maximum.

REPRODUCTION IN THE PRESENT FAMILY

The difficulty with data about reproduction has not been resolved even now: data were not available until very recently. Only since the late 1980s has the situation been gradually improving. There are the following sources of data: Vital Civil Registration, Censuses, and Sample Surveys. The General Statistical Office (GSO) is the only institution authorised to release official statistics on population and vital statistics. Demographic data based on the household registration and vital statistics systems are released by the GSO every year. Nevertheless, according to many observers (Vu Qui Nhan, 1991), this source of data is not reliable due to underreporting of deaths and births.

The Census of 1979 was generally estimated as unreliable. The latest Census was carried out in 1989. It is believed to have been carefully conducted and reliable, particularly in comparison to the previous one; the GSO estimates the error rate to have been about 3 per cent (Vu Qui Nhan, 1991: 147). However, according to some foreign experts (Banister, 1993: xii) both the 1979 and 1989 Censuses slightly undercounted the population. Since statistics about the birth control programme are not quite accurate, the survey is the best source of data on this issue. The 1988 Vietnam Demographic and Health Survey (VNDHS 1988) was the first nationwide sample survey conducted with high reliability.

The following study is in part based on the analyses which different authors carried out using the results of the VNDHS 1988 and the 1989 Census 5 per cent sample result. On the other hand, the study also uses the results of different sociological surveys and interviews. Their reliability will be evaluated when possible.

LONGING FOR CHILDREN

The first remarkable feature in this respect is the strong desire of almost all couples to have children. This is especially true of women.

According to the Vietnam Demographic and Health Survey in 1988, among 4,172 women aged 15 to 49 there was not one woman who did not desire to have children (Vietnamese Government, 1990: 31).

From time immemorial, reproduction has been the most important function of the Vietnamese family. The social character of reproduction was particularly emphasised. Childless couples were considered to have committed a very serious sin to their lineage. The causes of childlessness were believed to be social ones (i.e., it was the result of bad behaviour in social life; or punishment for immoral behaviour or for the sins committed in their earlier existence, and so on), rather than the biological ones (e.g. a disease leading to infertility). To put it another way, there has been a moralisation of reproduction – meanwhile the present birth control programme places great emphasis on the medical aspects of birth control, with little or no concern to the social aspects, as we shall see later.

Nevertheless, it was women who were believed to be responsible for reproduction. It may be said that women's role expectations in reproductive life were quite clear: to bear children. Moreover, most women in the traditional society had few other social roles outside their family. The majority of them were not permitted to study or take examinations – which was the only way to become upwardly mobile at the time. As noted earlier (see Chapter Three), rural women were barred from the membership in their villages (Wiegersma, 1988: 53), i.e., they were not even regarded as citizens. Their identity was defined so closely in terms of the home and family that they lost their own names and the way of counting their age. As Gourou (1936/1955: 208) pointed out, even the male individual had no need of official identity; 'often a man will be called *bo cu*, father of his son, *bo di*, father of his daughter.'

This was especially true of women. After marriage, in usual conversations they were called after their husbands (or their first sons). In both cases, the married woman's own name disappeared in everyday life. If someone called her by her own name, she would take it as a mark of disrespect. This meant that women gained their own identity through the family roles; the family was a primary, if not the single, source of identity for married women.

Since 1945 many women have been given better educational and employment opportunities and live on a relatively equal basis with men. Many others though, especially those living in the countryside, have failed to reap these gains. However, for both groups the family continues to provide them with identity, albeit to different extents. Whereas in some modern Western societies, for instance in America, there is so-called voluntary childlessness among some career women, in Vietnam people cannot even imagine that. Whereas these American women evaluate both career commitment and child-rearing in terms of economic costs/rewards and social costs/rewards when making the decision to be child-free (Sharon, 1986), it is commonly believed in Vietnam that: *Chim troi ai de dem long, nuoi con ai de ke cong thang ngay* [It is not easy to count the feathers of birds in the sky; similarly, the money, time, and energy spent on rearing one's child are immeasurable], as a folk-song puts it. That is exactly what Robertson means when he states that in reproduction, ordinary people do not behave like neo-classical economists who calculate the production of hats or cars.

> The rationale of child-raising is set about with complex qualitative issues that are not readily amenable to individual calculation, and instead become lodged in the folk wisdom of culture.
>
> (Robertson 1991: 72)

A woman in Vietnam who does not have any child often feels like 'a failure as a woman'. Women's identity is still defined very closely in terms of home and family, of their motherhood. In the well-known novel *Manh dat lam nguoi nhieu ma* [The piece of land with many people and a lot of ghosts] by Nguyen Khac Truong (1990/1991: 282) a married woman's own name is forgotten after her marriage. From then on, she is named after her husband, then her first child, then even her first grandchild. When she is suddenly called by her own name, she stands transfixed as if it is the naming of someone else, not her. If her own name is called by her immediate relatives, she understands at once that it certainly is not a pleasing call; on the contrary, something serious must have happened.

This is also confirmed by sociological evidence. In a survey in Cong Hoa commune, Nam Thanh district, Hai Hung province, right from the beginning there was an interesting difficulty. Using the list of female interviewees that was made with the help of the commune's administrative committee, local interviewers could not identify who their interviewees were. The reason was that the list was made according to the own names of the women; while in everyday life those women were called according to the names of their husbands or their first sons. More interestingly, when asked about their age, the above-mentioned women could not answer directly. Instead they had to count like this: 'I gave birth to my first child when I was ... years old; now (s)he is ... years old; that means that I am ... years old' (Bui The Cuong, 1992). This can be seen in many other areas as well.

In this sense, motherhood is still an indispensable, if not basic, part of female identity. If they have no child, women have the 'feelings of personal insufficiency' – to borrow the words of Giddens (1991: 65). So in a sense, children provide parents, especially mothers, with an essential part of their identity.

Another factor to be considered is the short time between marriage and the birth of the first child. In urban areas, according to a survey in Hanoi in 1983, 70.7 per cent of young wives become mothers after only one year of marriage (Trinh Thi Quang, 1983). In Van Nhan commune, Ha Son Binh province in 1990, more than half of the women surveyed had their first child within the first year of marriage. Those who have the first child after two years of marriage are very rare, and this was generally the result of some problem with the fertility, not a deliberate delay (quoted in Mai Huy Bich, 1993: 93).

A survey conducted among 411 mothers with children under 5 years of age in five communes of Tien Hai district, Thai Binh province, in 1992 shows that 53.9 per cent of non-Catholic women have their first child within one year of marriage, 27.7 per cent within a one- to two-year period, and non-Catholic women in general have their first child much earlier than the Catholic ones (Hoang Thi Hoa *et al.*, 1996: 14). There are some inaccuracies in this study. Moreover, the sample includes only mothers who have children under 5 years of age, i.e., it excludes other mothers, but it reveals the latest state of affairs.

We have no available data about the use of contraceptives among newly-wed couples, but we may put forward a supposition that it is rather uncommon. Couples tend to want to have their first child straight away. The above data have shown clearly that the so-called extended 'honeymoon' period is quite short for the overwhelming majority of couples. In fact, when greeting and talking to newly-weds a few months after their marriage, people often ask: 'Have you got any good news?' Parents, especially on the husband's side, wait with great impatience for their first grandchild. Couples who show no sign of the first pregnancy after one year or more are often suspected of having a fertility problem. That is why newly-wed couples, especially the eldest daughters-in-law, are eager to have the first child very soon to demonstrate their fertility.

PREFERENCE FOR SON(S)

While longing for the first child in general, parents particularly want it to be a boy, but there can be no doubt that the strong prejudice against having girls which is found in China is not a Vietnamese custom: on the contrary, the birth of a daughter is welcomed. In the traditional peasant family, a daughter was especially appreciated if she was the first child, because she would be a great helper to her parents with the household chores. That was why a Vietnamese proverb went: 'Having a piece of fertile land and a fertile female buffalo is not as valuable as having a daughter as your first child'. Another proverb goes: 'It would be better to have both glutinous rice and ordinary one'; i.e., people like to have children of both sexes. For that reason some families with many sons still long for a daughter. There is a popular saying which people often say to the parents' of new-born daughters: *Co hoa mung hoa, co nu mung nu* [Let us rejoice, whether buds or flowers]. That means that the birth of a child is a happy event, regardless of the sex of the new-born.

However, it is obvious that preference for son(s) is very strong. Foreign researchers have made a comparison that in Vietnam, the importance of having male children is stressed more than in Thailand and Burma (Goethals, 1991). It cannot be denied that in this respect, the Vietnamese family is similar to the Chinese one (Lang, 1946: 46). People, especially in the countryside, prefer to have sons, regardless of their social status: from ordinary people to officials, from non-members of political affiliation to Communist Party members. A chairman of the administrative committee in An Hiep commune, Quynh Phu district, Thai Binh province, whose job was to persuade people in his locality to implement the family planning programme, said: 'If the authorities tell us the right way to have sons, there is no problem' (Vuong Xuan Tinh, 1994: 28). In other words, he takes for granted that people prefer sons; the problem of overpopulation arises only for that reason. The preference for sons is so strong that parents who have a new-born son in the commune pull fire crackers to celebrate, or they slaughter one or two pigs for a celebratory feast for all members of their lineage (ibid.: 27). In other words, the birth of a son is happily greeted by the whole family.

By contrast, a couple with two or more daughters and no son feel disappointed. In the press there are often stories about how men who are waiting for a son react to their new-born daughters (this has not been given any attention by sociologists). For instance,

Nguyen Tri Thuc (1995) tells us about his relative who already had four daughters. When the relative's wife became pregnant again, the husband prepared well in advance for the celebration in the hope of getting a son. He carefully reared some chickens in preparation for the feast that he would give if the infant turned out to be a boy. The baby was born but it was a girl; his hopes dashed, he released the chickens and the event was not celebrated. This case is not unique – similar stories abound, especially in the countryside.

Other people who have no son feel worried, even ashamed. A large-scale survey on family planning in Hanoi, Hai Hung (and one province in Southern Vietnam) showed that out of the 5,010 women questioned, 70.2 per cent stated the absolute necessity of having male children (Mai Huy Bich, 1991). A survey conducted in Quyet Tien commune, Kien Xuong district, Thai Binh province, asked 100 women and 88 men how they felt about having no son. Even allowing for an understandable reluctance to admit their true feelings on so sensitive an issue, 65.5 per cent of women admitted feeling worried and ashamed. This was a much higher percentage than among the men (Doan Kim Thang, 1985).

Why is there this differentiation in the degree of guilt felt by the wife and husband? This derives from a tradition whereby the blame for not having a son generally becomes attached to the woman. It is usually believed that there must be something wrong with the wife. Her position in the family would then be rendered insecure, no matter how well she performed her duties as a wife and daughter-in-law. In the previous chapter, we saw how, according to the pre-1945 law, failure to give birth to a male child was the first of seven grounds which would allow a man to repudiate his wife. Nonetheless, that was *de jure; de facto* 'when a husband cannot obtain a male heir from his wife, he takes a second wife' (Gourou, 1936/1955: 219). Whatever he did, she felt her marital status was threatened. The situation remains little changed in many areas now. It is the impact of this traditional view that in part explains why women bear sole responsibility for all the reproduction problems, including contraceptive use, as well as failure to produce a son. That explains the extra burden of shame that many women admitted feeling because they had no son. Thus having children, especially sons, means a more stable marital status for women.

The preference for a son is strong among single mothers too. As explained in Chapter Two, recently a growing number of single women have begun to risk the century-old social disapproval of having children out of wedlock. Their situation has been gradually accepted, and official policy allows them to have one child. According to Le Nham (1994: 103), in An Hiep commune, Quynh Phu district, Thai Binh province, this phenomenon called 'asking for a child' is not rare: altogether among eighty-five unmarried women aged over 30, there were twenty-one who asked for a child. That is a marked change.

However, there is one unchanging fact: the preference for a son. In the commune, unmarried women even pay men in kind (paddy) to have sexual intercourse with them so that they may become pregnant. It is taken for granted that if the woman has a son, the man expects an extra payment, in fact twice the amount he would have received for a daughter (200 kg paddy for a son against 100 kg for a daughter). More interestingly, villagers who reported such stories also think that it is absolutely normal that payment for a son would be higher (Le Nham, 1994: 105). Although those stories were told by villagers and not the women involved (because it is quite difficult to interview them about this sensitive issue), there is no reason to doubt their accuracy. And this also means that if an unmarried woman has a daughter, she will be very likely to break the legal limit, and continue to ask for another child, until she gets a son.

In brief, the preference for a son reminds us of a traditional proverb: 'If you have a son, you can say you have a descendant; but you cannot say this, even if you have ten daughters.' The importance attached to having son and the frenetic drive to have at least one male descendant have led many families into conflict with the government's birth control programme.

THE VIETNAMESE GOVERNMENT'S BIRTH CONTROL PROGRAMME

The Red River Delta has long been subject to population pressure. However, the results of the 1960 Census made clear to the policymakers the urgency of the population growth problem (while agricultural land is limited). This, combined with the real possibility of widespread availability of contraception, made them more aware of the urgent need for a lower birth rate. A government policy to control rapid population growth has been implemented in the Delta since 1962, but the programme was not compulsory then, and most kinds of contraceptive supplies were hardly available. Moreover, the second Indochina war made clear the need for manpower, and on the other hand made it impossible to implement the birth control programme. Since the beginning of Vietnam's economic crisis (the late 1970s) the need for birth control and limited reproduction has become more and more urgent.

Authorities have escalated the demands on people to control their fertility. Oversimplifying this matter, they thought that if contraceptive supplies were available, people would seize the opportunity to practise family planning. Like many other developing countries, Vietnam has a high birth rate. The population growth rate was 2.2 per cent in 1980, and the population is still growing at about 1.9 per cent a year according to one source (Banister, 1993: xi). The authorities once set a target rate of 1.7 per cent. However, later they realised that many families were resisting the introduction of birth control. Thinking that the propaganda apparatus had not done enough, they launched propaganda campaigns to persuade people to implement the family planning programme. They tried to point out the disadvantages of having too many children, and the advantages of limiting birth. By so doing they made great efforts to persuade people to make an economically rational choice in reproduction.

More than that the authorities linked the biological reproduction to education and social reproduction by promoting the maxim: fewer but healthier and better-educated children. They said the move from a non-contraceptive to a contraceptive family would create favourable conditions not only for simply bringing children into the world, but also for ensuring their future by means of education and a higher standard of living for the whole family as well as the nation. A large family is associated with the past, backwardness, and ignorance, while a small family is linked to modernity, enlightenment, and civilisation (Gammeltoft, 1997a: 73). Again the authorities have juxtaposed tradition and modernity, and defined tradition as something bad and modernity as something good.

Nevertheless, the desired results failed to materialise. The authorities needed to take more drastic action. In 1983 the two-child policy was promulgated. This policy was occasionally forced upon people at the local level. The new Law on Marriage and the Family, implemented since January 1987, states:

Article 2: 'A couple has the duty to produce children in accordance with a plan';

Article 11: 'Wife and husband have the obligations to be faithful to each other, to respect, care for, and help each other to make progress and practise planned parenthood together'.

(Banister, 1993: 24)

In late 1988 the Vietnamese government specified financial and work penalties to be meted out to couples who had more than two children. The media reported strong enforcement measures including required IUD use, financial penalties, job loss, and even physical intimidation (ibid.: 24). It would be safe to suggest that the extent to which these compulsory measures are taken varies from locality to locality, but they are quite common in many places. Although this is again a borrowing of China's family policies, i.e., the Chinese one-child policy that was introduced some nine years earlier (Goodkind, 1995), the Vietnamese version is clearly less strict. How does the birth control programme affect the family's reproduction?

THE SOCIAL REALITY OF BIRTH CONTROL

Knowledge of contraceptive measures and means – a precondition for their use – is widespread among married women of reproductive age. According to the VNDHS, when asked to name ways to avoid pregnancy, almost 94 per cent of women who had ever been married were aware of at least one modern method. The best-known method is the IUD (intra-uterine device), followed by abortion, female sterilisation, male sterilisation, and the menstrual regulation. Less than half the female respondents knew about pills and condoms, and a similar minority percentage knew about the rhythm method and withdrawal. It is not surprising that urban educated women are more aware of modern methods than rural illiterate ones. That is the situation generally of the whole country. Compared to their sisters in the South, women in the North are more aware of the IUD (89.1 per cent and 94.1 per cent respectively), but less aware of the pill, condom, and female and male sterilisation (Vietnamese Government, 1990: 37).

As for contraceptive use, again it is the urban and more educated women who are more likely to be using contraception than the rural, less educated ones. However, the most popular method in the North is the IUD (47 per cent) while it is used only by 17 per cent in the South (ibid.: 41). It must be said that the birth control programme is poorly funded; the only widely available contraceptive technique is the IUD, especially in the North. According to a perceptive observation made by many researchers (Banister, 1993: 22), the programme has promoted only the IUD, to the exclusion of other methods. Significantly, this method is an exclusively female one; it is one in which the woman alone assumes total responsibility.

However, not all women feel that this technique is suitable and it can cause a great many health problems. Almost two-thirds of 206 women in a survey in Dong Minh and Dong Hoang communes, Thai Binh province, said that they had experienced side-effects of the IUD which they described variously as weakness, abdominal pain, backache, headache, and irregular, prolonged, or heavy bleeding. Interestingly enough, to check that, the authors of the survey asked the staff at the inter-communal clinic, and were informed that only 5 per cent of their clients suffered from side-effects (Johansson *et al.*, 1996: 63). This very low figure is no doubt derived only from the extreme cases of women who had to have their IUDs removed because of bleeding and pain. It almost certainly excludes those with less severe feelings of malaise or discomfort, who would not necessarily have reported their condition to the clinic. However, women also said that their husbands, and men in general, show little concern about female problems associated with the use of IUD. A woman in the survey commented: 'If the IUD does not suit you, or if you do not have the IUD, then you get pregnant. And the only way [out] is abortion. Men are irresponsible!' (Johansson *et al.*, 1996: 63). Asked about the effects of the IUD on his wife's health, a man replied:

> I do not know. It is women's business. Women speak about it themselves. Of course we are also responsible for their health, but we are so busy with our business, fishing for example!
> (Johansson *et al.*, 1996: 63)

As one respondent remarked, when the IUD proves to be unreliable and a woman gets pregnant, there is only one solution – abortion. Recently abortion rates have increased dramatically. For example, in Thai Binh province, from 1985 to 1989 the rate more than doubled from 330 to 707 abortions per 1,000 live births. In 1990 the abortion rate reached 850 and then doubled by September 1992 (1,700 abortions per 1,000 live births) (Le Thi Nham Tuyet *et al.*, 1994b: 74). Those are just the official statistics. A survey conducted in 1992 among 228 women who had had abortions during the previous year in the same province made the rather surprising discovery that the majority of these women were not young and inexperienced; on the contrary they were aged between 30 and 40, with two or more children (ibid.: 79). Having an abortion for them was an alternative method of birth control, not a never-to-be-repeated emergency measure, as it often is in the West. Twenty-five per cent of these women had gone through two abortions already; about 10 per cent had undergone three or more (ibid: 80). A 34-year-old woman had even undergone five abortions over four years (ibid.: 83).

It is predicted from the survey that if the trend continues, there will be twice as many abortions as births annually in the near future. Young women will go through more abortions than deliveries during their reproductive period. Their health will therefore suffer much more than it does now (ibid.: 88). The data presented above may underestimate the true numbers, since the survey's sample derived from the files of health-care networks which certainly missed cases of private abortions. However, one of the survey's findings is confirmed by the results of another survey of 2,088 women having abortions in Hanoi and Thai Binh. This proves that the majority of women undergoing abortions are married: 91.9 per cent and 99.5 per cent respectively in the two locations (Goodkind, 1994: 349).

Abortion rates vary from province to province, but the highest ones in the country were found in the major urban provinces (Hanoi, Hai Phong), in the densely populated provinces in and around the Red River Delta, as well as in Ho Chi Minh City and the Mekong Delta in the South. The 1992 total abortion rate for the country was at least 2.5 per woman. As one researcher estimates, that is the highest rate in Asia and is unusually high by international standards (Goodkind, 1994: 342, 350).

The rising abortion rate is a profound change. Until very recently a traditional view of abortion was still held, which regarded this practice as murder. In the eyes of many Buddhists, it was considered highly immoral and was roundly condemned. Although the present regime has legalised abortion, initially it took a long time for it to gain public acceptance. Moreover, having an abortion was not only costly, but also problematic because until very recently medical staff were obstructive and unhelpful to women seeking abortion. Now things have changed totally, since it has become an alternative method of birth control, which is a worrying trend. What about the results of birth control and contraceptive use? That is the next section's topic.

A SMALLER FAMILY

Needless to say, contraceptive measures and techniques bring fundamental changes to family life. In the traditional society there was little opportunity to limit the size of one's family. Although in some areas, women after giving birth practised the custom of *ba kieng* [three abstinences: abstaining from some foods, abstaining from sexual intercourse, and avoiding heavy work] the purpose was to space out the births of children, not to limit birth directly. Moreover, a lot depended on the man and on his ascetic control over his sexual impulses.

Modern contraception creates all kinds of new opportunities: to control the number of children and the spacing of pregnancies (to allow a great time period between the first and second child, for example); to pursue an education, job, or career training; to improve people's standard of living and, most importantly, their children's future. For many educated people, especially in big cities, modern contraception has been warmly welcomed. As a result, the fertility rate of the urban population is much lower than that of rural people. According to one source, by 1986–87, urban women had a total fertility rate of only 2.2 births per woman, compared to 4.6 births per woman in rural areas (Banister, 1993: 30).

Many women in the countryside also use modern contraceptive methods. Here are the interview notes about the life plan of a peasant woman in Thai Binh province in 1992, who was aged 23 with a 3-year-old child, and was using contraception. Asked why she had not yet given birth to her second child, she revealed that she was on a five-year family planning programme. She had already made the decision to have a second child five years after the first one. Replying to the next question: 'Why five years and not earlier?', she said: 'Too many births create big problems ... I have decided that I will have my second child when I have built a house for my family, big or small!' (Le Thi Nham Tuyet *et al.*, 1994a).

Such evidence leaves little doubt that women like this appreciate the new-found opportunity to regulate their fertility and plan their lives, in order to improve their standard of living: all advantages which the older generations never enjoyed. As a result of this, some important changes have occurred. An indicator of this change is the decline in the total fertility rate of women. In Vietnam as a whole, until the early 1970s, women were still bearing more than six children on average. However, since then this rate has declined: in the late 1980s the average was down to about four (Banister, 1993: 27).

Among respondents of a study conducted in Dong Minh commune, Tien Hai district, Thai Binh province in 1992, there was a peasant woman who was among the first ten women to have volunteered to try out an IUD in 1968. She said that family planning then was not compulsory as it is now. A medical team came to the commune, and women were invited to have a gynaecological examination. They explained that women who were suffering from a disease would be treated, and those who wanted to space births could have an IUD. At that time she had already had four sons; her life was difficult because of her large family, but they could do nothing. That was why when the team came, her husband who had been working in Hanoi advised her to have the IUD, and she agreed. After getting it, she was very enthusiastic. She kept it for some years, then went to the doctor and had it removed. Her health was good all the time she used the IUD. After having it removed she gave birth to two more children. Other women in the test continued to use the IUD right up to the present.

Many women who did not seize the opportunity to have the IUD and practise family planning at that time were jealous to see how successful it was proving for this woman. Her sister-in-law was one of them. During her interview, this woman complained that if family planning had been introduced earlier, the difficulties which her large family had faced would have been reduced:

> We had a hard life. Why didn't they introduce family planning before? We had no choice! Now the women can decide how many children they want'.
>
> (Johansson *et al.*, 1996)

Contraception seems to create a necessary condition for young couples to fulfil their dreams: to build a house of their own, to protect their health, and to improve their life. A 25-year-old woman said that after her marriage, she and her husband discussed the question of having children. They agreed to have just two children, preferably boys. If they had two girls, then they would try again for a boy. If the third child was another girl, then they would stop there and not try again.

> Now that we have the two boys we wished for, we will stop child-bearing and make a good life for ourselves and our children, first of all to build a spacious house to live in.
>
> (ibid.: 62)

We see here the connection between limiting the size of the family and house building. This case also underlines the preference for sons, which we dealt with earlier in this chapter.

In brief, modern contraceptive practices have effectively reduced fertility, and many people, particularly in urban areas, welcome it (even when no strict birth control programme has been imposed). Consequently, family size has been declining since the 1970s. By the end of 1988, when the birth control programme had been tightened, the total fertility rate had fallen to just below four births per woman (Goodkind, 1995: 91). Due to these profound transformations, the family has become smaller. On the other hand, as has been shown, the implementation of the birth control programme also produces a lot of problems, particularly for women who bear the brunt of the birth control responsibility. It has also led to a number of health problems for women, as many suffer from the side-effects of the contraceptive devices.

So far we have looked at the changes in reproduction mainly from a demographic point of view. In terms of quantitative demographic data, it seems that the government's target of a maximum of two children per couple will be difficult to achieve. That is what a demographer, using the data from the VNDHS, has stated. His argument is that of all women aged 20–24, nearly 20 per cent had already had at least two children (Vu Qui Nhan, 1991: 149). He meant that those women would have more children during their duration of marriage.

However, the demographic perspective does not tell us the whole story about the difficulty of the two-child policy. Nor does it explain why those women are likely to break the limit. As the woman quoted above said, she was 'lucky' (in the Vietnamese view) to have two boys. If she had given birth to two daughters, what would have happened? She said that she would have tried for a third child. Her case speaks for those who have sons, but it also says something about people who have no son: they would continue to try for a boy. In other words, the son preference is an obstacle to the birth control programme. That will be the next focus of our study, because we need to understand not only the changed and unchanged features of reproduction, but also the meaning and importance which Vietnamese people attach to reproduction.

SOLUTIONS TO THE BIRTH CONTROL PROGRAMME

The two-child limit has really put great pressure on many couples, and as a result it has deeply affected the attitude towards daughters. Before the birth control programme, as noted earlier, all babies were welcomed, especially the arrival of a daughter as the first child. Now because of the limit, many parents feel anxious if the first child is a daughter. They want to have a son as the first child to be sure that their dream has already come true. Then they need not worry which sex the second child is – they won't need to break the limit. If they have a daughter as the first child, and next have a son, they are viewed by public opinion as successful because they have children of both sexes. Moreover, a daughter as the first child will be the indispensable helper according to the tradition. However, they have to go through an uncertain period between the two births. Therefore the birth of the daughter as the first child is generally less welcomed than it was before the introduction of the two-child policy.

For those couples who already have two daughters but no son, the situation would be totally different. Unfortunately, we do not have any data about this family type, but we know that many educated people in urban areas have come to terms with the idea of never having a son.[1] On the other hand, many couples longing for at least one son have made use of the solutions that were predominant in the traditional family, and some of which are contrary to the government's birth control policy and the 1987 Law of Marriage and the Family. This creates a conflict between the interests of society and those of the family. This also brings many problems to the couples concerned. The possible solutions open to the couples are set out below.

The wife continues bearing children

The first solution is that the wife continues to bear children until at least one son is born, no matter how many children that may entail. In many cases, the more they try, the more they fail; their efforts result in only more daughters. A folk saying describes them as *khat nuoc* [being thirsty]. When choosing this solution, couples have to cope with problems of not only having more mouths to feed, but also of role conflict. Here is one concrete case.

> In the study in Dong Minh commune, Tien Hai district, Thai Binh province (1992), there was a 29-year-old peasant woman, who had just given birth to her third child, a daughter again (she already had two daughters, born in 1985 and 1987). It was said she felt very unhappy; when her husband came to take her and the baby home from the commune's health care station, she cried throughout the trip. Everybody felt sorry for her. Her family had to pay a fine of 200 kg of paddy imposed by the commune administration on those who broke the two-child limit: this put them into debt because they did not have enough money yet to buy paddy. During the interview she was very sad. She said that she was well aware of the two-child limit and did not want to go through too many births.
>
> When she was two months' pregnant for the third time, the head of the Women's Union branch and the head of her village tried to persuade her to get an abortion, but she refused. The reason was that there were too few people in her family at the moment. Her father-in-law had died in the front-line during the (American) war; moreover her husband was an only child so her mother-in-law was reliant on him. In her words,

'I told the above people that I would not get an abortion. Anyway, I must have the third child, regardless of its sex' (quoted in Mai Huy Bich, 1993: 27–28). It was clear that she had experienced a conflict of roles, which in the end was resolved in favour of the family through her decision to bear a third child.

It was her mother-in-law who was the most coercive element in persuading her to try for a third child. At last, four years after having the second child, the daughter-in-law was pregnant again in 1991. As we saw, the result was yet another daughter. When asked: 'You already had three nice, healthy granddaughters; will you push your daughter-in-law to bear more?', the old woman said: 'I do not know what to do now'.

(Ibid.: 28)

What happened to this couple tells us a lot about the conflict arising from the opposing role expectations. Like men, women now have their social roles outside their families, too: as citizens, as members of the Women's Union, and as members of agricultural co-operatives, etc. As wives and daughters-in-law, they are expected to bear more children, but everywhere outside their family they are expected to observe the two-child limit, or suffer the legal consequences. However, those who have not yet had a son are really under pressure from their family to carry on trying for a boy. Such couples find it difficult, if not impossible, to conform simultaneously to the two distinct sets of role expectations. Thus the role conflict emerges.

When role conflict emerges, social systems provide some mechanisms for dealing with it (Ebaugh, 1988). Many people, like the above couple, give priority to the family roles and sacrifice the others. The above husband is an example.

> Another man was a 50-year-old father of four grown-up daughters. Longing for a son, he withdrew from the Communist Party to resolve the role conflict, and to implement his dream. In the Vietnamese society even now this is seen as an enormous loss of status. Many people would still like to have his position because of its excellent benefits. His villagers said: 'How could he resolve to lose everything after so many years serving in the armed forces?' Nevertheless, that was not all. He had to pay a fine of 800 kg paddy. However, in considering the pros and cons, the man found that the advantages of leaving the Communist Party role outweighed the disadvantages. Finally the long-awaited son was born;

the family slaughtered a pig to celebrate. According to Le Nham (1994), not only his relatives, but all the villagers, including those not invited to the feast, shared with him the happiness of having a son.

In the case of rural women, not all roles in their repertoire are equally important to their identity. Faced with a role conflict, many of them tend to give priority to the family roles. That means that even now the family role and motherhood are still central to their identity.

Thus the desire to have a son is one reason why many couples infringe the two-child limit. This is confirmed by statistics and sociological surveys. In Thai Binh province, third-child births comprised 21.7 per cent of all births in 1989 and 24 per cent in 1990 (Vuong Xuan Tinh, 1994: 27). These are the official statistics of local authorities based on birth certificates. Considering the number of people who break the two-child limit and thus cannot get a birth certificate, we may suppose that the real rate is higher. According to many studies, for instance in Hai Van commune (Ha Nam Ninh province), Tam Son (Ha Bac province) in 1990, a majority of respondents said that they would accept the two-child limit provided they already had at least one son. This is borne out in the research data: among eighteen families with three children in Van Nhan commune, Ha Son Binh province in 1990, most broke the limit in order to try for a son (Nguyen Huu Minh, 1991). Despite the two-child limit and the sanctions imposed on those who break it, the perceived need for a son is a determinant factor in the birth rate of Vietnamese families.

In An Hiep commune, Quynh Phu district, Thai Binh province, many people are ready to pay a fine of 800 kg of paddy (a considerable amount for such a poor country as Vietnam) just to have a son. They would even accept the non-allocation of a share in the communal rice field (Vuong Xuan Tinh, 1994: 27). Of course this applies only to couples who enjoy a reasonable standard of living. This is witnessed by an interview with a 30-year-old woman from Dong Minh commune (Thai Binh province) who had two daughters:

> All the people in the village advise her to give birth to another child! Maybe the third child will be a boy; do not worry, your family's economy is good enough to pay the fine for the third child!
>
> (Johansson *et al.*, 1996: 62)

The more people have improved their standard of living after the socio-economic reforms of 1986, the more difficult it is for the government to control their birth rate. A woman with four daughters declared: 'I shall not stop giving birth to children until I get a son. No penalty can exhaust my reserves of paddy'. Earlier her husband had withdrawn his Communist Party membership to avoid the Party's sanction that would be imposed when she gave birth for the fourth time (Le Nham, 1994). Better economic conditions have created a great challenge to the government's birth control programme. The fact that these people can be punished for breaking the limit, but still receive the sympathy of other villagers, makes the programme's implementation more difficult.

Moreover, the lack of a son can also have a detrimental effect on the husband–wife relationship.

> A family with three daughters in An Hiep commune, Thai Binh province, had been quarrelling continually because the wife was suspicious of the husband having affairs with other women to get a son. The husband even beat the wife. Later she had a son; she was really excited and happy and thereafter the couple lived in harmony. The husband said: 'Now that we have both ordinary rice and glutinous one, there are no longer quarrels and tears in the family.' Villagers noticed that after having a son, the woman was no longer quarrelsome or jealous; moreover she had stopped watching her husband secretly.
>
> (Le Nham, 1994)

Cases like this are quite common in rural Vietnam.

Taking a concubine

As we have just seen, the lack of a son can cause marital conflict. Some wives are forced to accept that their husbands will take a concubine. This is the traditional measure which Gourou already mentioned. Before 1945 polygamy was an institution designed, among other things, to guarantee a male heir. Of course, it was not the case that every man practised polygamy. Whereas rich and upper-class men took many concubines, poor men could not afford to do so. Many poor men could not even afford the bride-price for one woman.

Gourou (1936/1955: 219) stated that only great poverty prevented men from taking concubines. The purpose and meaning of polygamy differed according to the man's social categories, but there was always one common aim: to have a son. Although the two new Laws of Marriage and the Family prohibit polygamy, it has not yet died out as a practice. Perhaps the most marked change in this institution is to be found in the residence arrangements. In the traditional family, co-wives usually lived close to each other. The sleeping arrangement between them is glimpsed in this excerpt of a folk-song lamenting the evils of being a concubine:

> When night-time comes the first wife keeps the husband
> And gives you a mat to sleep alone in the outside room [...].

Scientific evidence affirms this description. 'Quite often the second wife lives in the same house as the first wife. In this case a special building is reserved for her' (Gourou, 1936/1955: 219). Another source confirms this observation: one man in Son Duong village (Vinh Phu province) lived with his two wives (two sisters) in a house at the village school (Luong Van Hy, 1992: 25). That was why it was very easy to collect information about polygamy. According to Luong Van Hy (ibid.: 73), the wealthiest Son Duong villager had seven wives altogether. The second wealthiest man, who also occupied the position of village head, had at least four wives, albeit without children. More precisely, in this case, it was because the first wife had had no son that the man took so many other wives. The above data are on upper-class men. Gourou (1936/1955: 219) provided us with some data about poor people: in a village – incidentally a poor one – he found four concubines out of 500 inhabitants.

Now that the law does not permit husbands to take concubines, the institution has become illegal. Husbands often make separate household arrangements for co-wives, and keep the details secret. For that reason, it is not easy to obtain relevant information. However, it is not the case that polygamy is very rare, as some demographers have stated incorrectly (Banister, 1993: 21). Not being quite familiar with a certain locality, one cannot know for sure about the prevalence of polygamy today. According to one source, in a village of Tam Dao district, Vinh Phu province, forty-four cases of polygamy were identified in the 1977–82 period, including a man with four wives, and four men with three wives each (Duong Thi Thanh Mai, 1985: 67). Probably there are further undisclosed cases.

The change in household arrangement of polygynous marriages is clear. Whereas a man before 1945 had both of his surviving wives and all his sons living with him in a single household, his nephew half a century later has three wives; each of them sets up a separate household upon getting married. One resides in his native village; the other two live in a village about 14 kilometres away, where the man resettled in the mid-1950s (Luong Van Hy, 1989: 744). This case is far from unique.

How do women feel when faced with this situation? In the traditional family, polygyny was taken for granted, although the women involved, especially the first wives, often felt hurt and the concubines felt unhappy. It was forbidden for women to be jealous. The official law considered jealousy to be one of the seven grounds whereby a husband might repudiate his wife. Nevertheless, women strongly opposed the practice of polygyny. Ordinary women would sing a folk-song to describe the evils of becoming a concubine: 'How terrible it is to become a concubine ...'. It was quite common for co-wives to beat each other (*danh ghen*) out of jealousy. That was why a traditional folk-song went: 'Each and every chilli is hot; each and every wife is jealous of her husband'.

Now that the new law is in place, can women prevent men from practising polygyny? That is not simple because men often take concubines secretly, without any ceremony, and without informing their first wives. Meanwhile they still have certain, often minimal obligations to their first wives. Of course there may be trouble for a man who has two separate households if one wife finds out about the other. Very often a first wife has to come to terms with polygamy. If she 'overreacted' (in her husband's view) to that, he would abandon her completely, and settle with the concubine. As for the legal solution, we have already seen in Chapter Two that despite the official opposition to polygyny, there is no legal recourse unless a female party to one of the relationships makes an official complaint.

It should be recalled that a lot of women, particularly in the countryside, do not even know their legal rights. Others may know, but do not dare to protest for fear of losing their husbands completely. In a society where wives abandoned by their husbands are made to feel ashamed, and spinsterhood is still a social stigma, it is not simple for women to oppose their husbands' polygamy, as is shown in the following case study.

 A 40-year-old woman, a salt-maker in Dong Minh commune, Thai Binh province, had five children, all of them daughters. She wanted to bear more children but her husband intended to take a concubine. In response to her opposition, he reasoned: 'Your mother had only two daughters; that was why your father took three wives. Even if I took a concubine now, I would still have fewer wives than he had.' Not knowing how to argue with him, the only thing she could do was to cry.

(Mai Huy Bich, 1993: 32)

Thus the absence of male progeny has remained the greatest worry for the wife, even though medical research has shown that the sex of the unborn child in part depends on the husband at the time of conception. As long as she has not given birth to at least one male child, the wife's position in the family remains insecure.

A survey in 1988 showed that in Dai Dong commune, Thach That district, on the outskirts of Hanoi, everyone interviewed stressed the need for a family to have at least one male child. It was discovered that all local men without male progeny had taken concubines with public approval, in spite of the legal prohibition. It was also explained that a wife without a male child is in a perplexing situation. She is on the horns of a dilemma; she must accept either a concubine or an adopted son. If her husband takes a concubine, whether it be either with the first wife's reluctant agreement or active encouragement, the first wife is expected by local custom to bring up the concubine's children as if they were her own, and her children must look after their half-brothers or -sisters. When the concubine's parents die, the first wife must hold proper funerals for them, just as she would for her own parents. Yet paradoxically, local women who have no sons say to one another: *Be con chong hon bong chau ho* [Better to carry the child that your husband has (after he took a concubine) than the adopted child] (Mai Huy Bich, 1993: 32). This means that they would prefer to raise a concubine's child rather than an adopted child. Why?

One reason is that if they accept the concubines, their husbands will not abandon them. Moreover, when the concubines give birth to sons, the first wives are regarded as social mothers of those sons. That is why in some areas, they are called 'senior mothers'. A son born of a concubine is duty-bound to show proper respect to his father's first wife. In that case, the first wives can keep their social prestige as women. If they adopt a son, the grown-up adopted son is often prone to usurp power in the family, misappropriate its property, and mistreat them and their daughters.

This is not all. An old woman in Dong Hoang commune, Tien Hai district, Thai Binh province, whose husband died in the South during the American war and left her as a widow with four daughters, now lives alone. In the past, whereas men who did not have a son took concubines, she and her husband did not do so. In fact, they were hesitant for a moment, weighing alternatives. If he took a concubine, he would be expelled from the Communist Party (both of them were Party members) which at that time carried a social stigma. They thought that as communists, they should set a moral example of observing monogamy according to the new Law of Marriage and the Family. So they gave priority to their role as communists over family considerations. However, now she thinks that they should have done the opposite. When the interviewer asked her how many people in her village had only daughters and no sons, she replied that nobody else was in the same situation. All the men who had no sons took concubines.

> You know, there were even men who withdrew from the Communist Party membership, and resigned from positions to take concubines ... It is a pity that it was only my husband who sacrificed everything for the Communist Party, for revolution by not doing so.
>
> (Mai Huy Bich, 1993: 33)

This elderly woman then came to regret that her husband did not take a concubine. The fact that, despite the all the communist propaganda, she thinks in much the same way today as others in her village means that the propaganda did not have a long-lasting effect. One has to be a woman to understand her feelings when faced with the option of polygyny. One has to be a Vietnamese woman to understand how dearly she would be ready to pay (coming to terms with polygyny) in order to have a son.

Adoption

As in the past, adoption is still one of the solutions for families who have no son. The adoption of children follows a different pattern from that in the West. There are two purposes of adoption: one is to continue the lineage, another is to secure additional manpower. In the former, the choice is limited within the husband's nephews because they belong to his lineage. It is only they who can be considered, and one of them is chosen as the adopted son. In the latter, the adoption of children who do not belong to the husband's lineage is merely aimed at securing additional labourers. The scope of choice in this case is not limited.

The desirability of sons is also evident here, especially if one compares the patterns of adoption of Vietnamese infants by Vietnamese couples and Western ones. A policy of maternity hospitals is to give priority to Vietnamese families who wish to adopt children, while there is also a supply of baby girls for foreign adoptions. As Goodstein (1996) points out: 'The availability of Vietnamese girl babies for adoption is the result of a nine-to-one preference for male babies among Vietnamese prospective adoptive parents' (Goodstein, 1996).

However, this way of coping with the lack of male childlessness varies from place to place. In Luong Dien village, Dong Co commune, Tien Hai district, Thai Binh province, all sixteen families (out of a total of 400) without male progeny over the past three decades (1954–84) have shown a preference for child adoption (quoted in Mai Huy Bich, 1991). In Dai Dong commune, as mentioned above, wives without male children have chosen the other alternative: to let their husbands take concubines. If blood relationships are emphasised, people prefer this one to adoption.

Other solutions

We do not know for sure whether other traditional solutions to this problem are still being used, or whether they may be persisting in a modified form. One of them was for women to go to places of worship and pray for a son. Since 1945 campaigns against religious superstition have been waged continuously; we do not have available data on whether this practice still persists. However, newspapers still report stories on this kind of activity. One by Nguyen Tri Thuc (1995) centred on a couple that already had four daughters. Being keen to have a son, they visited various places of worship to pray for a son, but all to no avail: the fifth child was a daughter again.

In the traditional family, if the all the above-mentioned measures came to nothing, the husband might accept that he was sterile (this was admitted only after he taken had many concubines, and they all proved childless). In such a case there was one last resort – for the wife to have sex with someone else so that she could get pregnant (see Chapter Three). This shows how strong the desire was to have a child (particularly a son) in the traditional family.

Lacking empirical evidence about this, one can only assume that in the contemporary family this solution is no longer applicable thanks to the establishment and expansion of the health-care network. However, in the award-winning novel *Ben khong chong* [River watering place of unmarried women] by Duong Huong (1991), knowing that her husband – a war veteran – was keen to have a child, but unable to do so, a female doctor secretly looks for sex with a stranger in the hope of getting pregnant. At the beginning the stranger thinks she is a prostitute; that hurts her feelings very much. She fails to get pregnant, but does not dare to repeat the experience. It is worth pointing out that Vietnamese critics and reviewers do not regard this episode as unrealistic. One commented that it is so touching and believable that it moves the reader to tears (Bui Viet Thang, 1991). Of course we should not demand from a work of literature the same level of accuracy as we would from a real-life case study. However, at least this story reveals that this solution to the problem of childlessness is still within the realms of everyday experience.

In sum, when a couple has no son, the most common solution seems to be either for the wife to go on bearing more children until at least one son is born, or for the husband to take one or more concubines. Although both partners face problems if they lack a son (men may feel that they are filially impious to their lineage, while women feel their marital status is threatened), in both cases it is the women who bear the main burden of striving for a son and in this sense, who suffer most. The traditional view that regards reproduction as exclusively woman's business is still firmly held, and strongly influences women's reproductive behaviour – and their sufferings if they fail to produce a son.

The burden of the practical implementation of the birth control programme then rests mainly on women's shoulders. That also produces health problems of different kinds for many women, even for those who have already had a son. Declining fertility is mainly due to the availability of female contraceptive measures, and to the acceptance and wide availability of abortion. To put it another way, it is women who pay dearly for the reduction in number of births.

Meanwhile, current social changes have led to men becoming less involved in the whole process of childbirth. One of these changes relates to the place of birth. In the traditional family, childbirth took place at home (whether the home of the mother or grandmother) and nowhere else, because of a common belief which held that birth brought bad luck to people around the mother. So the mother was surrounded by her family; the husband somehow witnessed the painful delivery, though he might not be allowed to witness the birth itself.

If it proved a difficult delivery, the husband had to help his wife in a symbolic way. For instance, he might have to shin up an areca palm and slide down the trunk; climbing a ladder set up erect by passing through the small space between two rungs (Toan Anh, n.d.: 33). The famous novel *Buoc duong cung* [The impasse] by Nguyen Cong Hoan (1938) tells a similar story. The husband 'went into the yard up to the dilapidated pigsty, took in both hands the stakes of the door and shook them until he snatched away one by one all the four of them' (quoted and translated in Nguyen Cong Hoan, 1989). Interestingly enough, the novel also describes a traditional practice whereby during her painful labour, the wife cursed her husband (using really bad language) for causing all her sufferings.

The husband for his part accepted all the abuse stoically without any reaction. It was accepted for a woman in the throes of labour to release all her pent-up feelings of anger, unhappiness and dissatisfaction on her husband.

However, during the period of the 1960s–80s, almost all women gave birth in health-care centres and hospitals. According to a survey conducted by Nguyen Thi Thin (1989) among sixty-six women, in Duc Tu commune, Dong Anh district, on the outskirts of Hanoi, 100 per cent of the women aged below 30 gave birth at health-care centres. By comparison, 80 per cent of the older generation (women who at the time of the survey were about 60 years of age) had given birth at home. The survey was carried out by an amateur and its data may not be totally accurate. Moreover it does not reveal the difference between the periods before and after 1945, since most of the 60-year-old women must have given birth after 1945, and in the same place (home) as previous generations. Nevertheless, the data at least reveal one definite change: since the 1960s the act of giving birth is routinely hidden from men's view. This means that few men have the chance to hear and see their wives in labour. Men are 'sequestered' – in the words of Giddens.

In his book Giddens (1991) deals with the changes in the modern world that have the effect of removing basic aspects of life experience, especially moral crises, from the regularities of day-to-day life. He uses the term 'sequestration of experience' to refer to connected processes of concealment that set apart the routines of ordinary life from the following phenomena: madness; criminality; sickness and death; sexuality; and nature. In the premodern world, these phenomena were not concealed. He examines this change in terms of its effects on self-identity, but that is not our concern here. Nor does he mention childbirth in the above phenomena. Nonetheless, to some extent we can apply his approach to the change we are examining now.

In the traditional family, the presence and symbolic help of the husband were comforting to the woman in labour; he was aware of her pains and fears. Giving birth is a very difficult, even dangerous moment in a woman's life. That explains the proverb: 'Pregnancy and delivery open the door to the tomb' (the woman in labour is exposed to complications that may cost her life). Nowadays though, the birth does not take place at home, but in hospitals or health-care centres, where medical facilities can be concentrated, and where those who are disqualified from participating in 'orthodox social activities' (Giddens' words) are sequestered. This sequestration of experience has some consequences in terms of the concealment from general view of a certain crucial life experience – giving birth. Men become alienated from a fundamental existential issue. Not really understanding the pain of giving birth, men are more likely to urge women to have more children to satisfy their own male motivations, no matter how much suffering this inflicts on the woman.

Due to the deterioration of the health-care system after the renovation policy, there has been a tendency towards home births since the early 1990s. However, there is no evidence to suggest that men are resuming the supportive role that they adopted in the past with regard to the wife's labour and childbirth.

MOTIVATIONS OF STRIVING FOR SON(S)

Why is it so important to have a son? Apart from the joys and satisfactions of parenthood, which should not be underestimated but can be applicable to daughters as well, one may explain the preference for sons from three different viewpoints: economic, care of old parents, and ancestor worship.

The economic value of son(s)

First, one may explain the strong preference for son(s) in terms of their economic roles, i.e. what the benefits and costs of having son(s) are. It is argued that it is rational for the bulk of the population to have large families to share in manual labour. Sons with their physical strength are a source of manpower. Moreover, compared to a daughter, who might be considered an unprofitable investment because she will leave the family when she marries, a son, when he marries, brings in a daughter-in-law, an extra labourer. This view is held by some researchers, especially after the recent reforms, when the family regained its function as production unit.

However, according to a survey in Cat Que commune, Hoai Duc district, Ha Tay province in 1990, only 37.5 per cent of respondents mentioned a son's economic role as the motivation for them to have sons (Le Ngoc Van, 1991). Some interviews held in 1991 in Di Nau commune, Thach That district, on the outskirts of Hanoi help to identify the economic role of sons. Local parents are expected, in conformity with a prevailing custom, to bear the main financial burdens in their sons' marriages, to help their married sons with building houses, and to provide them with some furniture. The more sons one has, the heavier one's financial responsibility towards them. In fact, many parents began to fulfil their duties in this respect well in advance, when their sons were very young; now those parents are old, but they have not totally discharged their obligations yet (Mai Huy Bich, 1993: 29). The economic burden of having one or more sons may be one aspect.

But what about the other aspect, the economic rewards of having sons? Interviewees also said that sons are no more economically productive than daughters. One respondent of the 1992 survey was a peasant woman, aged 41, who had four children of both sexes, and who lived in Dong Hoang commune, Thai Binh province. She said 'Sons do not produce more than daughters; on the contrary, the latter sometimes prove to be better than the former in economic activities' (Mai Huy Bich, 1993: 29). So it is not generally agreed that sons always produce more than daughters; but they do consume much more than daughters. In other words, the cost of having sons may very well outweigh the benefits. Given that fact, what is the motivation behind the preference for sons?

Care for old parents

It may be explained that the patrilocal model and its variant play a role here. As in the traditional family, contemporary marriage requires the bride to leave her parents, and go to live with the groom's family. The crucial point was not the residence model, but the social security system related to this model. From then on the wife's main duties of care for the older generation are towards her parents-in-law, not her natal parents (Toan Anh, n.d.:153–154). It is necessary to emphasise this point because of the general prevalence of village endogamy not only in the traditional family, but also in the contemporary one (of course at different levels). This is confirmed by both folklore and scientific studies.

In the traditional family, village endogamy was common. There was even a saying in some localities: *Lay cho trong lang hon lay nguoi sang thien ha* [Better to marry your villager, who might be lowly like a dog, than a person of high social status, who is from outside your village] (ibid.: 202). Different studies reveal the same thing. According to Luong Van Hy (1992: 57), available data reveal that the rate of village endogamy in the pre-1945 rural communities reached at least 80 per cent. The author does not specify how he gets the rate, but he states that this pattern persists into the present era. In Viet Hung village, Vinh Phu province, all but one of the thirteen marriages registered in the first half of 1987 were endogamous. Even in the village of Bat Trang (which is well-known for its ceramics factories and is situated near to Hanoi), households have to employ a large number of villagers throughout the district because of labour shortages, but 59.4 per cent of the 320 registered marriages in the 1985–87 period were endogamous (Luong Van Hy, 1989: 747).

The survey 1992 in Dong Minh and Dong Hoang communes, Thai Binh province, showed similar results. Almost two-thirds of 206 women married men from the same communes; one-third were born in nearby communes then moved to their husband's commune; only five women (2 per cent) married men from other districts (Le Thi Nham Tuyet *et al.*, 1994a: 60). The high degree of village endogamy allows for the considerable physical proximity of couples to both sets of parents. However, after marriage, the daughter's main responsibility is towards her parents-in-law.

Available data paint different pictures about the family's generational structure. In a commune of Ha Nam Ninh province, 9 per cent of families are three-generational (Luong Van Hy, 1989: 750). In the two communes of Thai Binh province, almost three-quarters of the families are two-generational households; therefore the percentage of three-generational ones is about 24 per cent (Le Thi Nham Tuyet *et al.*, 1994a: 58). Some estimates put the three-generational family rate at 20–35 per cent, or even at 40 per cent (Luong Van Hy, 1989: 750). However, those estimates must be interpreted with great caution because we do not know whether or not the following factor has been taken into consideration: a young couple might live under the same roof as the parents-in-law, but cook and eat separately, i.e., they have a separate budget. They might consider themselves either a separate household or a shared household.

Thus the nuclear family is common. One thing we must not forget is that although married sons frequently live in their nuclear families, they keep up a close relationship with their parents, both giving and receiving help on a reciprocal basis. That is due to two factors. First, until very recently, the household registration system bound people to their village or city of their birth, i.e., there were many new limits on where married sons in the countryside could live. They could not move wherever they liked, therefore they often established the households of their own not far from their natal home, in their area of their birth. Second, it should be emphasised that at present the family is still the only institution providing old people with care, and young couples with help. Chapter Two dealt with the acute shortage of a child-care network. In this sphere, not to mention other domains, grandparents remain indispensable helpers. As for their needs, it must be said that no systematic attempt to resolve one of the biggest problems of reproductive process (care for the elderly) has ever been made on a societal basis.

In cities, retired people still have to earn their living because of inadequate pension provisions: in 1990 over 60 per cent of 238 retired people in Hanoi confirmed this (Bui Nguyen Phuong Linh, 1993: 17). In rural areas, during the collectivisation period, the elderly received some welfare from the co-operatives (a fixed amount of paddy for every crop). However, since the renovation policy, this very limited welfare has been reduced considerably, into an insignificant amount. They receive from the co-operatives just a piece of land, which is smaller than that allocated to able-bodied workers, and several kilograms of paddy per month (ibid.: 19–20). In An Dien village, Hai Hung province, in 1991 (ibid.: 18), old people revealed the sources of their income as follows:

Table 5: Source of income for old people in An Dien village, Hai Hung province, 1991

Source of income	Percentage of respondents
Farming	95.7
Breeding (livestock)	53.2
Financial assistance from children	38.3
Gardening	21.3
Assistance from cooperatives	10.6

Source: Bui Nguyen Phuong Linh, 1993

The survey reveals that the elderly have to attain an unusual degree of self-reliance in order to survive. Nonetheless, as the author points out, the old people are often unable to carry out the farming tasks themselves, even though this is the main source of income for the overwhelming majority of them. Instead, they have to ask for their children's help (ibid.: 19) which means that children play a crucial role in supporting them, either in cash or in practical help with farming. When the old get sick, it is only their spouses and children who take care of them.

On the one hand, the patrilocal pattern and its variant are continuing to be taken for granted. During the American war, although the need for manpower was enormous, the government accepted a rule according to which a son, if he was the only one of his family, was exempt from military service. He was allowed to stay at home to take care of his parents.[2] This continuation of the pre-1945 custom in soldier recruitment (Phan Ke Binh, 1915/1992: 152) bears testimony to the importance of the son's role. Asked where they live after marriage, Vietnamese village women think that is a very strange question. They reply: 'With our in-laws of course, where else would we live?' (Wiegersma, 1988: 248).

The fact that patrilocal pattern and its variant are taken for granted is confirmed by another case: in order to reduce the conversion of agricultural fields into private land for newly formed households during the late 1980s, the administration of a village decided not to grant requests for new household land until a couple had more than three daughters-in-law in the same residential unit (Luong Van Hy, 1989: 750). At present, patrilocal residence and its variant are being affected by the contemporary circumstances, due to collectivised land, overpopulation, and residential shortage. However, married couples still retain a close relationship with the husband's parents.

Recently two researchers (Hirschman and Vu Manh Loi, 1994) conducted a survey and rejected the existence of the patrilocal pattern (they did not see its variant), which they identified with the Confucian family. Nonetheless, their reasoning is not convincing. First, they did not ask where couples lived after marriage; they put their questions this way: 'When you were growing up, did you ever live in the same village or neighbourhood with either your father's or mother's family?', and: 'When you were growing up, did any of your grandparents or other relatives live with you?' They found that 80 per cent of respondents in a Red River Delta village never lived with relatives. The researchers were not aware, or did not take into consideration, that they asked only about the moment when the respondents 'were growing up' (an indefinite period), not earlier. It has to be recognised that the family is a process, not a static structure, and as such the residential group formed by that process varies according to the stage in the development of the family cycle.

Second, their sample included 'all persons between the ages of 15 and 65 in every household'. This means that they questioned not only married people, but also unmarried ones; not only young people, but also the elderly. For a number of respondents, to answer the above questions is to recall the remote past, related not directly to their marital experience, but to the presence or absence of their relatives. Even if their memory was accurate, that would not guarantee the reliability of their data. Moreover, this heterogeneous sample was then compared to the Chinese data for women in the 15–49 age range who were married, or who had once been married. Each woman in the Chinese survey was asked: 'whether she lived with her own husband's parents after marriage, and the length of this co-residence' (Lavely and Ren, 1992). In the end the researchers reached a conclusion about the absolute difference between the Chinese family and the Vietnamese one! In other words, those researchers compared things that are so different that there is no comparison between them.

As a matter of fact, newly-married couples in rural areas often start their marital life in the husband's family for many reasons. In order to create a household of their own they need substantial economic resources, which are not always forthcoming during the first stage of the family cycle.[3] As the data provided by Vo Phuong Lan (1994) have shown, a great many young couples initially co-habit with the husband's parents until, with the help of the parents and other close relatives, they are able to acquire a separate dwelling.

A second reason for the patrilocal residence pattern is the emphasis in Vietnamese society on the continuance of lineage through marriage. The newly-married couple is very much a part of the kinship system, and they have to be able to perform the tasks allotted to them. By living with the husband's parents, they begin to understand the system of which they are part. Some period of time later, both sides agree to the division of the household. The survey conducted in Dong Minh and Dong Hoang communes, Thai Binh province, confirms that.

In this survey, the question was put directly about where the couples lived after marriage. The overwhelming majority among 206 married women (93.7 per cent) said they started married life in the husband's family (Vo Phuong Lan, 1994: 31), so only the remaining 6.3 per cent established separate households immediately after marriage. There was often a transition period when the young couple continued to live under the same roof as the husband's parents, but did their cooking separately. In the fullness of time they then built their own houses (for instance, after the birth of the first child), usually in the same compound as that of the husband's parents.

One of the women described her own household formation: after she got married she went to live with her husband's parents. Initially they would all eat together. Six months later, the young couple had their own cooking area, but still lived under the same roof as the parents. After two years, the couple was given a plot of land to construct their own house:

> We could build a small two-room house with thatched roof, just enough for us to live in. Now we have bought bricks and tiles to rebuild our thatched house into a brick-walled one.
>
> (Le Thi Nham Tuyet *et al.*, 1994a)

This is a typical household formation pattern. However, if their grown-up children were asked the same questions as the ones put by the two researchers, they would reply that there were no extra-nuclear relatives living in their family when they were growing up. The reason is that the stage during which their parents co-habited with the grandparents was over; and the results would lead the researchers to incorrect conclusions about the residence pattern.

On the other hand, even if sons live separately, or far away from parents, strong intergenerational bonds are still maintained. The continued importance of kinship outside the nuclear family derives from the fact that this kinship provides the main, if not only, means of support and service which they cannot obtain elsewhere. This support is necessary not only in critical life situations (sickness, death, the problems of old age, taking care of young children of working mothers, and so on), but also in everyday life. The exchange of aid is important in shaping family behaviour. An examination of the rights and duties that subsist between sons' families and their parents is essential to a good understanding of the behaviour of its members.

Probably Hirschman and Vu Manh Loi understood the Vietnamese nuclear family from a Western-centred viewpoint, as being isolated: it does not form an integral part of a wider system of kinship relationship. They have reduced the relationship between parents and married sons to the only indicator 'seeing parents'; they have not taken into consideration the reciprocation of services. In other words, the researchers have not understood what is behind the visits, *viz.* their deeper significance. Thus in their eyes the inter-relationships between the Vietnamese nuclear family and relatives outside it are seen only in terms of quantitative frequency of contact (the couples from the nuclear family see their parents on a daily or weekly basis). In this way, the difference, if any, between the Vietnamese nuclear family and the Western one has been obscured.

For instance, in the late 1950s Willmott and Young conducted research in Woodford, a largely middle-class London suburb, and found that, although kin were more geographically dispersed compared to the less affluent/poorer Bethnal Green, fairly regular contacts were maintained. In Woodford, 30 per cent of married people had seen their mothers on the previous day compared to 43 per cent in Bethnal Green (Willmott and Young, 1960: 33). A comparison of these data with those presented by Hirschman and Vu Manh Loi, tells us little, if anything, about the difference between the English and the Vietnamese context and culture. 'But perhaps the most fascinating set of questions, sociologically speaking, deals with the question of meaning', as Morgan (1985: 163) has said. In this regard, it is clear that sociologically the meanings attached to the visits are not the same even if the frequency of visits is identical. In their meetings Vietnamese couples may discuss with extranuclear relatives (their parents) about very important issues of their own. In other words, to understand the behaviour of people it is essential to use the approach that gives the researchers an access to the meanings that guide that behaviour. As Hammersley and Atkinson (1983: 9) point out, this cannot be done by following standardised procedures.

Thus in the study of Hirschman and Vu Manh Loi, data have been collected but the need to understand their socio-cultural characteristics has been somewhat neglected. These researchers have criticised other scholars, who wrote about patrilocal customs in Vietnam, for having 'only a very limited body of empirical data available' but tending 'to rely on impressionistic evidence to make broad generalisations'. In my view, how to avoid reducing the subtle theoretical concept to a crude indicator is the most serious problem here. Moreover, how to avoid overemphasising the quantitative approach at the expense of the qualitative one is no less important.

Even so, it cannot be denied that more than 75 per cent of Vietnamese respondents with living parents saw them daily or at least weekly; and men seemed 'to keep in closer contact with parents than women' (Hirschman and Vu Manh Loi, 1994). However, the above researchers do not explain why; neither do they want to recognise that patrilineage is still more emphasised in Vietnam at present. Moreover, they state: 'This gender difference should not obscure the dominant pattern that both men and women maintained a high level of contact with their parents.' Not understanding fully the meaning of 'contact', those researchers have identified contact with the caring responsibility and the giving of practical help. They are not aware that daughters may keep in regular contact with their parents, but cannot take care of them to the same extent as they must of their parents-in-law. If it is the case that both men and women assume a high degree of care for their parents, parents who have only daughters would not be lonely. By this assertion, those researchers have denied the loneliness of people who have no son (which I shall deal with later).

As mentioned earlier, in the Vietnamese view it is sons, not daughters, who are expected to be responsible for old parents. In fact the sons themselves may not personally assume the care; often this role is handed over to their wives. Sons may live separately, or far away from parents, but they are still responsible for them. This remains little changed even in the age of mass migration. Villagers in An Hiep commune, Thai Binh province, point out that if something happens any time in one's family, one just sends a telegram; however far away one's son may live, he will be back very soon. Nevertheless, it takes a long time for one's daughter to do so, as she has to ask for permission of her husband's family, and that depends on the family's actual conditions. Even if a daughter wants to visit her natal parents, she has to get the permission of her husband's family (Le Nham, 1994).

For that reason, having no son can be a cause of old people's loneliness.

> The old communist woman (mentioned above) lost her husband during the American war, and has four daughters, but now lives alone. The interview with her and her daughters shows her situation. When the interviewer asked why she did not live with one of her four sons-in-law, her first daughter who was also present in the interview said that according to a common belief,
>
> > Your son is your blood relation. He may quarrel with you, but after that everything is all right. As for a son-in-law, he is not your blood relation; how can you live together with him?
>
> Replying to the question: 'What about your daughters? Do they want you to live with them?', the old woman said:
>
> > They asked me to do so several times, but I told them: 'That is your wish, but your husband's view is not so. How can I bear the situation in which I live with my son-in-law, and during every meal there will be many more tears than rice in my food?'.
>
> (Mai Huy Bich, 1993: 33–34)

This interview was a group one, thanks to which we know not only what the old woman thinks of her actual circumstances, but also her fears as to what she imagines might have happened had she gone to live with one of her daughters. She has a complex about having no son; she imagines her unhappiness if she were living with her sons-in-law. Nevertheless, her loneliness is only too real, not imagined.

Her case is far from unique. Many people feel the same way as she does, but to different extents. It is common for old people to have a complex about living with their son-in-law, no matter however good he may be. As for your own sons, however badly they may treat you, you still feel more comfortable living with them. That in part explains why people like to have sons as their main, if not only, source of security in their old age. While relatively young during the child-bearing period, parents are already thinking about their coming old age; this is why they want to have sons.

It could be said that if people in the modern Western family take rather a narrow view of reproduction as not being related to old people, that is because the situation there is quite different from that in Vietnam. For both, reproduction has remained a vital process. However, the modern Western family has had 'considerable success in transferring responsibility for the organisation of reproduction out into the public realm presided over by the modern state' (Robertson, 1991: 128). Meanwhile, the Vietnamese one is left to its own devices in coping with the basic challenges of reproduction, and is still heavily dependent on its own security mechanism. To put it in a simple way, old people in Vietnam up until now have had to rely on their children, above all their sons.

On the other hand, not all sons take good care of old parents. Folk experience has summed that up in a popular saying: 'One mother can raise ten children, but ten children cannot even feed one old mother.' The following fragment from an interview with an elderly woman, her husband, and her relatives in Dong Minh commune, Thai Binh province, in 1991, bears this out.

 In their opinion, when considering whether a son or a daughter cares better for their parents, it must be recognised that in both sexes there are those who care for their parents well.

> Nonetheless, it is unusual for a daughter to look after parents ... People place great hope in the male children because they continue the lineage. However, many people suffer much more from having sons than do those who have daughters .... The tradition is that old people should live with their sons, but many sons treat their parents badly.

Nevertheless, they all suppose that it is absolutely necessary to have both glutinous and ordinary rice, as the saying goes. In the words of the woman's husband, 'if you do not have any son, in the future, when you die, there will be nobody who kow-tows before your coffin'.

(Mai Huy Bich, 1993: 30)

This group discussion reveals that there is no guarantee that sons will take good care of old parents; 'Many sons treat their parents badly', a relative of the woman puts it. So why are people keen to have sons? Probably they hope that their sons might not be too bad. Moreover, the discussion also casts light on one of their motivations. The man's answer shows that if you do not have sons, 'there will be no body who kow-tows before your coffin' when you die. In another interview, an elderly woman had three sons who died in the war. She was living with her youngest son, but did not have a grandson at the time. She said:

> People have to be aware of their line of descent, and continue it. Who practises ancestor worship? Daughters cannot do that. In spite of the likelihood that sons may ill-treat you, it is absolutely necessary to have sons.
>
> (Ibid.: 31)

A man in another interview said: 'When someone is keen to have sons, nobody thinks of the sons' economic contribution; the main thing one thinks of is one's lineage' (ibid.: 28). All these interviews reveal that a vital motivation in the striving for sons is that only a male child can fulfil the duties of ancestor worship.

The son's role in ancestor worship

What is ancestor worship? Why is it so important? What is the link between it and the family? How do people worship their ancestors? To answer these questions is to venture beyond the topics of reproduction and family, into the realm of Vietnamese culture. It is impossible to understand the Vietnamese family without understanding the Vietnamese culture. To explain reproduction, we have to look at the last stage of the life course, at the parents' death, i.e., the last rite of passage for them.

Ancestor worship is based on the conception of lineage. In the Vietnamese view, lineage is a human community, but one of a special kind that could be called a diachronic and generational community. This community stems from a remote ancestor, whose name may be either recorded in the lists of ancestors or transmitted orally. A Vietnamese folk-song goes: 'Men have ancestors, just as trees have roots and rivers have sources.' This line of descent extends through the present into the future. In this sense, the lineage is more than a group of individuals; it is a continuing entity carrying on from generation to generation.

The importance of the community called lineage in comparison to the individual person lies in the following point. In a patrilineal lineage, a man is not an independent person, an individual in the full sense of the word, but a member of a given lineage. He is the personification of this lineage at present. His existence is only a link in the communal chain. He must remember his ancestors, practise ancestor worship, and continue his lineage by having at least one son to guarantee that someone will fulfil in the future his present obligations. It is only a male child who can ensure the continuation of the lineage in two senses; first, only he can practise ancestor worship. This cannot be done by female descendants who are treated as members of their husbands' families, and are not allowed to have access to the ancestral temple. Second, it is only a son who can ensure the continuation of the bloodline because of the prevailing patrilineage. If a man should die without male progeny, his whole lineage, including his ancestors and his unborn descendants, would die with him.

Why is ancestor worship so important? In Vietnam, it is believed that death does not mean a complete end to everything. By contrast, the soul lives on after the body's death. Moreover, after their death, people maintain ties with their descendants in a certain way. To some extent, the narrowing interaction is probably the most marked difference between death and life.

Let us examine a concrete link in the communal chain of the lineage – the parent–children relationship. The parent–child dependence continues after the death of the parents. Death does not release a son from his duty to his parents; it merely alters the form of this duty. His duty of worship to his parents starts from their death. In the funeral procession, sons of the deceased wear straw hats and walk on canes, while daughters and daughters-in-law lie in the courtyard in the path of the coffin. At his father's funeral, the son wears coarse material and walks on bamboo cane. At the mother's funeral, he walks on an erythrina cane and walks backwards before the casket. It is essential to have at least one son who walks on cane before one's coffin. The graveside must be known and remembered well by the family members. It must be taken care of and cleaned annually during the Thanh Minh Festival (the third lunar month).

A Vietnamese is socialised into old age and death by attending the funerals of others, and by preparing his own coffin. He knows in advance exactly what will happen to him after his death. Having at least one son helps to alleviate the fearful feelings of death, and to reduce the most traumatic experience of the human condition.

Sons must continue their obligations of worship to their dead parents. One of the fundamental purposes of ancestor worship is to ensure the happiness of dead parents in the afterlife. While alive, parents are served and respected; when dead, they are served and worshipped. Their other-worldly existence needs the same things as this worldly existence does. If the parents need food, clothing, shelter, and money when they are alive, they would continue to need that when they are dead. By practising ancestor worship, children supply their dead parents with these essentials. In celebrating death anniversaries of their parents, children 'transfer' goods from this world to the next. This transfer is achieved by burning. Paper clothes and paper money (specially printed notes for afterworld use) could all be sent on to the dead parents in this way. Real food is not burnt, but merely offered to the dead parents.

Dead parents need the worship of their children in order to be comfortable and happy. A soul with no descendants is doomed to eternal wandering in the World of Shadow because it would not receive homage. Children who do not observe the sacrifice are considered as committing a serious crime of impiety. They are not dutiful because the souls of their dead parents have to make a precarious living as wandering beggars.

However, the relationship between dead parents and their children is mutual interdependence. For their part, dead parents are believed to become the protectors of their descendants. In return for the sacrifices and services of the living, the dead parents render such blessings to their descendants as are in their supernatural power. Moreover, they might warn their children about some impending unhappy events so that their children could escape. To request intercession for success in business or on behalf of a sick child, sacrifices are offered, and prayers are said to the souls of the dead parents. To give their supernatural support, the dead parents are informed on occasions of family joy or sorrow, such as weddings, birth of a new-born child, success in an examination, or serious sickness or death (Mai Huy Bich, 1991).

Such an outlook on life and death exerts a profound influence on the family, determines many of its characteristics and makes its structure very close. While in this world, people live with their family and lineage members, their villagers; but after death, they are believed to interact with their living family members only. It is believed that it is only the blood ties that can help to pave the way for the communication between this world and the next. That is why ancestor worship is carried out first and foremost in the family. Moreover, only sons can get access to the souls of the dead parents. If a couple has no son, then their daughters, especially the eldest one, can worship them; but that is not a good solution. Pham Dinh Ho, a Confucian scholar of the nineteenth century, even believed that the spirit of a dead man would not accept offerings from women and their descendants (Yu Insun, 1990: 84).

The interaction between the dead and their living family members is not limited to the periodic annual occasions of ancestor worship (death anniversaries, New Year, Thanh Minh Festival, the 15th day of the seventh month according to the lunar calendar, and so on), but can also occur on other occasions that are often marked by rites of passage. These rites help people in the transition from one stage to another in the life-cycle. This transition is exiting one role and assuming another simultaneously. Although an incumbent may get some anticipatory socialisation into the new role before exiting the old one, the transitions are very difficult (Ebaugh, 1988). To overcome their difficulties in every rite of passage, offerings are prepared for the purpose, among other things, of informing their ancestors about the event. They want the ancestors' blessing for the occasion.

Ancestor worship requires the installation of an altar table in the home. Within many Vietnamese homes, in the very centre of the house, there is an altar dedicated to the ancestors. Moreover, it is imperative to perform sacrifices before the altar on the important occasions mentioned above. The practice of worship is based on the principle of male members of the family, on the eldest son. In the traditional family, he had to bear all expenses for celebrating death anniversaries. That was why he received the greatest part of property handed down by his parents, mainly land called *huong hoa dien* [land for incense and fire]. However, that does not mean other sons are excluded. In principle, they have to go to the eldest son's house with their families to attend the ceremony, although they can place a very simple altar in their own houses.

To sum up, we can say that one of the main meanings of reproduction for Vietnamese people is to bear sons who will be able to practise ancestor worship. How do the recent social changes affect ancestor worship? In the past, according to Dao Duy Anh (1938/1992: 229), every family had an ancestral altar in the centre of the house. That may not be an exaggeration because everyone did their best to get an ancestral altar at home, however poor they were, and however simple it might be.

Since 1945 though, government policies have been introduced to discourage the practice of ancestor worship. On the one hand, the land collectivisation programme deprives families of ancestral cult funds, i.e., lands for incense and fire. On the other hand, the government issued numerous directives against idealism and superstition. It is unknown what evidence the Norwegian researcher Tønnesson (1993: 57) has in mind when he supposes that Confucianism and communism have ancestor worship in common.

In fact the communists promote atheism and materialism as the official ideology. For a very long time, they strictly criticised those members of their Party who practised ancestor worship. Campaigns against idealism and superstition were launched continuously in the name of national salvation and wartime economy, as well as so-called socialist reconstruction after the American war. A new ritual system according to which every ritual must be simplified was imposed to replace the old one. A common change was that in many villages, during funerals, sons no longer wore straw hats and walked on cane; daughters and daughters-in-law no longer lay in the courtyard in the path of the funeral procession (Luong Van Hy, 1993: 282).

That is not all. Following the instructions of the propaganda apparatus, and in many cases at their own instigation, many families arranged a so-called 'fatherland altar' in the very centre of their houses instead of the ancestral altar. Some houses have both types of altar. This fatherland altar may include the national flag of Vietnam and a portrait of Ho Chi Minh. Different sources mention this new development. In Hoai Thi village, Ha Bac province, in 70 per cent of the households of the eldest sons the ancestral altars disappeared; pictures of the deceased were also absent. However, many households had large pictures of Ho Chi Minh in central positions, instead of the ancestral altar (Luong Van Hy, 1993: 275). This is a moderate estimation. Hoang Van Chi (1964: 34) even claimed that a photograph Ho Chi Minh was placed on every family altar; perhaps the author somehow exaggerated.

In spite of that, after 1975 and the end of the American war, the traditional ritual system was gradually restored by the people. In Tam Son commune, Tien Son district, Ha Bac province in 1983, 79 per cent of questioned families said they kept an ancestral altar at home and regularly performed the acts of worship. In Dong Co commune, Thai Binh province, 99.8 per cent of the interviewed families formally marked the ancestral anniversaries in different ways (Trinh Thi Quang, 1984). If the data are correct, they bear witness to the persistent vitality of ancestor worship. After the communist regime launched its renovation policies in the late 1980s, ancestor worship began to regain its public support.

Why is ancestor worship so vital and persistent? There are many explanations. Some people consider it to be a religion unto itself. If so, it must have those characteristics inherent in every religion; but in fact, there are no such characteristics in ancestor worship. Moreover, almost all religions in the world are undergoing secularisation, but that seems not to be happening to ancestor worship. On the contrary, it is being adapted to contemporary life, even modernised.

Since land for incense and fire is no longer available to defray the expenses of the death anniversaries and the feast gatherings, contributions are required from brothers' families. On the other hand, people use the new, modernised paraphernalia in death anniversaries, instead of the traditional ones. In the past, paper replicas offered to ancestors for other-world use included blankets, mosquito nets, clothing, trunks and hampers, trays, and bowls (Phan Ke Binh, 1915/1992: 36). At present, people buy and offer paper motorcycles, even special US dollar notes to their ancestors. These can be seen in markets everywhere. People who migrate far away from their native villages or become upwardly mobile still practise ancestor worship. In other words, ancestor worship has a different meaning to Vietnamese people from that of a religion.

There is another explanation, for which I am indebted to my father, who was a Confucianist scholar, and then a holder of the Franco-Vietnamese *certificat d'études élémentaires*. He wrote in his will that ancestor worship is what distinguishes human beings from other animals. To put it another way, human beings are different from other animals in that human beings know who their ancestors are, and they practise ancestor worship. Ancestor worship is culture understood in the sense that it makes us human. Probably this explanation is more correct than the one interpreting ancestor worship as a religion, because the latter looks at ancestor worship from an outsider's point of view, but the former actually succeeds in capturing the real meaning which the involved people, the Vietnamese, attach to ancestor worship.

In this sense, ancestor worship does not undergo secularisation. By contrast, people care about it regardless of their level of education or social status. When they are quite poor, they may tend to neglect it, but the more people improve their standards of living and social status, the more strongly they feel about human dignity, and the more they remember their ancestors. Furthermore, in a society where people rely mainly, if not solely, on their kinship network, not the society or the state, they often attribute the improvements of their standards of living to their ancestors. This traditional way of thinking has continued well into the socialist era.

A former landless peasant in Son Duong village sums up his thoughts in the following epigram written on the ceiling of his house: *On to tien xay nha moi, nho bac dang co ngay nay* [Owing to ancestors, the new house is constructed; thanks to the Party and Uncle (Ho), the present conditions are achieved] (Luong Van Hy, 1992: 219). Although the official propaganda indoctrinates people with a sense of gratitude only to the Communist Party and its leader, not to their ancestors, the old beliefs remain strong. The epigram embodies the traditional gratitude to one's ancestors and the new spirit of the socialist era.

People who forget their ancestors are looked down upon by public opinion. According to Vuong Xuan Tinh (1990), members of a lineage that used to be so poor that they lost their lineage records, now forget the death anniversares of their shared ancestors. That is a collective shame; the whole lineage is publicly humiliated. That is far from unique. People may be pushed by poverty to migrate far away from their native villages, but when they have stable lives in new places, they would certainly think of their ancestors, go back to their native villages, and make arrangements so that they can practise ancestor worship properly in the new place.

To ensure security in old age as well as the proper worship after their deaths, parents first need to have a child, preferably male. Then they need to maintain a close relationship with their children. The main aims of socialisation have been to teach children to respect, obey, and take care of living parents, and to worship dead parents as best they can. A common concept about a good child has been *ngoan*, i.e., the one who obeys and does what its parents tell it to do. The concept of *hieu* [filial piety] in the traditional family was the highest ideal of being a good child. Filial piety meant that children should be ever mindful of the services done for them by their parents, be dutiful to compensate for their parents' sacrifices, and obey their parents' wishes. Jamieson (1993: 17) has captured well this meaning of filial piety: 'Children were made to feel keenly that they owed parents a moral debt (*on*) so immense as to be unpayable.' Children were in debt to their parents in everything, no matter how much they might have accomplished, no matter how wretched they might be. Success only increased the debt. Therefore children were supposed to please their parents all the time and in every way (ibid.: 17–23).

In addition to the concept of 'filial piety', the folklore has tried for centuries to make children aware of how heavy their moral debt to their parents is. In the traditional family, educated people made use of a list that summed up parents' sacrifices to children as *cu lao chin chu* [parents' nine labours]: birth, nursing, caresses, weaning, feeding, education, supervision, care, and protection. Ordinary people used the folk-song: *Cong cha nhu nui Thai Son, nghia me nhu nuoc trong nguon chay ra* [Your father's merit is immense like Thai Son mountain, and the moral debt to your mother is endless like the water from its source]. In brief, from the earliest period of socialisation, the child was told that eventually he would grow up, marry, and produce children, but he would also support his old parents. That was the way he repaid his moral debt to his parents to some extent. In turn, parents often did their best for children in both direct and indirect senses. They offered their children all kinds of help, both financial and practical.

In a sense, the generational hierarchy and the concept of filial piety, and the core importance attached to the parent–child bond are explicable in terms of the need to assure adequate services for old parents and their afterlife existence, to restrain the 'natural' desire of young people to move out, and set up independent units of their own. Given that meaning of having children, and the undeveloped state social security systems, the lost traditions of filial piety and the somehow loosened parent–child bond during the last half century period have been worrying. This is not only on moral grounds, but also in terms of the concern about relieving the pressures that reproduction processes put on human beings. It is more worrying if one looks at neighbouring Taiwan, where throughout the decades of 1960–80, filial piety was maintained with the government's encouragement (Yi, 1993). Meanwhile, the level of economic development of Taiwan is much higher than that of Vietnam, and the state security network there is also more developed (Chang Chih-Ming, 1988).

CONCLUSION

Each gender has its motivations and aspirations in having children. For women, children are an indispensable part of their identity, their comfort, and the guarantee of stable marital status. For men, children also provide a sense of identity, their fulfilled duty to ancestors, etc. On the other hand, both genders have this in common: male children are the providers of security in old age for the parents, as well as proper worship after death. If the concern about security in old age is common for parents in many parts of the world, the concern about an afterlife existence is specific to Vietnam (and some other countries in the so-called East Asian cultural world).

In the eyes of family members it is not simply due to their wish for more manpower in their family that the peasants long for the birth of a son. Neither is it simply due to the custom that a married couple lives with, or near, the husband's parents and takes care of them, though the last factor is quite essential. The cause of the strong preference for sons goes beyond the usual economic and psychological motives. The male child, in the eyes of his family, assumes an overwhelming importance in economic, religious, practical, and symbolical fields, and last but not least in terms of his role in continuity of the lineage. In this sense, giving birth to a son means continuity to people, while a daughter does not. The conception of continuity in the lineage not only reflects a mystical view of the world; on the social plane it separates one lineage from others.

The above facts give an idea of the difficulties and opposition which the campaign for birth control has been facing. People, especially the husbands, are not independent individuals who may set a limit to the number of children they want to have, particularly when they do not have a son. They feel that they are only a link in the chain of the lineage and are responsible for ensuring its continuation. Many people, including women, unwilling to be burdened with a large family and conscious of the necessity of family planning, would have preferred to set a limit to the number of children they should have, even in the absence of male progeny. Then they have come under pressure from the family community that urges them to carry on having children until a son is born, or to accept polygyny.

Thus the present family produces fewer children than the pre-1945 did; this change is undeniable. However, this is a burden borne mainly by women, and is in part due to the government's birth control programme, which has become stricter and stricter. On the other hand, the preference for son(s) is so strong that it causes a lot of problems to the official policy-makers who are trying to steer society towards the concept of a smaller family.

Thus, the movement towards a smaller family in Vietnam is not merely a cognitive, technical, economic, or psychological problem as in many other societies, but also a socio-cultural problem. It is not likely that lower fertility will be achieved once wealth is more evenly distributed and social security systems well established. In

Vietnam, in order for this fertility to be possible, the individual must be liberated from the tight control exercised by the community (including both the diachronic, generational one and the synchronic one that consists of people around the individual at present) with regard to his/her reproductive behaviour.

In terms of the government's birth control programme, although great efforts are being made to persuade couples to recognise the advantages of family planning for themselves and the whole society, and although severe measures have been implemented to limit birth rates, the desired result has not been achieved yet. The main reason is that the programme does not fulfil the family's interests, especially in the late stages of the life course. Personal reproductive decisions are deeply shaped by the concerns about long-term security in old age and death. If supporting social institutions are non-existent, or cannot reassure parents in these respects, most parents will continue to try to safeguard their own welfare by bearing and relying on children.

NOTES

1 In January 1993, in my neighbourhood, which consisted of social scientists working at the National Centre for Social Sciences and Humanities in Hanoi, there were among nine families three that had two daughters each, but no son. Two other families had one daughter each and no son. The rest had both sons and daughters or all sons. The three families, like many educated people in the same situation in urban areas, came to terms with the fact that they only had daughters.

2 My thanks to Rita Liljeström for reminding me of this fact. Although I cannot ascertain its reference from Sweden, it was well known in the North of Vietnam during the American war.

3 A Canadian researcher has inaccurately supposed that 'in the North, the capacity to form an independent household is a condition for marriage' (D. Belanger, 1995. 'Household Structure and Family Formation Pattern in Vietnam'. Unpublished paper). If that had been true, many young people would not have been able to marry, because they would not have been capable of forming an independent household upon marriage. In fact, as we have seen from evidence, unlike their counterparts in some modern Western society, in Vietnam's countryside the capacity to form an independent household is not a condition for marriage (that may be true of people in urban areas, see Chapter Three). By contrast, a great many young people in rural areas marry without being able to form independent households. With the assistance of close relatives as well as their own efforts, they gradually establish households of their own later. Others may very well be urged by their relatives to marry when they reach the marriageable age, regardless of their capacity to form an independent household.

Conclusions

We have examined the changes that the family in the Red River Delta has been undergoing under the impacts of the social transformations during the last half century. Now we shall summarise them and draw some conclusions.

If our knowledge about the traditional family is correct, and the evidence about the contemporary family is reliable, we may say that the changes are remarkable in many respects. Parental power was stated in the Gia Long Code and practised in the traditional family. Today freedom in marital partner selection has not only been recognised on paper, but has become a reality for a wide range of young people: those living in urban areas far away from their family of origin; those who have liberal parents; those who are well-educated; and to a lesser extent, those in rural areas whose parents more or less recognise children's choices. For the overwhelming majority of young people, unlike their pre-1945 forerunners, at least they have some say, albeit limited, in this issue.

Women's status has improved significantly both inside and outside the family. A dramatic change has been the freedom to choose their own marriage partner, and hence to enjoy a marriage based on love. This has strengthened the conjugal ties and has placed the partners on a more equal footing. Contraception and the birth control programme have both reduced the number of children. Thanks to that, families can invest more of their resources on improving their living standards and their children's education. The socio-economic transformations have tended to drive young people from their homes, and to some extent loosen the parent–child bond.

Nevertheless, one can hardly attribute the family changes to industrialisation, as it has been stated in sociological literature. In his influential study, Goode (1963) has stated that on a world-wide scale there has been a move towards the so-called conjugal family. He has attributed the change to a factor named 'industrialisation' that he uses in a very wide meaning. Among the factors related to industrialisation (freedom of geographical and social mobility, freedom of young migrants in relation to their elderly parents as well as their employers, etc.) he has considered a social factor, i.e., the freedom to use one's talents and skills in improving one's job, to be the prime criterion or measure of industrialisation. Obviously, if we follow him by labelling the social changes during the last half century as 'industrialisation', we find it difficult, if not impossible, to place the Delta accurately. The reason is that most of the phenomena of industrialisation mentioned by him have not appeared yet in the Delta.

Unlike Goode's definition of industrialisation as a liberating factor, in the Delta until the late 1980s and early 1990s freedom of migration has been very limited because of the household registration policy. There is no limit on mutual rights and responsibilities between employers and employees outside the workplace. By contrast, the government through the state-run factories and workplaces became the new agent of control, along with the old one (parents and kinsmen), over young people's lives, including their choice of spouse and family issues. In Goode's view, under industrialisation, individuals are evaluated in terms of their own talents and skills, not birth, and so on; but in the Delta, that is often not the case. The family background as a prime criterion for recruitment and promotion, and the keeping of personal files on all state employees are examples of that.

THE STATE'S ROLE IN CHANGING THE FAMILY PATTERNS

Given such a character and the low level of industrialisation in the Delta, and the significant changes the family has undergone, we need to examine other factors and other kinds of major social transformation that may explain the transformation. In other words, we need to link the family change first of all to the social transformations designed and instigated by the state, the government's socio-economic programmes, i.e., the state's role.

The government has stated openly its position towards the family. In the first Vietnamese Constitution (1946) the government declared its position: The state protects the rights of mothers and children. The state protects marriage and the family' (White, C. P., 1989: 179). In the latest (1992) one that is elaborated: The family is the cell of society. The state protects marriage and the family' (Tønnesson, 1993: 16). However, the most important thing is that the state has been willing to intervene to create the so-called 'good' socialist family in that 'only good families can make up a good society, and a good society makes the families still better' (The 1987 Law on Marriage and the Family). Moreover the state has had its guiding principles about how to rebuild the old family and to establish the new one. That is the Marxist theory of the family and the socialist development project. The family changes in the Delta are inseparable from that.

Like its comrades in the Eastern European countries in the Soviet bloc (Dahlström, 1989) the ruling party in Vietnam has changed considerably its understanding of the family. From a negative assessment of its role, hence a positive evaluation of the state's role, they have adopted a more or less positive evaluation of the family and its certain forms combined with a recognition of the necessity for the state's intervention. Nonetheless, the core of the understanding is kept. Based on a sharp contrast made between the existing society, the family included, and its concept of the so-called socialist one, the state insists that the new socio-economic system demands a new family. The family as well as other parts of society must change to become good, and socialist. The family has to transform itself to contribute towards changes in other parts of the society. The state has put into motion many family alterations.

Thus the change in the family is seen not as a simple consequence of social upheaval, and socio-economic transformation, but as a necessary condition for the so-called socialist revolution to be successful. It must be a product of intended reforms, including strong ideological motivation, and deliberate measures according to the Marxist theory of the family and the so-called socialist line of socio-economic development. As we have seen throughout this study, that is the guiding principle of all reforming measures taken by the government. We shall just mention some of those differences/opposites in the state's dichotomy.

The usual method of agricultural production for many generations was regarded as closely related to private property ownership, i.e. to be of an exploitative, oppressive character which must be uprooted. Land and agriculture were collectivised. That is one of the most radical changes the family has ever undergone, not just in this century, but in the course of history. Though the peasant family has recently regained its role as a productive unit, land is still owned by the state. Time will tell whether this reform is sufficient or not, and how the lack of ownership rights affects the peasants' attitude towards long-term investment on the land.

As we saw in Chapter Four, the 'rationale' of child-raising and the number of children a couple decides to have, are not only dependent on the availability of contraception, or on whether they adopt a 'careless' or 'irresponsible' attitude towards birth control. A large family was also the product of 'folk wisdom' (in Robertson's phrase, 1991: 72) of culture in the form of customs. However, that may now be viewed by the state as too many, and demonstrating unreasonable behaviour. For many couples, contraception and birth control have created for the first time the possibility to limit the size of their immediate family and to improve standards of living. This was unimaginable only some decades ago. For others, birth control also leads to some difficult role conflicts and family contradictions that the previous generations never encountered.

The common way parents socialise children is seen as lacking a wide perspective of class position and national interests. Parents must take a much wider view beyond their family, 'bring up children to become useful members of society' as the official position has put it (1987 Law on Marriage and the Family). Filial piety, the cornerstone of traditional morality, is neglected in the present family. It should be moved out of the family, and widened to apply to the whole society.

Family members emphasise ancestor worship as a way of life. If the Confucian scholar's interpretation quoted in Chapter Four is accepted, then ancestor worship is to be regarded as what distinguishes human behaviour from that of other animals, i.e., it demonstrates the superiority of humankind. However, the government blames it for promoting idealism and superstitions. The state sees the reciprocal ceremony system, which served to strengthen the group solidarity and communication between dead family members and the living ones, as superstitious and costly, therefore it has to be simplified.

In an effort to safeguard the long-term interests of their old age and death as well as the continuity of lineage, parents have traditionally assumed the rights and responsibilities of arranged marriages for their children. In many cases young people accept that as natural. Considering young people's emotions, the government encourages free choice of marital partner by children. If they find themselves in dispute with their parents about that, young people can turn to different social organisations for help.

Realising women's importance in society and the need for their liberation, the state supports and encourages the women's liberation movement, which has brought about considerable achievements. This change is undeniable.

In brief, the state wants the family to turn into something quite different from, if not opposite to, the usual forms it has taken. Thus the government has in fact designed the most radical family revolution. In this regard they have done the opposite to Confucianism. The traditional Confucian society with its familism saw the family as the cornerstone of society, which must be kept intact.

> In this respect Confucianism may be viewed as a familial religion, and it seems that no other cultures have placed such emphasis on the family as have the Confucianist cultures of East Asia.
> (Insook Han Park and Lee-Jay Cho, 1995: 117–118)

Everyone's family duties were 'honouring one's parents, remaining faithful to one's spouse until death, managing family affairs well' (Nguyen Khac Vien, 1974: 26). By contrast, the socialist regime with Marxism as its official ideology insists that the family must be transformed because of its basis on private property ownership. Class position must permeate everything, including kinship (the parent–child and husband–wife bonds).

As for the whole population, the difference and/or opposite between Confucianism and communism is seen mainly in the intergenerational relations within a family as well as the relations between the family and society. That is to say, it finds expression in what I name the temporary and spatial dimensions of the family.

The government's attitude towards ancestor worship reveals a lot about the difference and/or opposite in family issues between Confucianism and communism. More than adopting ancestor worship, Confucianism in Vietnam brought about a deeper meaning to it (Mai Huy Bich, 1991). In the pre-1945 family, ancestor worship was a fundamental feature. It was a concentrated expression of almost all the main characteristics of the Vietnamese family. We see here on the one hand the communitarian character of the family in which each and every individual member was just a link in the intergenerational chain. The lineage's interests were put before those of individual members. On the other hand we also find the hierarchy between the generations in which parents dominated over children. The younger members were expected to take care of, to worship the older ones, and to continue what the older ones had left behind. Ancestor worship also revealed the hierarchy between genders according to which male was more important than female.

Women were supposed to serve men's continuum of lineage by producing children, especially male ones. Moreover, the crucial values and norms of family life found expression in ancestor worship: respect for the previous generations, the elderly, filial piety, stability, and continuity, etc. Furthermore ancestor worship helped people to get a sense of their origin, roots, and their human dignity.

In the traditional family, the practice of ancestor worship turned a family's members into people of an assembled faith. What was done in ancestor worship could only have been performed by people who were both kin and committed in their joint faith towards one another. It could not be performed by doubting or unbelieving individuals, or by those who were not kin. The very act of worship not only set together a group of people with the same kinship ties and faith, but it also set them apart from others (because the latter did not believe in the sacred power of somebody else's dead ancestors).

But ancestor worship meant more than that. We have analysed the beliefs and practices underlying ancestor worship in Chapter Four. The attempts made by some researchers to identify ancestor worship with a religion have led us to Durkheim's (1995: 44) definition of religion in which he distinguished between the sacred and the profane. If applying it to ancestor worship, we may say that it was the ancestors who were regarded as sacred, and ancestor worship did not deal with the supernatural, the miraculous, and divinity. The objects of those beliefs and practices related to ancestor worship (which acquired a sacred status) were none other than one's ancestors. It was their death and the joint belief of their living descendants that set them 'apart and forbidden' (in Durkheim's phrase). Firmly believing that dead ancestors were 'set apart', and forbidden, the living descendants observed a custom named *kieng ten*. According to the custom, children so respected parents that they made parents' names a taboo, not to be mentioned. If they had to say some words that were the homophones of their parents' names, they deliberately mispronounced the words. They even wanted their visitors to do the same. A visitor was expected by this prevailing custom to discover the taboo names right from the beginning of his visit to a family in order to avoid them (Phan Ke Binh, 1915/1992: 27). By the same token, the most serious insult is one aimed at the target's ancestors or respected relatives. It can be literally translated from Vietnamese into English as something like 'Your father!', 'Your mother!', and 'Your ancestors!' (Vuong G. Thuy, 1976: 20). Thus the belief behind ancestor worship made kinship sacred.

As for the government, promoting materialism and a modern scientific outlook, they instigated the fight against everything that is labelled as idealism. As we have seen, the folk belief in existence after death comes under fire. That has deprived dead parents, ancestors, and kinship in general, of sacredness. Nothing is sacred, everything is profane. In short, communism and Confucianism are quite different in this issue.

The second (spatial) dimension of the difference and/or opposite between Confucianism and communism is that, in the Confucian view, the family and society were similar. The family was a microcosm of society; society was an extended family; and the difference between them was only one of size, not nature. The saying by one of Confucius's eminent disciples: 'I know of almost no man with filial piety who challenges authority' (Nguyen Khac Vien, 1974: 36) means that filial piety also served to maintain the social order; family virtues were also the social ones. The Confucian saying *tu than, te gia, tri quoc, binh thien ha* means one should improve oneself, then manage one's family affairs well. This in turn paves the way for a proper governance of the country and the maintenance of peace in the world. 'In other words, the country is but a large family, and if one cannot manage one's family, one cannot do the same with one's country' (Le Thi Que, 1986: 3).

By the same token, if somebody mistreats his (her) parents, (s)he is definitely a bad person to everyone, and a bad member of the whole society. The reason is that if (s)he mistreats the people closest to him (her), how can (s)he be kind to anyone else? This argument of a Confucian scholar at the beginning of this century (Phan Ke Binh, 1915/1992: 27) gives voice to a prevalent opinion in society at large at that time. Thus the way to reform was to proceed from the family to the wider society/country.

Meanwhile under the communist government, family virtues in general have not been paid enough attention in the public arena, in the school curriculum for instance. By contrast, only the virtues of being a good citizen have been emphasised. Recently there has been an opinion that these virtues are overemphasised at the expense of family ones (Ngan Tam and Tran Thi Lien, 1985; Dinh Hai, 1987; Mai Huy Bich, 1993: 61).

Therefore one may assume that either the family values are underrated or the 'good citizen' ones are also applicable to the family. As a matter of fact, many people believe in the second option. Trying to persuade a girl to marry a young military officer, whom she did not know very well, her parents and villagers told her:

'He's a second lieutenant, a Party member, he has been decorated several times ...', 'The boy is all right ...' (Ngan Tam, 1988: 49). The assumption is that if a person is an exemplary citizen, (s)he is certainly a good family member.[1] If my arguments are correct, we may say that, contrary to Confucianism, in communist eyes the opposite seems to have been true: exemplary citizen qualities in society are applicable to family life.[2]

Thus Confucianism is viewed by the communist government as the ideology of overthrown feudalism, and must be rejected. 'In fact, Confucianism was more than just conservative; it turned squarely towards the past' (Nguyen Khac Vien, 1974: 36). Meanwhile, the socialist revolution is believed to be the most radical one in history of mankind, therefore it must oppose all the existing structures. It has only been the recent renovation policy, and the overseas attempts to attribute the successful economic developments of the neighbour Confucian countries to Confucianism (Mineo Nakajima, 1994) that has led to a re-examination of Confucianism in Vietnam (Vu Khieu, 1990).

With such a concept of the desirable family, the state has called for legal changes, and promoted the two Laws on Marriage and the Family. The state has made the socio-economic and cultural policies, taken the necessary measures, including the promotion of the ideology of the new family as well as what Goode (1963) names a political force, to reform the old family and establish the new one. For example, realising the urgent demand for free choice, the two Laws on Marriage and the Family have recognised free choice as one of the main principles. As for political force, it is applied by local authorities together with different organisations (the Women's Union, Youth Organisation, etc.) to guarantee young people's free choice.

All this has changed the family considerably. *So it is undeniable that the state has played an enormous role in changing the family patterns.* That is the first conclusion of this study.

The last half-century has witnessed the expanded role of the state both as a vehicle and an instigator of family change. The state is capable of creating a new taboo in marriage and plays the role of not only the go-between in the traditional family and the matchmaking or dating service of modern marriage, but also of the significant others who give marriage certificates, and witness the wedding ceremonies. In the marriage of the state employees in urban areas, it is the workplace authorities that sign the documents testifying that the involved people are eligible to marry. A representative of the workplace is often chosen as the master of the wedding ceremony. Workmates usually take an active part in performing the ceremony. It is the state that sets the birth limit for each couple, gives birth certificates, and tells parents how to bring up their children. It is the state that grants divorce and death certificates.

In short, the state's role is pervasive. We can see more clearly this role in changing family patterns if we keep in mind the limited extent of the factors that are often said to have contributed enormously to family change: migration and mobility (Goode, 1963) and the development of welfare institutions (Robertson, 1991). Moreover, the state itself places limits on rural–urban migration. In other words, the state is capable of changing the family patterns not only of migrants, but also of other population groups even without large-scale migration as well as welfare-institution building.

Nevertheless the state's role is seen not only in changing family patterns, but also in the persistence of some features of the traditional family, and in this sense, in setting the limits on the family change, especially with regard to the gender issue.

HIERARCHY AND THE LIMITS OF FAMILY CHANGE

However far away children live from their parents, their bonds and mutual support (as well as those between siblings) are emphasised. The freedom of marital partner selection is very limited: in the overwhelming majority of cases, the compromise between the arranged marriage and free one has been adopted. It takes the form of either 'children's choice, parents' approval/disapproval', or 'parents' introduction and/or selection, children's say', etc. The conjugal ties may in some ways have become stronger thanks to the above changes, but the intergenerational bonds are still robust and predominate over the conjugal ones. Women may enjoy a high status outside their homes, in some cases even higher than that of their husbands. Nevertheless, divorce is still considered highly undesirable, therefore women often feel obligated to appease their husbands, to avoid hurting their masculine pride.

If the conjugal family is one largely characterised by gender equality and closeness (as Goode has seen it) then the movement towards this model within Vietnamese society requires the eradication of male dominance. Although patriarchy is universal (Giddens, 1989: 169), there can be no doubt that it varies greatly from society to society. In the Delta the movement presupposes first and foremost that equality in general has to be recognised in the society.

Nonetheless, in this respect, the Vietnamese society with its communitarian character has shown its specific way of perceiving the Western ideas of equality and liberty. In the active search for national independence since the pre-1945 period, those concepts were understood not in terms of individual benefits, but as collective rights in the relations between the Vietnamese and their colonial masters (Luong Van Hy, 1992: 94).

One may suppose that similarly, the concept of gender equality is very likely to be understood in a limited sense. This way of understanding the Western concepts prevails not only in the pre-1945 period, but also in the later developments up to now. Equality and liberty as individual rights and benefits have been neglected. The Confucian heritage with its hierarchy between generations, ages, and genders is unfavourable to younger people and women. However, only the issue of gender inequality has been called into question; the others have not. They are taken for granted. I would like to place great emphasis on Jamieson's penetrating remark that in Vietnam, hierarchy itself has been made 'part of the intrinsic structure of the universe, a state of affairs that was both "natural and unalterable"' (Jamieson 1993: 16).

The strength and vitality of hierarchy may be explained in terms of the Confucian influence, which for centuries emphasised stability, order (against instability and chaos), and hierarchy as a guarantee of that state of affairs. Applied to family issues, for instance, freedom from parental control in marital partner selection, encouraged by the communists since the early 1930s, implies a breaking down of the established hierarchy of parents and children. According to one source, this was unimaginable for a majority of the population. That was why 'for most Vietnamese of the time, the idea of basing marriage on love alone and advocating free choice of partners without prior approval by parents was scandalous' (White, C. P., 1989: 176).

That is not a thing of the past. While many old norms and values have been shattered, the above norm has been maintained. Breaking the established hierarchy is still the most serious and unforgivable offence (behaviour called *hon lao* in Vietnamese means a great disrespect), no matter for what reason and how right that person may be. It should be pointed out that when dealing with equality, the leadership of Vietnam also retains the traditional norms and values. The President of the Women's Union has stated that it is necessary to reject 'the mistaken idea that equality means not maintaining the family hierarchies (*ton ti trat tu*), that equality means that everything in the family should be equally shared, etc'. In her words, constructing a family of equality means continuing 'the good aspects of the Vietnamese family from previous times until now: respecting one's elders, yielding to the younger, harmony and loyalty' (Gammeltoft, 1997b: 8).

Applied to the family, this also means that a woman may achieve an equal, or even higher social status than her husband, and more or less succeed in changing the traditional gender hierarchy. However, when the hierarchy between generations and ages is not challenged, and if she is younger than he (according to the acceptable pattern), she is still in a lower position in the family hierarchy than he is. We have noted the way contemporary couples address and treat each other based on the model 'older brother–younger sister' (*anh em*). We can see how hierarchical it is by quoting a common saying *quyen huynh, the phu* [the power of the father and older brother is undeniable].[3] In other words, women may be liberated in one respect, but are caught in the trap of hierarchy in another. The problem is not only that hierarchy is a long-established and deep-rooted norm, while equality is a newly-established one. The problem is also that hierarchy is perceived as universal, whereas equality has been recognised as particular in the sense that it is applicable in some domains, and not in others (outside the home, not inside, as we shall see later).

Thus hierarchy is multiform; if only one of the three hierarchies (gender) is challenged, inequality in the others will find a way to re-establish itself in gender relations. All this has laid the foundations for the second conclusion that *although the idea of social equality is put forward in some respects, the traditions of hierarchy still continue unabated in others*. As a consequence, whatever fundamental changes the family in a Confucian society may have undergone, as long as the underlying key norms and basic values in society (hierarchy) remain unchanged, it is unlikely that a more radical family change in favour of women can take place. Without further comprehensive social transformations that pave way to equality – that is, as long as equality is not recognised as an individual right – the resolution of the gender issue will not be achieved.

CONFUCIAN LEGACY PLUS MARXIST BIAS ON THE GENDER ISSUE

As we have seen, gender hierarchy and patriarchy, i.e., male domination, are deeply rooted in the Vietnamese culture, especially due to the Confucian heritage. In the traditional family it was taken for granted, even made a 'heaven assumption', i.e., the sacred thing. It is widely believed that 'it is against the order of heaven for a man to be under the political authority of a woman' (Eisen, 1984: 19). During the last half-century this belief has remained little changed. It is only in the light of this that we can understand why, after the American war, demobilised veterans forced women, who had been promoted earlier, back to their homes.

The reason is not simply that wars are exceptional situations which demand extraordinary measures; when the wars are over, the 'normal' state of affairs in man–woman relations needs to be restored. The real reason, as C.P. White (1989: 187) explains, is that men, particularly officers, felt it a slight to their wartime service if they had to work under the managerial control of women cadres.

We saw in Chapter Two how husbands whose wives are in higher social position than they are have taken measures to maintain their domination inside the family. They insist that it is the husband who is the boss at home, no matter how high the wife's social position may be outside it. This shows that when men are unable to stop women's progress, they try to limit that success; to make it particular, not universal. In the eyes of men, women's achievements must be of limited applicability, especially not in the home. Equality as the norm that the wider society promotes and supports has to stop at the gates of the house. Here, the line between the public and the private is drawn in men's favour: women's success is rated only in the public not the private domain. The home has been made the man's domain. This is what I call 'privatisation' of the family.[4] It is a way to uphold the traditional status quo not just in this gender issue, but also in other family respects. Consequently, many rural women complain that they have had rights only outside the family, not inside it (Gammeltoft, 1997a: 204–205).

Meanwhile, influenced by Marxism, the communist government has not recognised how entrenched male domination is within the society. We have noted that Marxism and Confucianism are opposite to each other in many ways. Nonetheless, Confucianism and communism also have something in common. A leading communist intellectual even emphasised the similarities between Confucianism and Marxism (Nguyen Khac Vien, 1974).[5] What concerns us here is the gender issue that is not dealt with at all in Nguyen Khac Vien's essay. The state's early attitude towards extramarital sexuality, especially of single mothers; the official expectations of women as the traditional housewives (while they also play the role of workers in social production) in order to release men from their villages to make revolution; the previous policy prohibiting the native traditional village festivals and so on are examples of what the communist government shares with Confucianism.

However, the essential thing is that while Confucianism accentuated male dominance, in Marxism the gender issue is of only secondary importance compared to the class one (Morgan, 1985; Landes, 1989). What concerns us most here is that when dealing with the gender, Marxism examines it in terms of class.

It must also be said that Marxism is introduced and interpreted in Vietnam mainly through the works of Marx, Engels, and Lenin. In those works of the founders of Marxism, the gender issue is often stated in terms of class relations. First is Engels' proposition that

> The first class antagonism which appears in history coincides with the development of the antagonism between man and woman in monogamian marriage, and the first class oppression with that of the female sex by the male.
>
> (Engels, 1972: 75)

Second, the class terms are used to describe and analyse not only the relations between men and women in the remote past but also in the family that was contemporary to Marx and Engels. In the propertied classes the husband is the bourgeois, and the wife represents the proletariat (Engels, 1972: 82). That exerts an enormous influence even on feminists. Like Marxists in general, Marxist feminists believe that class ultimately better accounts for women's status (whereas socialist feminists dissatisfied with that have come to a conclusion that gender and class play an approximately equal role in any explanation of women's oppression) (Tong, 1989: 39).

Consequently, it is believed first that it is the ruling classes that are the primary oppressors of women as working people. Men are merely the secondary oppressors of women as women. Male–female relations in marriage are exploitative in precisely the same way as those in employer–employee relations. Nevertheless, as some researchers point out, 'for all similarities, exploited workers do not suffer in the same way as do oppressed wives and/or prostitutes' (Tong, 1989: 64). Second, gender and class structures are intertwined, but that is not taken into consideration by Marxists. Men in oppressed classes and women in oppressing classes are overlooked.

Third, it is believed that because man's control of woman is rooted in his control over property, so the oppression of women will cease only with the dissolution of the institution of private property

(Tong, 1989: 49). One example of that is the proletarian family in which all the foundations of male domination (private property) have ceased to exist. Because large-scale industry has transferred the woman from the house to the labour market and the factory, and makes her the breadwinner of the family,

> the last remnants of male domination in the proletarian home have lost all foundation – except, perhaps, for some of that brutality towards women which became firmly rooted with the establishment of monogamy.
>
> (Engels, 1972: 80)

Similarly, when class oppression is eliminated, gender oppression also disappears: if anything is left, it is only in a residual form.

Thus in the way Marxism treats the gender issue there has been what I call a gender bias – in the sense that it has mixed up gender with class, by identifying men with oppressing classes, and women with oppressed classes. Gender has been obscured by class. Thus Marxism does not specify men as the dominating gender, therefore it is to some extent in favour of men. Probably it is from those propositions that the gender issue has been put in class terms by Vietnamese communists.

Applying this approach to Vietnam, the government sees the gender problem in relations between Vietnamese women on the one hand, and (mainly male) colonialists, imperialists (due to the French and American domination), and feudalists on the other. Apart from national independence, they have overemphasised the class struggle approach at the expense of the gender perspective (and kinship as well). By defining colonialists, imperialists, and feudalists as the obstacles to the women's liberation movement, the government failed to deal with men and patriarchy in this issue.

By the same token, women are seen as a part of the oppressed nation, and of the working class, not as a specific social group. The release of the Vietnamese people and the working class from the yoke of the oppressive forces is also understood as liberating women. Since that moment onward, die-hard 'feudal' attitudes, that is to say, the vestige of their overthrown class enemy, are mainly blamed for any manifestation of gender inequality. After the wars for national independence, the persistence of feudal patriarchal ideology was considered the most formidable obstacle to women's liberation. Gender domination has been confused with 'feudal residue'. As Mies (1986: 190) puts it, 'this means the problem is seen as an ideological and not a structural one'. In other words, the resolution of the problem is viewed as just a matter of time, patience, and a continuance of the ideological struggle. It does not require the rejection of the structural subordination of women, nor substantial structural transformations.

It should be mentioned here that, immediately after the American war, when the country was reunified, many men from the North, being disappointed and even fed up with the gender equality movement there, found their lost paradise in the South. In the remark of a Western researcher, 'they prefer southern women who are said to be more "traditional" in their deference to men and devotion to their husbands' (Pelzer, 1993: 317). The researcher questions this widely held view by doubting whether southern women are actually more traditional than their northern counterparts due to the American cultural influence and aid. However, before the American troops invaded on a large scale (1965), another author had already pointed out that women in the North were far less shy in society, i.e., less traditional than their sisters in the South (Hoang Van Chi, 1964: 144).

The validity of this widely held view by men could be debated, but its existence is certain, and men's disappointment as well as nostalgia for the lost paradise are certain too. That is a new sign of men's reaction and resistance to the women's liberation movement. It should be taken seriously by the leadership if they are really committed to continuing the movement whereby national enemies are swept away, and the class enemies are overthrown. Nonetheless, that is not the case.

Since the renovation policy, many traditional patriarchal traits have been restored. Little has been done to prevent that, partly due to the trade-off between economic efficiency and social equality, and partly because insufficient attention is paid to the interaction between class, age, and gender, etc. (Truong Thanh Dam, 1995). As a result of all this, a great number of women openly express their discontent. To quote a peasant woman: 'In other countries husband and wife are very equal, it is not like in Vietnam. In Vietnam, one has to endure like this, so life is very miserable for women in Vietnam' (Gammeltoft, 1997a: 214). The quoted study points out that women do not passively endure the hardships and injustice, however. By contrast, they are actively and consciously striving to negotiate and affect the existing social relations in different ways. According to the study, women send out the signals of distress that permeate their daily life in four different ways:

- confiding in other women, i.e., talking about and sharing stressful experiences with their peers;
- 'foot-dragging', i.e., doing what their mothers-in-law and husbands expect, but only in a slow and sullen way;
- abstaining from food, i.e., losing their appetite and refusing to eat together with other members of their families; and
- somatic expressions, i.e., using physical weakness and bodily tension to express their social and moral conflicts and imbalances.

As for the last way, the researcher has noted that women express the disturbing feelings through their bodies rather than through verbal idioms; that is to say physical symptoms become a language for the expression of distressful social experience. 'In the absence of more direct forms of power, being physically weak may therefore be a very effective strategy for women to exert influence on their social surroundings' (Gammeltoft, 1997a: 240–248).

However, all those ways do not directly challenge the gender hierarchy. They just constitute some passive resistance. The other remark of the researcher has been more convincing. Most women seem to come to terms with the fact that having to please one's husband or being obedient and respectful to his parents are the difficult but more or less unchangeable facts of life. 'This is just the way things are and these are the conditions which all women share. Being a woman means having to endure ...' (ibid.: 186). Therefore the only thing a woman can do to change her inferior position is to wish she were a man (ibid.: 171). That means she repeats what Ho Xuan Huong, a feminist poetess, did over one hundred years ago.

Thus the state as the instigator of change should have done much more in this issue. Nonetheless, they blame only the residue of a feudal system for gender inequality. They do not recognise the responsibility of men and the existing socio-cultural structure for it. Moreover, they reject the so-called bourgeois feminism, insist that one must look at women's issue from a class viewpoint, and emphasise only national interests and class consciousness-raising activities in the women's liberation movement. In brief, the communist government has failed to recognise the deep roots of patriarchy. As a consequence, they instigate the women's liberation movement in some ways, but assist the masculine domination in others, even if this is sometimes simply by passive acquiescence. The point is that to achieve gender equality, the issue must be treated on its own terms, not in national or class terms. Gender should not have been mixed up with other issues, although it may or may not be necessary to examine them together.

The bias has had far-reaching consequences on the potential for change within the family. Patriarchy of the Confucian type is one of the main obstacles, but the communist government's gender bias has made it more difficult to see and resolve the gender problem at its roots. That is why the country could not have progressed at a faster pace in the path to gender equality. Researchers have noted the revival of religion since the late 1980s (Tønnesson, 1993: 30–34; Dang Nghiem Van, 1995). That includes the renaissance of Confucian ideas and may pose another problem here.

That also means that *however narrowly the concept of gender equality is understood, to achieve it in a Confucian society that has adopted Marxism, as Vietnam has done, requires a redoubled effort.* That is our third conclusion.

Then the next question arises: Does Confucianism or Marxism exert a stronger influence on the Vietnamese society in this issue? Though the Confucian influence varied from class to class, it was so widespread that there existed even a concept of 'popular Confucianism' to capture its impacts on the lower classes. Women themselves, even among the peasants, also absorbed its ideas of gender hierarchy. 'Women internalised submissive norms almost to the point of believing them to be natural law' (Marr, 1981: 191). Thus everybody was influenced by the Confucian idea of hierarchy to different extents. To quote a Japanese researcher, today almost everyone in a sense is a Confucian although no one claims so (Fumie Kumagai, 1995: 137). As for Marxism, there has been so far no study of its influence. One can only speculate that it is more visible among those who are indoctrinated and familiar to the Marxist theory: Communist Party members, officials in the governmental apparatus, and educated groups, etc. For the rest, if it survives at all, it is in a diluted form. If that speculation is correct, however, it is the leading group that is most influenced by the Marxist bias on the gender issue, while it is also under the impact of the Confucian hierarchy. To intervene when changes within the family have negative consequences, or when the speed of positive change is not fast enough, the state has to be able to evaluate the pace and direction of the transformation. In this regard, it is hard to assume that the state can recognise the problem, and to continue driving the whole society towards gender equality.

THE DIRECTION OF CHANGE WITHIN THE FAMILY

As noted earlier, in sociological literature, family change in this century is often regarded as a movement towards the so-called conjugal family. This family has transferred many of its functions to welfare institutions (Robertson, 1991), therefore it has far fewer obligations and rights to its extranuclear relatives. The emphasis is now more on the conjugal bond (Goode, 1963). In this regard it is difficult to say the family in the Delta is moving towards the conjugal form in the sense Goode has understood it, though the basic factors which Goode mentions (migration and neolocal marriage, some version of the ideology of the conjugal family, and political force) have obviously been put into motion.

Some features of the traditional family patterns are stable because other social transformations have not created the necessary and sufficient conditions for the family to adopt the conjugal form. The first expression of that is the weakness of welfare institutions that help to relieve what a researcher has named 'reproduction's pressure' (Robertson, 1991), therefore to reduce the need for mutual assistance between generations (parents and children), brothers, and sisters. Robertson's idea is that the process of reproduction is a thorough-going source of disturbance in human lives. It places us as defenceless infants, raises us to creative maturity, and eventually cripples us with age and kills us. The progression from birth to death takes us from complete incapacity to adult capacity, and back to complete incapacity. Thus there have been some 'periodic internal pressures' (ibid.: 27), or 'cyclical reproductive pressures' (ibid.: 33) on individuals as well as households. To survive as infants, we are chronically dependent upon our parents, who in turn hope that we, as their adult children, will take care of them later when they are old and incapacitated. By overlapping in this relationship, the two curves describing each person's degree of dependence mitigate each other.

As for the small household, in order to survive, it has learnt to deal with the ups and downs of the reproductive cycle in different ways: squeezing more effort from its own able-bodied members; setting aside savings in the fat periods in order to buy its way out of troubles in the lean periods; and drawing assistance from the wider network of the family and community, or from welfare programmes organised by the state, etc. (Robertson, 1991). In the light of this finding, the family has been the base of the social organisation of reproduction, and the extended kin network is one of the ways to cope with the ups and downs of reproduction.

It is here that we see an important difference between the Western family and the Vietnamese one. Since medieval times Europeans have been seeking ways of securing their old age independently of family networks. By the end of the nineteenth century most people in the continent depended for support in their old age on savings accounts and pension funds rather than on their own children. 'This has meant that people can expect to be provided for in their old age whether or not they have children of their own' (Robertson, 1991: 69).

The striking contrast between modern Western societies and the Vietnamese one is that the latter has produced relatively few public institutions to support old people; moreover, they are not effective. We saw in Chapter Four how for old people in Vietnam the main source of help is their children. And in the Vietnamese view, parents have to rely on children even after their death. For their part, children need parents' help, too. Parents' assistance is required not only when children are young and dependent, but also in marriage, to help them establish their own households, to take care of grandchildren, and other difficult situations. In brief, there have been so far very few non-familial institutions to relieve the pressures of the reproductive process. As a consequence, Vietnamese parents and children have to continue relying on each other.

To quote Castillo, we may say that even in the pre-1945 period, the family was already 'residentially nuclear but functionally extended' (quoted in Jones, 1995: 189). In this regard, no considerable change has occurred. Unlike the Western societies examined by Robertson, in the Delta the essential importance of reproduction can be seen in keeping the family's role to cope with reproduction's pressure, not in shaping modern welfare institutions. Moreover, it could be suggested that the strategic means to keep the family and kinship network are wide-ranging. They include not only the great respect for the elderly, a belief in their wisdom, the age hierarchy, filial piety, and ancestor worship, but also the deepest concern, help, care, and sacrifice that the older generations in the family offer to the younger ones. In the pre-industrial world, the task of relieving the pressure of reproduction was fulfilled in organising mating, fertility, ageing, and mortality, as Robertson has seen it, but in the Delta this has been carried much further. By giving one's ancestors a sacred status, by creating the popular belief in the continual mutual interdependence of close relatives, even after the older generations' death, i.e., the interdependence of both living and dead relatives, one hopes to guarantee some well-being for both older and younger generations.

Nevertheless, in the Delta it is not likely that the nuclear family would curtail its relationships with extranuclear relatives even if welfare institutions were developed. Experience of the other Confucian societies, for instance Taiwan (Mei-Lin Lee and Te-Hsiung Sun, 1995: 107–112), has shown that institutions for elderly people tend to be used by only those who are unmarried or have no children, i.e., who are the most unfortunate in the Confucian view.[6] By contrast, the family is still preferred due to its blood relationships and emotional environment.

The most crucial thing is that as long as people still attach a great importance to ancestor worship, i.e., the care for the previous generations and other life of their own, no social institution can act as a substitute for children. The ceremony reform in the Delta demonstrates that non-familial institutions (co-operatives, work teams) may participate in the simplified ritual for a dead person by giving some help, but did not, and could not take care of what is believed to be his/her afterlife. This can be done only by his/her children.

If by the conjugal family we mean the emphasis on emotional ties in the relationship between husband and wife, it is also hard to say that the family in the Delta is moving in this direction. However, the part that emotion plays in spouse selection is undoubtedly increasing. Chapter Three has demonstrated that marital bonds have not yet become the centre of family relationships; much more emphasis is still placed on intergenerational bonds. An old mother in the novel *Mua la rung trong vuon* [Leafshedding season in the garden] tells her married son: 'My dear, if your wife dies, you will have another one by remarrying; but if your mother dies, you will never be able to have another mother!' (Ma Van Khang, 1985). That sums up well, at least in attitude, the comparative weight of each bond: the irreplaceable bond, not the more intimate bond, should be more highly valued (Mai Huy Bich, 1988). Lack of companionship and gender separation are still visible.

As for the ideal family that the state promotes, i.e., the official ideology of the new socialist family (as official documents put it), it is not the conjugal one in the sense defined by Goode. The reason is that it required that conjugal ties and love must not be so close that they can distract couples from revolutionary duties. In this respect, despite the new regime's claim of the sharp contrast between itself and other regimes in that it recognises 'genuine love' (Le Duan's phrase), the new regime is no different in its view that passionate love is a danger to social order and duty.

As defined in the introduction to the 1987 Law on Marriage and the Family, the ideal socialist family should contribute to the construction of a good society, achieve good relations with that society and lead a good life. To compare, we may recall the so-called *gia dinh ne nep* [respectable family with decent manners] in the traditional period. Its internal relations were emphasised: hierarchy and harmony within the family were strictly observed (Tran Dinh Huou, 1991).

Of course the ideal type of the so-called socialist family is not in reality the perfect model just because the government has declared it to be progressive and positive, nor because it has declared the existing family to be backward, negative, and so on. On the contrary, if traditions are often regarded as folk wisdom and natural, it is because of the sharp contrast made by the state between the traditional family and the so-called socialist one that the latter is likely to be seen by some groups as anti-natural. If we keep in mind one of the five criteria of the 'Five Good' movement in the period 1961–65, the contents of the New Cultured Family campaign since 1975 (see Chapter Two) as well as the criteria for recruiting state employees until the late 1980s (see Chapter Three), we can see that a good (i.e. strict) observance of state policies is emphasised over and over again. That is to say the family at least should obey the government. So the state has made a virtue out of conformity to the government policies. (We shall see later that apart from rewarding those families that obey the state's policies, there is also some discrimination against those who do not).

It is beyond any doubt that the concept of a good life (to include the family), promoted by the state, is in some respects just that. It aimed at prosperity and well-being for the majority of population, and a great many families benefited from it. On the other hand, the concept did not always work well in practice. For example, collective agricultural production beyond the family was positive in one sense, but negative in another. Although it benefited families of soldiers and disabled war veterans, or female-headed households that were not small in number (White, C. P., 1989: 188), its advantages were limited for many other people. Even for those who benefited most directly, the model was not always good: it was helpful only as long as they needed some minimal security. If they wanted something over and above this, i.e., to improve their standard of living, even though they worked hard, they often felt underpaid.

Promoting free choice, encouraging the conjugal bond and accepting divorce also means putting the parent–child bond at risk. Class endogamy and solidarity may bring spouses close to each other in some ways, but not necessarily in one of the crucial respects of marital life: gender relations. Having fewer children may create favourable conditions for family life in some ways. However, as long as the security in old age and afterlife existence of parents are concerned, it offers little comfort. Furthermore, the attack on ancestor worship also tends to undermine the family and kinship to the extent that vital functions previously performed by the family may be neglected. The simplification of ritual ceremonies also has its pros and cons. It has reduced considerably not only the family celebrations of rites of passage, but also the interrelations between the family and its wider network. In other words, behind the old ceremonies there were certain social needs that the simplified ones were unable to satisfy.

We saw in Chapter Two that in response to the state's accusation of wasting resources on costly ceremonies, people argue that they are spending their own money, not that of the state. This is another example of what I have previously called the 'privatisation' of family issues, and poses a problem for the state. A sharp line is drawn by family members between the public sphere and the private one. In the eyes of those family members, the private sphere is a protected zone in which they can act freely with respect to their personal interests. By so doing, they try to set some limits on the state's intervention. They are ready to keep and defend those limits by all means and at any cost. Thus the 'privatisation' of family life is the way to escape from the state's pressure, and the shell to protect the status quo of the traditional family. Facing the pervasive state that seems not to recognise privacy, family members have to make use of the shield 'the private'. The state, however pervasive and paternalistic, may very well fail in its intervention, if it does not consider the line between the two spheres.

Therefore families perceive and react in different ways to the changes wanted by the government. In brief, the state's impact on the family has been uneven in different groups. Devoted Communist Party members may have been more enthusiastic about observing the state's policies than the rest of population. Nonetheless, one may say that the benefits from the state's socio-economic programmes and more than five decades of socialist indoctrination and ideological training have had certain effects on the family. Therefore most families follow the changes in certain areas and on certain occasions (i.e. when the changes suit their interests) but not in all domains. There are good reasons though for families to observe the state's policies, because local authorities frequently discriminate against families that do not conform. Often those families will suffer from these sanctions for generations.[7]

Conclusions

Consequently some families may conform to the state's policies in order to achieve a good family background so that they can leave this benefit to their children and grandchildren. Thus the tradition of 'accumulating virtues, storing up merit' that we saw in Chapter One has taken a new form in the socialist era. Conforming to the state's policies is one way to avoid harming succeeding generations, and to guarantee a promising future for them.

In brief, if following the ideal patterns, the traditional family has changed for both better and worse. That derives from the state's evaluation of the existing family as well as their view of the ideal one. The forms of the traditional family decried by the state came into being not because of the general ignorance, as the state supposes, but because behind the visible irrationality, there lay a kernel of wisdom and appositeness. Consequently, the present family is not entirely shaped by the ideology and the socio-economic and cultural programmes of the government. Many 'undesirable' (from the state's point of view) features still exist in the family, while other desired elements have still to become established. In other words, the state's role is not unlimited.

However, the leadership seems to have supposed that the ordinary families are 'hindered by *ignorance* and/or *inertia* from perceiving and pursuing their own true interests' (to borrow the words of Therborn, 1990: 376). They also believe that it is only the leadership itself who knows best what is good. Insisting on their concept of the good life, this paternalistic position goes against the idea that there are many conceptions of the good life (Dahlström, 1995: 71).

The interplay between the ideals and reality of the family leads to the current renovation policy. That is the way the family 'makes history'. That is not insignificant if one bears in mind that a state armed with Marxism – supposedly the apex of human thought – in a Confucian society is doubly paternalistic.

To sum up, we may say that the state's vision of how the family should change is largely based on the Marxist theory of the family. It is beyond doubt that Marxist theory in general has been very helpful in solving some problems in Vietnamese society. For instance, it must be said that there was a class problem in the Vietnamese society at the time the communist government started their first socio-economic programmes (in the mid-1950s). Therefore the theory has something to contribute. Nonetheless, the problem is that in some cases the class struggle matrix is overused at the expense of the family and kinship, which is one of the cornerstones of the Vietnamese society.

On the other hand, the rejection of young people's choice of marital partner on the ground that it does not observe class endogamy, and the encouragement of class endogamy by some state-run workplaces create a new problem, rather than resolving the existing one (lack of freedom in mate selection). In Chapter Three we saw the case of a woman who was deceived by a polygamist man disguising himself as a class comrade. At least this has demonstrated that class solidarity cannot solve the gender issue. Meanwhile, the gender issue remains one of the acute problems of the Vietnamese society. Nevertheless, influenced by the above Marxist bias on the gender issue, the state, as the vehicle and instigator of change, has failed to recognise and resolve the issue to the extent that it had hoped.

Therefore the transformations carried out according to the view of how the family should alter, have achieved some notable successes in crucial areas (e.g. freedom of marital partner choice as well as gender equality), but those changes have not gone far enough. In the meantime the changes pose new problems in other respects (e.g. the parent–child bond is loosened when pressures of reproduction are not relieved considerably).

Thus we may say the present family in the Delta bears the features of both traditional and socialist traits. The fact that the peasant family has regained its productive function, and that the family in general has had to resume the caring function after the renovation policy, proves that unlike the progressive change proposed by some theorists (Goode, 1963) family shifts may include some reversals. That is evidenced too by the restoration of many traditional features since 1987. *The more the families improve their standards of living due to the present renovation policy, the more independently they can build up their family life: restoring traditions, absorbing some Western influence, or adopting some combination of both.* That is our fourth and last conclusion.

NOTES

1   One may argue that, due to the privileges which state employees, military officers and Communist Party members receive, such a prospective spouse is in great demand on the marriage market, i.e., the pragmatic calculations have their weight here, but that is not the case in this story.

2   In fact, that is not the case. The good citizen in the above story turns out not to be a good husband, and their later painful divorce demonstrates that citizen qualities do not coincide with the family ones, as is often expected.

3   The relations between older siblings and younger ones are always hierarchical, never equal. That is why they are used to mean the unequal

CONCLUSIONS

non-familial relations. For instance in each and every traditional village there were powerful families called *ho dan anh* [families of senior brothers, or senior families], and powerless ones called *ho dan em* [families of junior brothers, or junior families] (Nguyen Tu Chi, 1980: 40).

4   This is not the place to consider whether the distinction between the two domains really exists in a communitarian society or not. Here it is enough to note that even if it did not previously exist, it is a reality now, with the state's intervention and the resistance of families. If anything, this trend is becoming more marked.

5   The mentioned similarities include the goal of liberation of the country; the non-religious emphasis on social organisation, not the afterlife; the virtues of courage and loyalty for gentlemen as well as revolutionaries; the concern with social discipline, not individualism; and the emphasis on morality and moral role of leaders, etc. Among the similarities between Confucianism and communism we can notice the following: they are both alien to 'bourgeois individualism which puts personal interests ahead of those of society' (Nguyen Khac Vien, 1974: 47).

That is not entirely accurate regarding communism. Confucianism was alien to individualism, and in favour of familism. To certain extent its familism put one's own family before one's society (Quang Dam, 1990). However, in the eyes of the communist government, (see Chapter Two), paying too much attention to one's own family is associated with individualistic behaviour, and must therefore be criticised. That is to say familism is identified with individualism and has become subject to official opposition. If this is correct, we have another indication of the contrast between Confucianism and communism, between the Confucianist familism and the Marxist theory of the family.

6   In the Confucian view, the most unfortunate people include four categories: *quan* [unmarried men or widowers]; *qua* [unmarried women or widows]; *co* [young orphans]; and *doc* [childless elderly] (quoted in Mai Huy Bich, 1993: 14). In brief, they are unfortunate because they have no family.

7   For instance, their children may have difficulties in gaining access to university. As we saw in Chapter Three, local authorities may not write a recommendation in the CV of somebody whose family does not conform to the state's policies and who wants to apply for a job in the state sector or a place at a university. In addition, if a young person's family does not conform, (s)he cannot become a member of the Ho Chi Minh Communist Youth Union. Until the mid-1980s, membership of that organisation was still regarded as one of the main criteria for selection to a university (Rubin, 1988: 60).

References

Agence France-Presse. 1995. 'Hanoi puts its tolls in Vietnam war at 3 million'. *International Herald Tribune.* 5 April, p. 4.

Banister, J. 1993. *Vietnam Population Dynamics and Prospects.* Institute of East Asian Studies. Berkeley: University of California.

Bao Ninh. 1991/1993. *The Sorrow of War.* London: Secker & Warburg.

Barry, K. 1996. 'Industrialisation and Economic Development: The Cost to Women'. In: Barry, K. (ed.). *Vietnam's Women in Transition.* London: Macmillan Press Ltd.

Belanger, D. & Khuat Thu Hong. 1995. *Marriage and the Family in Urban North Vietnam, 1965–1993.* Paper presented at the Annual PAA Meeting, San Francisco, April 1995.

Beresford, M. 1988. *Vietnam: Politics, Economics and Society.* London: Pinter Publishers.

Binh Minh. 1991. 'Ve quan he hon nhan trong gia dinh nong thon hien nay' [On marital relationships in the present rural family]. In: *Nhan dien gia dinh Viet nam hien nay.* Ha Noi. Ky yeu hoi nghi.

Bui Nguyen Phuong Linh. 1993. 'Nguoi gia o Viet Nam hom nay: mot vai nhan xet ban dau' [The elderly in Vietnam today: some preliminary remarks]. *Xa hoi hoc* no. 1, pp.14–22.

Bui The Cuong. 1992. 'Nguoi phu nu cao tuoi o nong thon' [Old women in countryside]. *Xa hoi hoc,* no. 2, p. 21.

Bui Tin. 1995. *Following Ho Chi Minh.* Memoirs of a North Vietnamese Colonel. London: Hurst & Company.

Bui Viet Thang. 1991. 'Ngon nguon cua nhung rang buoc' [The origin of restraints]. *Van nghe,* no. 12, p. 7.

Buttinger, J. 1967. *Vietnam: A Dragon Embattled.* Volume I: From Colonialism to the Vietminh. New York: Frederic A. Praeger.

REFERENCES 255

Chaliand, G. 1969. *The Peasants of North Vietnam*. Harmondsworth: Penguin Books.

Chang Chih-Ming. 1988. 'Changing Relations Between Traditional and State Social Security in Taiwan'. In: Benda-Beckmann, F. von, K. von Benda-Beckmann, E. Casino. F. Hirtz, G.R. Woodman and H.F. Zacher (eds) *Between Kinship and the State. Social Security and Law in Developing Countries*. Dordrecht, Holland/Providence, RI, USA: Foris Publications.

Chu Khac. 1986. 'Phu nu nong thon co thuc hien duoc quyen binh dang voi nam gioi khong?' [Is gender equality achieved by rural women?]. *Xa hoi hoc*, Vol. 13, no. 1, pp.48–52.

Dahlström, E. 1989. 'Theories and Ideologies of Family Functions, Gender Relations and Human Reproduction'. In: Boh, K., M. Bak, C. Clason, M. Pankratova, J. Qvortrup, B.J. Sgritta and K. Warness (eds). *Changing Patterns of European Family Life. A Comparative Analysis of 14 European Countries*. London: Routledge.

——— 1995. *Social Theory and Evaluative Reasoning. A Meta-theoretical Testament*. Research Report from the Department of Sociology. University of Gothenburg.

Dang Canh Khanh. 1991. 'Ve su phan tang xa hoi o nong thon hien nay' [On social differentiation in countryside at present]. In: *Kinh te xa hoi nong thon Viet nam ngay nay*. Ha Noi: Nha xuat ban tu tuong van hoa.

Dang Nghiem Van. 1995. 'Religion and Beliefs in Vietnam'. *Social Compass*. Vol. 42, no. 3, pp. 345–365.

Dang Nguyen Anh. 1991. 'The position of women in two rural communes'. In: Liljeström, R. & Tuong Lai (eds). *Sociological Studies on the Vietnamese Family*. Hanoi: Social Sciences Publishing House.

Dao Duy Anh. 1938/1992. *Viet nam van hoa su cuong* [A general history of the Vietnamese culture]. Nha xuat ban thanh pho Ho Chi Minh.

Dieu Tan. 1991. 'Co dau bep' [The female cook]. In: *Con mua dau mua*. Toronto: Langvan.

Dinh Hai. 1987. 'Ba muoi nam sach Kim Dong' ['Kim Dong' Publishing House is thirty years old]. *Van nghe*, nos. 25–26–27.

Do Thai Dong. 1991. 'Modifications of the traditional family in the South of Vietnam'. In: Liljeström, R. and Tuong Lai (eds). *Sociological Studies on the Vietnamese Family*. Hanoi: Social Sciences Publishing House.

Doan Kim Thang. 1985. 'Thai do cua nguoi nong dan doi voi viec sinh con trai va con gai' [The peasants' attitude towards the births of male and female children]. *Xa hoi hoc*, no. 4.

Duong Huong. 1991. *Ben khong chong* [The river watering place of unmarried women]. Ha Noi: Nha xuat ban tac pham moi.

Duong Thi Thanh Mai. 1985. 'Van de hon nhan qua khao sat thuc te o mot so noi' [The issue of marriage: Empirical research in a number of localities]. In: Vien Xa hoi hoc (eds). *Tinh yeu, hon nhan, gia dinh trong xa hoi ta.* Ha Noi: Nha xuat ban khoa hoc xa hoi.

Duong Thu Huong. 1987. *Ben kia bo ao vong* [Beyond illusions]. Ha Noi: Nha xuat ban Phu nu.

—— 1988/1994. *Paradise of the Blind.* Novel. New York: Penguin Books.

Durkheim, E. 1995. *The Elementary Forms of Religious Life.* Transl. K. E. Fields. New York: The Free Press.

Ebaugh, H. R. F. 1988. *Becoming an Ex. The Process of Role Exit.* Chicago: The University of Chicago Press.

Eisen, A. 1984. *Women and Revolution in Vietnam.* London: Zed Books Ltd.

Engels, F. 1972. *The Origin of the Family, Private Property and the State.* New York: Pathfinder Press.

Fforde, A. and Paine S. H. 1987. *The Limits of National Liberation.* London: Croom Helm.

Filimonova, T. N. 1992. 'The Problem of a Family and an Individual in the Novels "Doan tuyet" and "Lanh lung" by Nhat Linh'. Paper presented at the Nordic Institute of Asian Studies Symposium on "Problems of literature, culture, society and history of Vietnam" in Egebjerg, Denmark, 20–23 August.

Fumie Kumagai. 1995. 'Families in Japan: Beliefs and Realities'. *Journal of Comparative Family Studies.* Vol. XXVI, No. 1, pp.135–163.

Gammeltoft, T. M. 1997a. *Women's Bodies, Women's Worries.* Ph. D. Thesis. Copenhagen: Institute of Anthropology, University of Copenhagen.

—— 1997b. '"Faithful, Heroic, Resourceful". Changing Images of Women in Vietnam'. Paper presented at the Third European Conference on Vietnam in Amsterdam, Holland, 2–4 July.

Geiger, H. K. 1968. *The Family in Soviet Russia.* Cambridge, Mass.: Harvard University Press.

Giddens, A. 1989. *Sociology.* Cambridge: Polity Press.

—— 1991. *Modernity and Self-Identity. Self and Society in a Late Modern Age.* Cambridge: Polity Press.

Goethals, P. R. 1991. 'Southeast Asia. The Vietnamese'. In: *The New Encyclopaedia Britannica.* Chicago: The University of Chicago. Vol. 14. Macropedia, pp. 202–203.

Goode, W. J. 1963. *World Revolution and Family Patterns.* New York: The Free Press.

—— 1982. 'Why men resist'. In: Thorne, B. and Yalom, M. (eds). *Rethinking the Family. Some Feminist Questions.* New York: Longman.

Goodkind, D. 1994. 'Abortion in Vietnam: Measurement, Puzzles, and Concerns'. *Studies in Family Planning,* Vol. 25, no. 6, pp. 342–352.

—— 1995. 'Vietnam's One-or-Two-Child Policy in Action'. *Population and Development Review.* Vol. 21, no.1 (March 1995), pp. 95–111.

Goodstein, L. 1996. 'Sexual Assault in the United States and Vietnam: Some Thoughts and Questions'. In: Barry, K. (ed.). *Vietnam's Women in Transition.* London: Macmillan Press Ltd.

Goody, J. and Tambiah, S. J. 1973. *Bridewealth and Dowry.* London: Cambridge University Press.

Gourou, P. 1936/1955. *The Peasants of the Tonkin Delta. A Study of Human Geography.* New Haven: Human Relations Area Files.

Hammersley, M. and Atkinson, P. 1983. *Ethnography: Principles in Practice.* London: Routledge.

Harris, C. C. 1983. *The Family and Industrial Society.* London: George Allen & Unwin.

Hiebert, M. 1994. 'Single mothers'. *Far Eastern Economic Review.* February 24.

Hirschman, C. and Vu Manh Loi. 1994. 'Family and Household Structure in Vietnam: Some Glimpses from a Recent Survey'. Paper presented at the annual meetings of Association for Asian Studies. Boston, Mass. 18–20 March.

Ho Chi Minh. 1977. *Selected Writings.* Hanoi: Foreign Language Publishing House.

Hoang Thi Hoa *et al.* 1996. 'Child Spacing and the Two-child Policy in Practice in Rural Vietnam'. In: Hoang Thi Hoa. *Family Planning and Reproductive Pattern in Rural Vietnam. A Study during a Period of Rapid Socio-economic Transition.* Stockholm: IHCAR, Karolinska Instutet.

Hoang Van Chi. 1964. *From Colonialism to Communism.* New York: Praeger.

Houtart, F. and Lemercinier, G. 1984. *Hai Van: Life in a Vietnamese Commune.* London: Zed Books.

Huynh Kim Khanh. 1982. *Vietnamese Communism 1925–1945.* Ithaca, N.Y.: Cornell University Press.

Insook Han Park and Lee-Jay Cho. 1995. 'Confucianism and the Korean Family'. *Journal of Comparative Family Studies.* Vol. XXVI, no. 1, pp. 117–134.

Jamieson, N. L. 1993. *Understanding Vietnam.* Berkeley: University of California Press.

Johansson, A. *et al.* 1996. 'Family Planning in Vietnam – Women's Experiences and Dilemma: A Community Study from the Red River Delta'. *J. Pshychom. Obstet. Gynecol.,* no. 17.

Jones, G. W. 1995. 'Population and the Family in Southeast Asia'. *Journal of Southeast Asian Studies.* Vol. 26. No. 1, pp. 184–195.

Khuat Thu Hong. 1991. 'Overview of Sociological Research on Family in Vietnam'. In: Liljeström, R. and Tuong Lai (eds). *Sociological Studies on the Vietnamese Family.* Hanoi: Social Sciences Publishing House.

Kleinen, J. 1993. 'Responses to Economic Change in a North Vietnamese Village'. Paper presented at the Nordic Institute of Asian Studies Conference on Vietnam in Copenhagen, Denmark. 19–21 August.

Landes, J. B. 1989. 'Marxism and the "Women Question"'. In: Kruks, S., Rapp, R. and Young, M. B. (eds). *Promissory Notes. Women in the Transition to Socialism.* New York: Monthly Review Press.

Lang, O. 1946. *Chinese Family and Society.* New Haven: Yale University Press.

Lavely, W. and Ren, X. 1992. 'Patrilocality and Early Marital Co-residence in Rural China, 1955–85'. *The China Quarterly.* 130. June, pp.378–391.

Le Duan. 1984. *Vietnam Social and Economic Problems of the '80s.* Hanoi: Foreign Language Publishing House.

Le Luu. 1986. *Thoi xa vang* [Echoes of time past]. Ha Noi: Nha xuat ban tac pham moi.

Le Ngoc Van. 1991. 'Tim hieu co cau, chuc nang quan he than toc cua gia dinh nong thon trong tinh hinh doi moi quan ly nong nghiep' [An examination of structure, function, kinship relations of rural family in the context of changing management of agriculture]. In: *Nguoi phu nu va gia dinh Viet Nam hien nay.* Ha Noi: Nha xuat ban khoa hoc xa hoi.

Le Nham. 1994. '"Asking for a child" practice at An Hiep commune'. *Vietnam Social Sciences,* vol. 1, no. 39, pp. 103–109.

Le Phuong. 1986. 'Tinh hinh ly hon hien nay va nguyen nhan cua no' [The current situation and some reasons for divorce]. *Xa hoi hoc,* no. 2, pp. 39–45.

Le Thi Nham Tuyet. 1975. *Phu nu Viet Nam qua cac thoi dai* [Vietnamese women through ages]. Ha Noi: Nha xuat ban Khoa hoc xa hoi.

——— 1991. 'Women and Their Families in the Movement for Agricultural Collectivisation in Vietnam'. In: Afshar, H. (ed.). *Women, Development and Survival in the Third World.* New York: Longman.

———, A. Johansson, Mai Huy Bich and Hoang Thi Hoa. 1994a. 'Women's experience of family planning in two rural communes (Thai Binh province)'. *Vietnam Social Sciences.* 1 (39), pp. 55–72.

———, A. Johansson and Nguyen The Lap. 1994b. 'Abortions in two rural communes in Thai Binh province'. *Vietnam Social Sciences,* vol. 1, no. 39, pp. 73–90.

Le Thi Que. 1986. 'The Vietnamese Family: Yesterday and Today'. *Interculture*, vol. XIX, no. 3. Issue 92.

Le Thi Quy. 1996. 'Domestic Violence in Vietnam and Efforts to Curb It'. In: Barry, K. (ed.). *Vietnam's Women in Transition*. London: Macmillan Press Ltd.

Liljeström, R. *et al.* 1988. *Migrants by Necessity*. A report on the living conditions of forestry workers in the SIDA supported Bai Bang programme. Stockholm. SIDA Evaluation Report, Forestry, Vietnam.

Luong Van Hy. 1989. 'Vietnamese Kinship: Structural Principles and the Socialist Transformation in Northern Vietnam'. *The Journal of Asian Studies*, vol. 48, no. 4, pp. 741–756.

—— 1990. *Discursive Practices and Linguistic Meanings. The Vietnamese System of Person Reference*. Amsterdam/Philadelphia: John Benjamins Publishing Company.

—— 1992. *Revolution in the Village. Tradition and Transformation in North Vietnam, 1925–1988*. Honolulu: University of Hawaii Press.

—— 1993. 'Economic Reform and the Intensification of Rituals in Two North Vietnamese Villages, 1980–90'. In: Ljungren, B. (ed.). *The Challenge of Reform in Indochina*. Harvard: Harvard University Press.

Ma Van Khang. 1985. *Mua la rung trong vuon* [Leafshedding season in the garden]. Ha Noi: Nha xuat ban Phu nu.

Mai Huy Bich. 1988. 'De tai gia dinh trong van xuoi nhung nam gan day' [The family topic in the recent years' prose]. *Van nghe*. 4 June.

—— 1991. 'A Distinctive Feature of the Meaning of Reproduction in Confucian Family Tradition in the Red River Delta'. In: Liljeström, R. and Tuong Lai (eds). *Sociological Studies on the Vietnamese Family*. Hanoi: Social Sciences Publishing House.

—— 1993. *Dac diem gia dinh dong bang song Hong* [Some characteristics of the family in the Red River Delta]. Ha Noi: Nha xuat ban van hoa.

—— 1995. 'Reproduction and Socialisation of the Catholic Family in a Vietnamese Commune'. *Social Compass*. Vol. 42, no. 3, September, pp. 367–378.

Marr, D. 1981. *Vietnamese Tradition on Trial, 1920–1945*. Berkeley: University of California Press.

—— 1995. *Vietnam 1945. The Quest for Power*. Berkeley: University of California Press.

Mason, M. S. 1994. 'Vietnam: Landscape of Memory'. *Christian Science Monitor*. April 1–7., vol. 86, no. 87.

Mei-Lin Lee and Te-Hsiung Sun. 1995. 'The Family and Demography in Contemporary Taiwan'. *Journal of Comparative Family Studies*, vol. XXVI, no. 1, pp. 101–116.

Mies, M. 1986. *Patriarchy and Accumulation on a World Scale. Women in the International Division of Labour.* London: Zed Book Ltd.

Mineo Nakajima. 1994. 'Economic Development in East Asia and Confucian Ethics'. *Social Compass,* vol. 41. no. 1, pp. 113–119.

Moise, E. E. 1983. *Land Reform in China and North Vietnam.* Chapel Hill: University of North Carolina Press.

Molander, C. 1977. 'Women in Vietnam'. Stockholm: SIDA Report (unpublished).

Morgan, D. H. J. 1985. *The Family, Politics and Social Theory.* London: Routledge & Kegan Paul.

Ngan Tam. 1988. 'How to Preserve Family Happiness'. *Vietnamese Studies,* vol. 18, no. 88, pp. 46–56.

—— and Tran Thi Lien. 1985. *Chuyen ke cua nguoi tham phan* [The stories of a judge from divorce court]. Ha Noi: Nha xuat ban Phu nu.

Ngo Vinh Long. 1973. *Before the Revolution: The Vietnamese Peasants Under the French.* Cambridge, mass.: MIT Press.

—— 1993. 'Reform and Rural Development: Impact on Class, Sectoral, and Regional Inequalities'. In: Turley, W. S. and Selden M. (eds). *Reinventing Vietnamese Socialism. Doi Moi in Comparative Perspective.* Boulder, Col.: Westview Press.

Nguyen Cong Hoan. 1989. 'Critical Moment'. In: *Vietnamese Studies,* vol. 23, no. 93, pp. 145–152.

Nguyen Hong Phong. 1977. 'Di san lang xa truoc cach mang' [Pre-revolutionary village heritage]. In: *Nong thon Viet Nam trong lich su.* Ha Noi: Nha xuat ban Khoa hoc xa hoi.

Nguyen Huu Minh. 1991. 'Bien doi kinh te xa hoi va kha nang giam chuan muc so con trong cac gia dinh nong dan Bac Bo' [Socio-economic changes and the possibility of a reduced number of children in peasant families in the North]. *Xa hoi hoc,* no. 4.

Nguyen Huy Thiep. 1988. *Tuong ve huu* [The Retired General]. Ha Noi: Nha xuat ban thanh nien.

Nguyen Khac Truong. 1990/1991. *Manh dat lam nguoi nhieu ma* [The piece of land with many people and a number of ghosts]. N.p.: Hong Linh xuat ban.

Nguyen Khac Vien. 1971. 'Directives and resolutions of the DRV government and the Vietnam Workers' Party on national education'. *Vietnamese Studies,* no. 30.

—— 1974. *Tradition and Revolution in Vietnam.* Berkeley, CA: The Indochina Resource Centre.

—— and Huu Ngoc (eds). N.d. *Vietnamese Literature.* Hanoi: Red River.

Nguyen The Anh. 1970. *Viet Nam thoi Phap do ho* [Vietnam under French domination]. Sai Gon: Lua thieng xuat ban.

Nguyen Thi Thin. 1989. 'Three generations of mothers under the same roof'. *Vietnamese Studies*. No. 23.

Nguyen Tri Thuc. 1995. 'Lai gai...' [A daughter once more]. *Phu nu Viet Nam*, no. 14, p. 11.

Nguyen Tu Chi. 1980. 'The Traditional Viet Village in Bac Bo: Its Organisational Structure and Problems'. *Vietnamese Studies*, no. 61, pp. 7–119.

—— 1991. 'Preliminary Notes on the Family of the Viet'. In: Liljeström, R. and Tuong Lai (eds). *Sociological Studies on the Vietnamese Family*. Hanoi: Social Sciences Publishing House.

Nguyen Tuan Minh. 1992. 'Dam cuoi khong dem tan hon' [A wedding without the nuptial night]. *Tien phong chu nhat*, no. 44.

O'Harrow, S. 1995. 'Vietnamese Women and Confucianism: Creating Spaces from Patriarchy'. In: Karim, J. (ed.). *'Male' and 'Female' in Developing Southeast Asia*. Oxford: Berg Publishers.

Parsons, T. and Bales, R. F. 1955. *Family, Socialisation and Interaction Process*. Glencoe, Ill.: The Free Press.

Pelzer, K. 1993. 'Socio-Cultural Dimensions of Renovation in Vietnam: Doi Moi as Dialogue and Transformation in Gender Relations'. In: Turley, W. S. and Selden, M. (eds). *Reinventing Vietnamese Socialism. Doi Moi in Comparative Perspective*. Boulder: Westview Press.

Pham Thi Thu Thuy. 1994. 'Bon muoi nam Ha Noi' [Hanoi for forty years]. *Tuan tin tuc*, no. 42.

Pham Van Khanh. 1988. 'Nen de dang vien lam kinh te ca the va tu nhan' [Allow party members to carry out individual and private economic activities]. *Tap chi cong san*, no. 10.

Phan Ke Binh. 1915/1992. *Viet nam phong tuc*. [Vietnamese customs]. Thanh pho Ho Chi Minh.

Phu nu Viet Nam [Vietnamese women]. 1992. 6 April.

Popkin, S. L. 1979. *The Rational Peasant. The Political Economy of Rural Society in Vietnam*. Berkeley: University of California Press.

Quah, S. R. 1993. 'Sociologists in the International Arena: Diverse Settings, Same Concerns?'. *Current Sociology*. Vol. 41, no. 1.

Quang Dam. 1990. 'Khong giao va gia dinh' [Confucianism and the family]. In: Vu Khieu (chu bien). *Nho giao xua va nay*. Ha Noi: Nha xuat ban khoa hoc xa hoi.

Robertson, A. F. 1991. *Beyond the Family. The Social Organisation of Human Reproduction*. Cambridge: Polity Press.

Rubin, S. 1988. 'Learning for Life? Glimpses from a Vietnamese School'. In: Marr, D. and White, C. P. (eds). *Post-war Vietnam: Dilemmas in Socialist Development*. Ithaca, N.Y.: Cornell University.

Schafer, J. C. and The Uyen. 1993.`The Novel Emerges in Cochinchina'. *The Journal of Asian Studies*, vol. 52. No. 4, pp. 854–884.

Scott, J. C. 1976. *The Moral Economy of the Peasant. Rebellion and Subsistence in Southeast Asia*. New Haven: Yale University.

Segalen, M. 1986. *Historical Anthropology of the Family*. Cambridge: Cambridge University Press.

Shaplen, R. 1986. *Bitter Victory*. New York: Harper & Row.

Sharon, K. H. 1986. 'Voluntary Childlessness: Toward a Theoretical Integration'. In: Skolnick, A. S. and Skolnick, J. H. (eds) *Family in Transition. Rethinking Marriage, Sexuality, Child Rearing and Family Organisation*. Fifth edition. Boston: Little, Brown and Company.

Ta Van Tai. 1997. 'Continuity and Change in Vietnamese Women's Role through the Ages'. Paper prepared for the Third EUROVIET Conference in Amsterdam, the Netherlands, 2–4 July.

Taylor, K. W. 1983. *The Birth of Vietnam*. Berkeley: University of California Press.

Therborn, G. 1990. 'Social Steering and Household Strategies: the Macropolitics and the Microsociology of Welfare State'. *Journal of Public Policy*, vol. 9, no. 3, pp. 371–397.

―― 1995. *European Modernity and Beyond*. London: SAGE.

Thuan Thao. 1994. 'Phan phu nu: hoi dap' [Questions and answers for female readers]. *Van nghe tien phong*, no. 449. Arlington.

Toan Anh. Date unknown. *Nep cu con nguoi Viet nam*. Phong tuc co truyen [Old customs of Vietnamese people]. Lancaster: Xuan Thu.

Tong, R. 1989. *Feminist Thought. A Comprehensive Introduction*. London: Routledge.

Tønnesson, S. 1993. *Democracy in Vietnam?* Copenhagen: Nordic Institute of Asian Studies: NIAS Report.

Tran Dinh Huou. 1991. 'Traditional Families in Vietnam and the Influence of Confucianism'. In: Liljeström, R. and Tuong Lai (eds). *Sociological Studies on the Vietnamese Family*. Hanoi: Social Sciences Publishing House.

Tran Hoai Anh. 1993. 'From Kitchen to Cooking Place'. Paper presented at the Nordic Institute of Asian Studies Conference on Vietnam in Copenhagen, Denmark, 19–21 August.

Tran Manh Hao. 1989/1990. *Ly than* [Separation]. Paris: Que Me.

Tria Kerkvliet, B. J. 1995. 'Village–State Relations in Vietnam: The Effect of Everyday Politics on Decollectivisation'. *The Journal of Asian Studies*, vol. 54, no. 2 (May 1995), pp. 396–418.

Trinh Duy Luan. 1993. 'Doi net ve nguoi ngheo do thi qua mot cuoc khao sat' [Upon a survey: some features of poor urban people]. *Xa hoi hoc*, no. 1.

Trinh Thi Quang. 1983. 'Vai nhan xet ve so con trong gia dinh' [Some remarks on the number of children in the family]. *Xa hoi hoc*, no. 4.

—— 1984. 'May van de quan he than toc o nong thon' [Certain questions regarding kinship relations in countryside]. *Xa hoi hoc*, no. 2.

Truong Nhu Tang, with Chanoff, D. and Doan Van Toai. 1985. *A Vietcong Memoir*. Vintage Books.

Truong Thanh Dam. 1995. 'Uncertain horizon. The Women's Question in Vietnam revisited'. Paper prepared for the conference 'Vietnam – Reform and Transformation'. Centre for Pacific Asia Studies, Stockholm University, Stockholm, 31 August–1 September.

Vietnam Resource Centre. 1974. *Vietnamese Women in Society and Revolution*. Cambridge. Mass.

Vietnamese Government. 1972. *History of the August Revolution*. Hanoi: Foreign Language Publishing House.

—— 1976. *An Outline History of the Vietnam Workers' Party*. Hanoi: Foreign Language Publishing House.

—— 1987. 'The Marriage and Family Law'. In: *Vietnamese Studies*. 1988, vol. 18, no. 88, pp. 28–45.

—— 1990. 'National Committee for Population and Family Planning'. *Vietnam Demographic and Health Survey 1988*. Hanoi.

—— 1990. 'Central Census Steering Committee (CCSC)'. *Vietnam Population Census 1989*. Sample Results. Hanoi.

—— 1990. 'Vietnam Population Census 1989'. *Ket qua dieu tra mau nha o* [Household sample census results]. Ha Noi: Nha xuat ban thong ke.

Vo Phuong Lan. 1994. 'A Study of the Reproductive Life of Women by the Method of Reproductive History Life Lines'. *Vietnam Social Sciences*, vol. 1, no. 31, pp.29–42.

Vu Khieu (chu bien). 1990. *Nho giao xua va nay* [Confucianism: yesterday and today]. Ha Noi: Nha xuat ban khoa hoc xa hoi.

Vu Manh Loi. 1991. 'The gender division of labour in the Red River Delta'. In: Liljeström, R. and Tuong Lai (eds). *Sociological Studies on the Vietnamese Family*. Hanoi: Social Sciences Publishing House.

Vu Qui Nhan. 1991. 'Fertility and Family Planning in Vietnam: Levels, Trends and Challenges'. In: Forbes, D. *et al.* (eds) *Doi moi: Vietnam's*

Renovation Policy and Performance. Department of Political and Social Change. Canberra: Australian National University.

Vu Tu Lap et al. 1991. *Van hoa va cu dan dong bang song Hong* [Culture and population of the Red River Delta]. Ha Noi: Nha xuat ban khoa hoc xa hoi.

Vuong G. Thuy. 1976. *Getting to Know the Vietnamese and Their Culture.* New York: Frederick Ungar Publishing Co.

Vuong Xuan Tinh. 1990. 'Van hoa lang' [Village culture]. *Van nghe,* no. 22.

—— 1994. 'The Need for Sons: Problems and Solutions'. *Vietnam Social Sciences,* vol. 1, no. 39, pp. 25–28.

Walder, A. G. 1986. *Communist Neo-Traditionalism. Work and Authority in Chinese Industry.* Berkeley: University of California Press.

Werner, J. S. 1997. 'Gender and Economic Reform in Vietnam'. Paper presented to the Third EUROVIET Conference. Amsterdam, The Netherland, 2–4 July.

White, C. P. 1989. 'Vietnam: War, Socialism, and the Politics of Gender Relations'. In: Kruks, S., Rapp, R. and Young, B. M. (eds). *Promissory Notes. Women in the Transition to Socialism.* New York: Monthly Review Press.

White, T. P. 1989. 'Hanoi: the Capital Today'. *National Geographic.* November, pp. 561–594.

Wiegersma, N. 1988. *Vietnam: Peasant Land, Peasant Revolution. Patriarchy and Collectivity in the Rural Economy.* Basingstoke: Macmillan Press.

Willmott, P. and Young, M. 1960. *Family and Class in a London Suburb.* London: Routledge & Kegan Paul.

Wolf, M. 1985. 'Marriage, Family, and the State in Contemporary China'. In: Kingsley, D. (ed.). *Contemporary Marriage. Comparative Perspectives on a Changing Institution.* New York: Russell Sage Foundation.

Woodside, A. B. 1976. *Community and Revolution in Modern Vietnam.* Boston: Houghton Mifflin Company.

Wurfel, D. 1993. '*Doi Moi* in Comparative Perspectice'. In: Turley, W. S. and Selden, M. (eds). *Reinventing Vietnamese Socialism. Doi Moi in Comparative Perspective.* Boulder, Col.: Westview Press.

Yi, Chin-Chun. 1993. 'Studying Social Change: The Case of Taiwanese Family Sociologists'. In: *Current Sociology.* Vol. 41, no. 1.

Yu, Insun. 1990. *Law and Society in Seventeenth and Eighteenth Century Vietnam.* Seoul: Asiatic Research Centre, Korea University.

Index

abortion 192–194, 198, 199, 207
adoption 205, 206
adultery 37, 48, 66, 112, 113, 162
age difference 141–144, 151
ancestor 19, 24, 27, 35, 54, 56, 111, 112, 117, 219–226, 234
~ altar 25, 27, 35, 87, 114, 151, 222, 223
~ worship 26, 53, 95, 111, 112, 151, 182, 209, 209--225, 232–235, 247–248, 250
arranged marriage 57–59, 61, 106, 108, 109, 115, 127, 140, 161, 177, 232, 237

birth control 182–185, 190–194, 197, 227–229, 231
bourgeois 48, 60, 132, 241
boy 12, 63, 70, 110, 135, 196, 197. *See also* sons.
bride 12, 27–30, 36–37, 42–43, 54, 105–106, 109, 111, 114–116, 124, 167, 180, 210
~ price 11, 30, 42–43, 54, 58, 111, 124, 201

brother 16, 42, 86, 110, 119, 142, 224
elder 20
younger 22, 26
See also sibling
Buddhism 5
Buddhist 21, 194

capitalism 4, 46, 48, 80, 84, 96
capitalist 10, 132
cause and effect 20
central-planning economy 76, 83, 84, 91, 100, 177
challenge (of reproduction) 218, 226, 246, 252
city 11, 12, 52, 57, 80—82, 96–99, 121, 124, 125, 150, 160, 178, 195
class 41, 71, 76, 80, 111, 178, 241–243, 245
~ approach 50, 76, 132
~ consciousness 69
~ contradiction 42
~ criterion 60
~ dynamic 17
~ endogamy 50, 135, 137, 138, 177, 178, 249, 252
~ enemy 50, 68, 75, 76, 132, 135, 156, 242, 243
~ issue 69, 100, 241

265

~ label 69
~ matrix 251
~ perspective 48
~ position 64, 73, 232, 233
~ relation 15, 16, 42
~ solidarity 178
~ struggle 45, 70, 71, 74, 76, 135
upper 8, 10–11, 32–33, 35–36, 38–39, 64, 104, 106, 110, 114, 123, 151, 201–202
~ viewpoint 60, 69, 177, 244
working 9, 10, 59, 60
co quan 133–137
collective community 17, 18
collectivisation 42, 45, 64, 76–79, 97, 99, 147, 212
collectivism 83
colonialism 9, 46, 47, 68
colonialist 17, 44, 68, 242
communality 18
communism 46, 48, 223, 233, 235, 240, 253
communist 16, 41, 42, 53, 60, 85, 95, 135, 137, 204, 205, 223, 238, 242
Communist Party 1, 17, 41, 44–47, 49–52, 57, 60, 62–65, 68–72, 79, 90, 134–136, 155, 188, 199, 201, 204, 205, 225
community 12, 17, 19, 20, 21, 24, 25, 56
companionship 40, 149, 150, 178, 248
compatibility 106, 130–134
concubine 10, 15, 34, 60, 99, 106, 113, 117, 120–123, 201–206
Confucianism 4, 5, 33, 116, 223, 233, 235, 236, 240, 241, 245, 253
Confucius 28, 29, 235

consumption 14, 48, 54, 79, 82–84, 99
contraception 58, 170, 183, 190, 192, 194–196, 229, 231
co-operative 14, 56, 64, 66, 70, 76–79, 92–96, 100, 199, 212, 248

death anniversary 24, 26, 221-225
decision 38, 39, 125, 127, 150–125, 228
descendant 20, 21, 26, 190, 220–222, 234
diachronic (generational) community 19, 20, 219, 228
dichotomy 4, 46, 231
double standard 36, 87, 116, 158, 165

engagement 54, 57
equality 41, 45, 48, 50, 58, 60, 62, 69, 70, 117, 140, 150–153, 178, 237–240, 243–245, 252

family (definition of) 2
~ background 71, 106, 125, 131, 132, 134–137, 139, 177, 230, 251
Confucian 13, 28, 29
extended 8, 31–33, 38, 150, 170, 235, 247
immediate 42, 232
matrilineal 26, 88, 103
natal 26
new cultured 45, 50–53, 56, 249
nuclear 3, 14, 22, 31–33, 211, 215, 247
one-parent 32

~ of origin 11, 22, 119, 125, 129
patrilineal 25, 26, 30, 31, 36, 88, 220
~ planning 58, 66, 70, 188, 189, 195, 196, 227, 228
semi-nuclear 32
stem 30
socialist 45, 47, 49, 231, 248, 249
traditional (definition of) 3–4
~ of procreation 22
fatherland altar 223
feudalism 46, 47, 62, 68, 236,
feudalist 60, 68, 155, 156, 242
fiancé 28
fiancée 28, 126
filial piety 16, 19, 23, 28–31, 41, 51, 105, 107, 109–112, 169, 225, 226, 232, 234, 235, 247. *See also hieu*
filial impiety 169
Five Good Emulations 52, 249
Five Teachings (of Uncle Ho) 51, 53
Four virtues 11
French influence 2, 7, 9, 10, 17

gender 22, 233, 238, 239, 241–244
~ domination 242
~ equality 62
~ hierarchy 155, 244, 245
~ inequality 68, 238, 242
~ issue 42, 69, 100, 178, 237, 239, 240–242, 245, 252
~ oppression 38
~ relationship 37
~ role 178
~ separation 33, 36, 38, 114, 149, 150, 178, 180, 248

groom 12, 27, 29–31, 37, 54, 106, 109–111, 114, 124, 158, 167, 180, 210

hierarchy 22-25, 41, 52, 73, 74, 96, 117, 143, 167–168, 226, 233, 237–239, 247, 1249
hieu 105, 109, 225. *See also* filial piety
Ho Chi Minh 44, 46, 51, 53, 59, 60, 62, 87, 223, 225. *See also* Uncle Ho
household
~ chores 67, 84, 98, 110, 116, 140, 147, 148, 152, 160, 188
~ registration 45, 80, 174, 175, 184, 211, 230
housewife 35, 36, 52, 83, 131, 132, 240
housework 33–35, 51, 67, 83, 140, 148, 151, 176

imperialist 68, 71, 242
incompatibility 30, 130
individual 17–19, 21, 25, 49, 78, 81, 83, 124, 130, 177, 227, 228, 230, 234
individualism 18
industrialisation 42, 45, 76, 80, 82, 104, 182, 229, 230
inequality 48, 143, 149, 152, 239, 244
inferior 22, 23, 34, 38
intellectual 14, 131, 140, 179, 240
intelligentsia 10
interaction 6, 23, 26, 90, 147, 149
intergenerational
~ bond 114, 115, 215, 237, 248
~ link 166, 170, 174, 176, 177

~ relation 113, 114
~ tie 169
interior 26, 40

kin 23, 42
kindred 14
kinship 2, 16, 23, 25, 26, 31, 41, 42, 60, 74, 215, 233–235, 250, 251
kinsmen 13, 16
kitchen 35, 36, 82, 83, 150, 155

landlord 10, 15–17, 21, 34, 38, 71–76, 121, 132, 157
land reform 45, 70–76, 99
Laws (on Marriage and the Family) 45, 54, 57–61, 125, 151, 177, 191, 198, 201, 205, 231, 232, 236, 248
Le Duan 46, 60, 64, 69
lineage 3, 16, 22, 26, 53, 105, 107, 110–113, 115, 119, 171, 172, 185, 205, 207
little sister 142–144
lower class 8, 32, 34, 36, 38, 40, 106, 115, 151, 245
ly lich 134, 135. *See also* family background

male dominance 237, 241
domination 33, 60, 178, 240, 242, 244
marital partner 49, 104, 111, 115, 121, 125, 128, 129, 132, 133, 145, 147, 163, 164, 177, 178, 229, 232, 252
market 8, 11, 12, 15, 33, 84, 92, 158, 224, 242, 252
marketplace 33, 68, 97
marriage partner 50, 105, 119, 122, 125, 133, 134, 138, 177, 229

masculine domination 33, 60, 244
Marxism 80, 233, 240–242, 245, 251
Marxism–Leninism 46, 47
Marxist
~ bias 239, 245, 252
~ theory 1, 6, 17, 41, 42, 47–49, 60, 76, 231, 245, 251, 253
mate selection 177, 252
maternal side 23, 26
matriarchy 33
middle class 8–12, 63, 80, 117, 119, 121, 141
modernity 4, 46, 191
monogamy 58, 157, 159, 205, 242
mourning period 112, 113
mutual responsibility 17, 74, 75

non-state employee 80–82, 84, 102, 132–134, 138, 139, 177

offspring 29, 32, 105, 112, 113, 183
older brother 22, 90, 131, 142–144, 239
older sister 22, 104, 142
open door 45, 85, 91
order
~ of birth 22, 130
~ of precedence 22, 25
ownership 1, 48, 49, 58, 83, 231–233
paternal side 23, 26
patriarchy 33, 61, 68, 156, 237, 239, 242, 244, 245
patrilineage 42, 177, 216, 220
patrilocal residence 27–31, 41, 212–214

polygamy 3, 26, 38, 57–59, 61, 62, 120, 135, 201–203
polygyny 3, 26, 34, 87, 99, 203, 205, 227
pressure (of reproduction) 218, 226, 246, 247, 252
private property 1, 42, 48, 49, 76, 231, 233, 241, 242
privatisation 240, 250
proletariat 95, 241
property 36, 48, 50, 58, 71, 76, 80, 85, 113, 117, 123, 130, 172, 204, 222, 241, 242

reciprocity 14, 167
registration (of marriage) 54, 55, 135
renovation 45, 55, 91, 92, 95, 96, 138, 139
reproduction (definition of) 181
residue 242, 244
rite 26, 157, 222
~ of mourning 26
~ of passage 14, 54, 56, 111, 167, 219, 222, 250
ritual 12, 14, 19, 24–26, 51–55, 95, 96, 98, 166
role conflict 198–200, 232

sacred 234, 247
senior mother 19, 21, 24, 204
seven reasons (for divorce) 111, 112, 118, 122
sexuality 6, 117, 154, 156–160, 165, 184, 240
sibling 2, 22, 25-27, 106, 118, 119, 143, 174, 237, 525
younger 22
See also brother, sister
single mother 87, 88, 240
sister 22, 26, 75, 110, 116, 118, 120, 202, 243

younger 22, 118, 144, 239
See also sibling
sleeping arrangement 114, 115, 170, 171, 202
social steering 45, 46, 49, 80, 85, 91, 100, 130
socialism 46, 155
sons (preference for) 182, 188–190, 196, 197, 209, 210, 227. *See also* boy
spatial dimension 233, 235
spouse selection 103, 104, 132, 140, 248
state 56, 77–78, 82, 84, 92, 133, 138–139, 177–178, 183, 225, 230–233, 236–237, 240, 244–246, 248–253
state employee 55, 61, 80–82, 84, 87, 94, 101–102, 131–134, 136, 138–139, 174, 176–178, 230, 236, 249, 252
superior 22, 23, 25, 34, 38, 42, 66, 109

temporal dimension 3, 233
term of address 23, 73
three obediences. *See* three submissions
three postponements 56
three submissions 11, 24, 33, 40
town 9, 10, 81, 82, 96, 97, 99
tradition 4, 7, 10, 16, 19, 28, 33, 42, 46, 59, 106, 127, 157–158, 174, 189, 191, 197, 218, 239
two-child limit 154, 191, 197–200

Viet (ethnic group) 4
village endogamy 210, 211

violence 155, 156
visiting marriage 174

wedding 9, 12, 27–30, 37, 43, 54–55, 107, 109–111, 113–114, 128, 149, 166–167, 170–171, 221
welfare 17, 89, 212
  ~ institution 237, 246–248
  ~ institution building 228, 237
wet-rice cultivation 32–34
wife-battering 58, 99, 155
wife-beating. See wife-battering
women's liberation 38, 45, 60, 62, 64, 65, 69, 70, 88, 98, 151, 157, 162, 232, 242–244

women's emancipation 38, 45, 60, 62, 64, 65, 69, 70, 88, 98, 151, 157, 162, 232, 242–244
Women's Union 47, 50, 59, 61, 62, 65, 165, 180, 198, 199, 236, 238
work
  ~ unit 133–134
  ~ place 55, 81, 83, 101, 134–139, 165, 166, 174–176, 178, 179, 230, 237
worship 111, 112

Youth Organisation 50, 54, 166, 171, 180, 236, 253
Youth Union 50, 54, 166, 171, 180, 236, 253

The Nordic Institute of Asian Studies (NIAS) is funded by the governments of Denmark, Finland, Iceland, Norway and Sweden via the Nordic Council of Ministers, and works to encourage and support Asian studies in the Nordic countries. In so doing, NIAS has published well in excess of one hundred books in the last three decades, most of them in co-operation with Curzon Press.

Nordic Council of Ministers